Globalization and the Third World

Also by B.N. Ghosh

THE THREE DIMENSIONAL MAN: Human Resource Development in Malaysia

ECONOMIC THEORY: Past and Present

FROM MARKET FAILURE TO GOVERNMENT FAILURE: A Handbook of Public Sector Economics

CONTEMPORARY ISSUES IN DEVELOPMENT ECONOMICS (*ed.*)

GLOBAL FINANCIAL CRISES AND REFORMS: Cases, Correlates and Caveats (*ed.*)

POLITICAL ECONOMY

DESIGNING SOCIAL RESEARCH

GENDER AND DEVELOPMENT (*co-editor Parvesh Chopra*), 2 vols

CONTEMPORARY ISSUES IN MACROECONOMIC MANAGEMENT

ECONOMIC DEVELOPMENT IN TURKEY: Some Contemporary Issues (*co-editor*)

GANDHIAN POLITICAL ECONOMY: Principles, Practice and Policy (*forthcoming*)

Globalization and the Third World

A Study of Negative Consequences

Edited by

B.N. Ghosh

Department of Economics, Eastern Mediterranean University, North Cyprus and Centre for the Study of Human Development, Leeds, UK

and

Halil M. Guven

Eastern Mediterranean University, North Cyprus

First published 2006 by
PALGRAVE MACMILLAN
Houndmills, Basingstoke, Hampshire RG21 6XS and
175 Fifth Avenue, New York, N.Y. 10010
Companies and representatives throughout the world

PALGRAVE MACMILLAN is the global academic imprint of the Palgrave
Macmillan division of St. Martin's Press, LLC and of Palgrave Macmillan Ltd.
Macmillan® is a registered trademark in the United States, United Kingdom
and other countries. Palgrave is a registered trademark in the European
Union and other countries.

ISBN-13: 978–0–230–00467–2 hardback
ISBN-10: 0–230–00467–9 hardback

This book is printed on paper suitable for recycling and made from fully
managed and sustained forest sources.

A catalogue record for this book is available from the British Library.

Library of Congress Cataloging-in-Publication Data
Globalization and the Third World:a study of negative consequences/edited by
B.N. Ghosh and Halil M. Guven.
   p. cm.
Includes bibliographical references and index.
ISBN 0–230–00467–9 (cloth)
1. Developing countries—Economic conditions. 2. Developing
countries—Social conditions. 3. Globalization. I. Ghosh, B.N.
II. Guven, H.M. (Halil M.).
HC59.7.G59 2006
337.09172′4—dc22   2005058947

10   9   8   7   6   5   4   3   2   1
15   14   13   12   11   10   09   08   07   06

Transferred to digital printing 2007

Contents

Part II Labour Market Distortions and Inequalities

List of Tables

List of Figures

Notes on Contributors

Samir Amin is Professor Emeritus and Director, Third World Forum, Senegal, Africa.

Tim Anderson is Lecturer in Political Economy, University of Sydney, Australia.

Nahid Aslanbeigui is Professor of Economics, Monmouth University, West Long Branch, New Jersey, USA.

Amitava Krishna Dutt is Professor of Economics and Fellow, Kellogg Institute of International Studies and Kroc Institute of International Peace Studies, University of Notre Dame, USA.

Partha Gangopadhyay is Associate Professor, School of Economics and Finance, University of Western Sydney, Australia.

B.N. Ghosh is Professor of Economics, Eastern Mediterranean University, North Cyprus, and Director (Hon.), Centre for the Study of Human Development, Leeds, UK.

Halil M. Guven is Rector and Professor, Eastern Mediterranean University, North Cyprus.

Ozay Mehmet is Professor Emeritus, Carleton University, Canada and Professor of Economics, Eastern Mediterranean University, North Cyprus.

Shyam Nath is Professor of Economics, University of Mauritius, Mauritius.

Phillip Anthony O'Hara is Professor of Global Political Economy and Governance and Director, Global Political Economy Research Center, Curtin University of Technology, Perth, Australia.

Mustapha Kamal Pasha is Professor and Chair in International Relations at the University of Aberdeen, Scotland.

Franco Praussello is Jean Monnet Chair Professor of International Economics, University of Genoa, Italy.

Johannes D. Schmidt is Director of Studies and Associate Professor, Research Center on Development and International Relations, Aalborg University, Denmark.

Raj Kumar Sen is Professor and former Head of the Department of Economics, Rabindra Bharati University, Kolkata, India.

Gale Summerfield is Director, Women and Gender in Global Perspective Program, Department of Humanity and Community Development, University of Illinois at Urbana Champagne, USA.

Kevin Honglin Zhang is Professor of Economics, Illinois State University, Normal, USA.

Xiaobo Zhang is Senior Researcher in International Food Policy Research Institute, Washington, D.C., Washington.

Introduction: The End of Geography and the Beginning of Conflicts

B.N. Ghosh

As a concept globalization is difficult to understand, more difficult to interpret and perhaps most difficult of all to appraise. Globalization marks the end of geography and the rise of conflicts and clashes both actual and potential between developed and developing countries. Its effects however, are often more misunderstood than understood. The output of literature in this new area in terms of theories, paradigms and opinionated discussion is indeed overwhelming. However, the impact of globalization on developing economies, as numerous research studies reveal, is not conclusive: studies show diametrically opposite conclusions on the same problem in the context of globalization in developing countries. For instance, many studies reveal that globalization (economic liberalization) has reduced income inequalities in less developed countries (LDCs), but many other studies conclude that globalization has infact increased income inequalities. It is this analytical inclusiveness that is the genesis of this book. It makes a fresh attempt to study the real impact of globalization on many critical problems of LDCs in the areas of labour, capital inflow, trade, technology transfer and many socio-cultural issues. Evidently no consistent attempt has so far been made to study globalization exclusively and the conflicts that it generates in LDCs. As far as I am aware, no systematic study explaining the negative consequences of globalization has yet been undertaken to gauge the plight of the poor economies. The present study, therefore, is necessary and is expected to make a contribution in the area of the political economy of globalization. The contributions in this volume are divided into four parts: clashes, conflicts and contradictions; labour market distortions and inequalities; capital, technology and finance; and trade liberalization and unequal competition.

Clashes, conflict and contradictions

Neo-liberal globalization gives rise to a number of contradictions such as, international integration and national disintegration, attempts to shield the domestic society and simultaneously exposing it, growth of regionalism alongside the growth of globalism, and so forth. The global political economy is in a long-wave downswing as negatives outweigh the positives; the contradictions are very strong. O'Hara explains in detail the contradictory dynamics of modern neo-liberal globalization, paying special attention to the positive and negative trends of globalization both of which are endogenously embedded in the global movement.

The basic purpose of O'Hara's chapter is to examine the principal contradictions of globalization arising partly as a response to the worsening economic performance of the mid–late 1970s, deepening in the 1970s–2000s under the impact of Reaganomics, Thatcherism, neo-conservatives, New Labour, businesses and economic libertarians. But have the efforts reversed the decline in performance? This chapter examines this question in some detail, by considering the critical issues of globalization. Attention is given to the contradictions associated with the conflicts between (a) global capital and labour, (b) global finance and industry, (c) global profit and the environment, (d) global culture and local culture, (e) global politics and local politics, and (f) global hegemony and rising terrorism. In each of these contradictory processes, positive movements of globalization are inextricably linked to the negatives, while the balance of the positives and negatives depends upon the position of nations and regions in the long wave. A critical view of these contradictory dynamics provides a holistic and practical view of the system that includes future governance measures to moderate the contradictions.

Is there any contradiction between the modern universal phenomenon of globalization and the historically specific tradition of Islam? Kamal Pasha examines the link between globalization and cultural conflict in the Islamic Cultural Zones (ICZs) by recasting the discussion on the topic in more historical terms. Repudiating presentist understandings, he sees cultural conflicts as a product of the working of internal political dynamics within ICZs, intensified by neo-liberal globalizing trends. The tradition–modern dichotomy is rejected in favour of a more complex logic implicating the confluence of cultural and economic dispossession. Under neo-liberal dispensation, struggles between privilege and want increasingly appear as a clash of cultures. Hence, cultural survival and the quest for dignity are inextricably interwoven with growing social inequality between the beneficiaries of the neo-liberal order and its victims. The principal aim of Pasha's chapter is to contextualize the role of Islam in a broader socio-political framework, challenging standard accounts of religious resurgence in the ICZs.

Pasha observes that neo-liberal globalization considers rifts within Muslim society as an expression of cultural contestation between tradition and modernity or a confrontation between Islam and the West. Islamic resurgence is fundamentally a reaction to neo-liberal globalization even though the resurgence has pluralistic causalities including local politics and conditions. The prevailing antithesis between globalization and Islamic resurgence is the manifestation of a clash of civilizations between an explosively liberal and rather slowly progressing cultural entities in the Islamic zone. The attempt to dominate the primordial cultural matrix of Islam by the so-called materialistic civilization unleashed by neo-liberal globalization is the root cause of Islamic resurgence. The fragmentation of the civil society and cultural invasion in the name of homogenization during the period of globalization and the decoupling of identity and territory that provides Islamism its transnational appeal have been responsible largely for this upsurge, instigated by the philosophy of domination–subordination that goes hand-in-hand with the political economy of modern globalization. The clash of cultures is also embedded in the growing economic disparities, marginalization and exclusion of cultural groups in the process of globalization. The clash of cultures in the course of time leads to the clash of civilizations in many cases during the period of homogenization and integration. This is the thrust of Chapter 3.

Chapter 3 dwells on the broader perspective of nineteenth-century globalization and modern globalization and examines the current civilizational disharmony in the world in light of Huntington's claims of clash of civilizations. Halil Guven explains that civilizations have both social and material components and that these two equally important aspects of civilizations are not being kept in balance during the period of neo-liberal globalization. The author argues that industrialized Western civilizations have developed advanced material civilizations, amassing enormous amount of wealth and with it the potential to dominate other civilizations. He asserts that globalization is providing the mechanism for such domination and creating accumulated civilizational disharmony and clash. However, if the media tools of globalization are used to launch an inter-civilizational dialogue, many of its pernicious effects can be eradicated.

The global or Western culture that globalization espouses ushers in an era of unwanted modernism in the pre-capitalist traditional societies, which creates a disembedded system. The superimposition of global reality in the context of traditional or conservative actuality of many developing countries immediately creates a clash of interest that has given rise to different forms of protests including the Islamic resurgence and many other regional insurrections. Globalization involves two types of alienation for these marginal groups. First, they are not associated with the process of globalization and, secondly, domestic states undergo decomposition and cannot protect their interests, or are inimical to them. A large number of countries in Africa today are in this marginalized category. Modern globalization is not based on any normative or moral culture. It is neo-liberal and not democratic. Western cultural hegemony is against any form of religious ideals or traditional culture.

Globalization as a sort of cultural imperialism may not face open and bloody clashes in all cases, but there would be a deep and sustained undercurrent of conflict. Western domination is not liked even by some modernistic nations such as Japan. On a different plane, in the perspective of modern civilizational determinism, religion seems to be the focal points for conflicts in the global system. To avoid this clash of civilizations, the chapter suggests a better diagnosis of the problems at hand (e.g., full examination of the impact of globalization on civilizations and cultures); a better dialogue among civilizations on an equal footing, as opposed to monologue and dictation from one to another. The chapter examines the whole lot of issues in the historical as well as country-specific context by invoking the critical cultural and civilizational conflicts that globalization entails.

The superimposition of global reality in the context of traditional or conservative actuality of many developing countries immediately creates clashes of interest that give rise to different forms of protest including the Islamic resurgence and many other regional insurrections.

There is an inherent and serious contradiction accompanying the process of globalization in many developing nations. On the one hand, these nations have experienced significant rates of growth of GDP that, in turn, have increased the pace of privatization and sales of state-owned enterprises and assets, and declining (real) tax revenues, incomplete reforms, corruption and inappropriate accounting practices have lead to huge debts. The debts are incurred in order to modernize economies, to extend the rate of quantitative growth beyond what is warranted by domestic savings. The conditions imposed on borrowings from so-called international organizations have reduced the resources of the state, which has become financially weaker during the period of globalization, and independent policy-making seems to be impossible. Many state governments in these countries are finding it difficult to service their debts, forcing them to adopt severe austerity measures. This has an adverse impact on the provision of local goods and infrastructure in the urban areas. In most of the developing world there has emerged a widening gap between demand for and supply of infrastructural services in urban areas, for example, urban water supply, sanitation, roads, basic public health facilities, primary schooling, housing and so on. This severe shortage of urban local goods and services begins to look like an urban crisis that is partly a spin-off from the indebtedness of state governments that forces them to cut back on all local expenditures. The chapter argues that the source of urban crises is an incorrect tax scheme that is propelled by the electoral motive of local governments. Therefore, this chapter calls for reforms of property taxes, implementation of property rights and introduction of Tiebout-type competitive forces in the provision of local goods in developing nations.

While governments in LDCs are providing more facilities to the corporate sector to attract FDI, the local citizens are deprived of many necessary goods and services. Globalization has been accompanied by privatization, decentralization and devolution of gubernatorial activities to lower levels of government. Does a lower level of government mean better government? Gangopadhyay and Nath's chapter reveals three far-reaching impacts of globalization on sub-national governance and local public goods. First, they demonstrate how globalization has created serious indebtedness for sub-national governments in India. Secondly, they explain how lower levels of government have failed to provide the *minimal* local goods and infrastructure to their citizens. Thirdly, they show how the governments have become less able to follow independent and correct fiscal polices. The chapter argues that some kind of urban crisis has accompanied globalization. Some reforms are needed to deal with such a phenomenon, but this requires a strong state, which modern globalization precludes.

Labour market distortions and discrimination

Globalization has been responsible for changing the nature of employment, job conditionalities and wage structures around the world, particularly in LDCs. One of the key features of economic globalization is the change in labour market dynamics that not only affect employment but also the job security and reward pattern as risks shift from corporations to workers. The dynamics of this process have many consequences: (i) the informal economy expands regardless of a country's state of development; (ii) transnational migration – voluntary or forced – grows rapidly; and (iii) gains and losses are redistributed and workers have to bear the brunt.

As corporations make more profits, most workers – women and men – seek jobs that are less secure and pay less. Aslanbeigui and Summerfield's chapter focuses on the gender-related conflicts that are very conspicuous in the changing labour market conditions in the context of the off-shoring that globalization entails. Offshoring is more popularly known as outsourcing. Focusing on a few critical countries that are most likely to offshore jobs, with India and China as the most likely sourcing countries, they examine the reasons for job offshoring. The major part of the chapter, however, is concerned with the consequences of the phenomenon, identifying winners and losers and labour market conflicts. Special attention is paid to the gender impacts of offshoring. The chapter explains gender dimensions of the most recent source of conflict between workers and firms and among workers in different regions of the world – the expansion of offshore or cross-border employment in services. It concentrates on the gender impacts of these changes in the US and India, with references to China. Given the dynamic, and therefore uncertain, nature of future labour market outcomes, the authors highlight the need for gender-conscious measures that increase human security globally.

One of the implicit issues in labour market conflicts during the period of globalization is the problem of inequality. The problem of rising inequality in many parts of the world is indeed a serious one as analysed by Zhang and Zhang. Developing countries are increasingly concerned about the effects of globalization on regional inequality. A recent study by the World Bank also expresses concern over the growing income inequality in poor countries as a result of globalization. This reinforces Zhang and Zhang's conclusion that greater globalization of a country is associated with higher income inequality within the country, which may be a significant source of internal conflict. This chapter develops an empirical method for decomposing the contributions of two major driving forces of globalization, foreign trade and foreign direct investment (FDI), on regional inequality and applies it to China. Even after controlling for many other factors, globalization is still found to be an important factor contributing to widening regional inequality. The chapter ends by investigating the role of factor market segmentations in aggravating the distributional effect of changing regional comparative advantages in the process of globalization.

Chapter 6 reveals that the increasing trend of regional disparity can be largely explained by the uneven distribution of factors of production and variations in the degree of economic liberalization in the different regions of the country. Evidently in China both domestic and foreign capital investments have been concentrated in the more developed coastal region, which records a faster growth in these areas. The study by Zhang and Zhang finds that, in the context of globalization, FDI and trade have played critical roles that have changed the overall pattern of regional inequality in China. The finding of their study is in contrast to theoretical predictions of the standard trade theoretic model that implicitly assumes integrated factor markets. The empirical findings of the authors can be supported by the fact that China's factor markets are rather segmented and segregated. This is mainly the reason for the uneven distributions of gains of globalization among the various regions of the country, and the growth in regional inequality is the obvious outcome. It is not simply the income inequality that has increased during the period of globalization, the labour market has also structurally changed in the developing world.

Chapter 7 attempts to examine how global restructuring has impacted on labour markets in the North and the South. Its point of departure is that the era of globalization has been marked by a transformation from welfare to workfare. Schmidt argues that globalization has had a huge impact on the deregulation of labour markets, which to varying degrees can be interpreted as moving towards varieties of flexibility with a concomitant removal of workers' protection, a lowering of social protection and a weakening of labour unions. This also implies a loss of social cohesion and individualization of human security.

What we are witnessing is a transformation of work arrangements in the North with an accompanying loss of the social relevance of the work-place and of work-based social organizations. Another measure is the extent of so-called 'a-typical' work such as part-time employment, fixed-term contracts and sometimes also self-employment. The process of global restructuring has also witnessed the collapse of stable social structures and traditional institutions in both North and South. The new phase of globalization is associated with the rise of 'disorganized capitalism', 'post-industrialization', 'risk' or 'network' society, all of which draw upon the changing nature of work and labour markets and, in some cases, it has led to some degree of flexicurity.

In the South casual work might simply be the price paid for flexibility, and also here trade unions have lost bargaining power owing to a whole array of reasons and a continuation of the neo-liberal thrust towards reduced protective regulation (sometimes called labour market deregulation) is seemingly the result. At the same time, deregulation and the withdrawal of the state have created a new reserve army of unemployed workers and a new trend towards informalization of labour markets. The chapter concludes by discussing various conflicts and resistances towards the impact of neo-liberal globalization by highlighting examples from Brazil, India and South Korea.

Another view of the sad plight of labour is brought out by Ozay Mehmet. In Chapter 8 he complains that in the age of globalization, surprisingly little attention has been paid to the employment impact of the huge flow of capital and technology. While Western culture and technique have become more mobile globally, the economic welfare of populations in developing countries has fallen behind. Workers in particular should be among the first beneficiaries of increased liberalization in global markets. However, there is doubt that this is in fact occurring. This chapter uses empirical data from four Asian countries (China, Thailand, Singapore and the Philippines) to test the hypothesis that FDI causes a 'race to the bottom' (RTB), that is, a downward pressure on wages in both the host and home countries' labour markets. In the host country, employment expands at subsistence wage levels with 'bad jobs' becoming the norm. In the process, there is a global impoverization of workers as FDI operates as a corporate tool, squeezing labour at both the home and host country ends of the labour market. The test is centred on the elasticity of demand for labour, an increased elasticity coefficient implying that globalization led by multinational corporations (MNCs) and based on FDI has indeed relocated low-wage jobs from high income countries to labour-abundant countries. This empirical study based on some of the East Asian economies comes to the conclusion that because of globalization the demand for labour has become more elastic, and exploitation of labour has indeed increased in developing countries. Is the RTB evidence temporary? As Mehmet reflects, in a corporate strategy of maximizing global profits, there is no reason to show why the RTB will be self-adjusting. In other words, it may not automatically correct itself. FDI, as in the case of footloose industries, will simply move internationally across borders always attracted by the magnet of cheap labour at subsistence wage levels. The assumption is that globalization has escalated the labour market conflict and clashes of interest.

Capital, technology and finance

Modern globalization is neo-liberal and not based on equity and justice: the majority of peasants do not find their place in the expansion of dominant capitalist globalization. Needless to say, the Farm Bill in the United States and the agricultural policy of the European Union violate the basic principles that the WTO is trying to encourage. An important issue – the agrarian question – is often overlooked by critics of globalization. Samir Amin observes that the right to access farm land is the fundamental condition of the continued existence of a peasant society. In a capitalist system the ownership of land is often transferred through the market, as a result of which most of landowners who have to sell their land become proletariat emigrants to towns. It is indeed very unjust suddenly to dispossess the peasants who made a life-long investment in the improvement of their land. To consider land as a form of merchandise, or what is known as commodification of land in the current sense of the term, as is practised in capitalist regions, is to spread the policy of enclosures the world over. This practice is not something new but is increasing with the expansion of global capitalism. There should be an alternative to modern globalization which aggravates the agrarian question and creates conflicts among the peasants.

The chapter critically examines various systems of land tenures and land reforms from historical perspectives drawing examples from Asia, Africa, Soviet Russia and Latin America, and finds that the combination of subsistence farming and production only for exports means that peasants are paid almost nothing for their products. Globalization today generates a huge amount of profit from socially useless production that is not destined to meet the needs of hundreds of millions of hungry people. The collective imperialism in the name of globalization interprets land reforms to mean the acceleration of privatization of land and nothing more. Indeed, privatization and marketization principles of globalization have brought havoc even to the most prosperous East Asian economies in the form of financial crisis.

In Chapter 10 Ghosh argues that global financial crises that occurred in the last part of 1990s were due to many factors that could be associated with globalization. Given the menu of globalization, financial crisis can be shown to be induced by such a system in developing economies. By examining the problem of East Asian economies in this context the chapter explains that dependent-type capitalism was mainly responsible for the financial crisis in these countries. Capital market liberalization was not necessary for these economies; they could have otherwise sustained a fairly high growth rate with their high savings rate. However, for the purpose of a very high quantitative growth rate, the required investment in excess of domestic saving was obtained by these countries through foreign borrowing, and they became heavily indebted. Borrowing was high because of the loan-pushing type of lending strategy operated by the international financial institutions. All these economies opened their capital account before reforming the financial sector and without strengthening the banking sector. Capital market liberalization is rather dangerous for nascent economies. Because of lack of proper knowledge about sterilization, the East Asian economies could not make their monetary policy effective and the money supply expanded beyond the warranted level. Excessive and unregulated capital inflow produced many types of macroeconomic vulnerabilities, such as high debt/reserve ratio, higher deficit in the current account and appreciation of the real exchange rate. The appreciation of the real exchange rate reduced exports, which aggravated the macroeconomic vulnerabilities and financial crisis was the natural outcome.

Increased capital inflow augmented capital intensity in production that possibly reduced employment and wages. Moreover, by increasing the production of exportables, higher capital inflow put the terms of trade against these countries, which led to the situation of immiserizing growth. A good amount of capital inflow in such countries was accompanied by hot money that contributed to short-term speculative bubbles; the bubbles burst with the sudden outflow of that money. The IMF put pressure on these countries for capital market liberalization, claiming that it increases economic stability. When these economies faced financial turmoil, the IMF advised them to raise the interest rate, and this erroneous advice converted the recession into a full-blown crisis. The Asian financial crisis teaches us a couple of lessons that are worth remembering in the days of neo-liberal globalization: first, capital market liberalization is not generally needed to obtain FDI for a country which has achieved macroeconomic stability (as in the case of China); and secondly, FDI is not necessarily beneficial all the time for all types of countries. The MNCs that provide FDI are also the agents of technology transfer.

For LDCs technology transfer in the framework of globalization involves a number of adverse effects, ranging from negative terms of trade changes to adoption of distorted specialization models based on a permanent catching-up process with technologies devised and produced by MNCs for the needs of developed countries (DCs). Praussello makes it clear that the clash of interests between MNCs and foreign investment host countries is inevitable. On the one hand, MNCs need to have full control of their proprietor technological competitive advantage, in many ways restricting technology transfers and maintaining LDCs locked in a low-level technology trap, simply imitating their dismissed outdated technologies. On the other hand, domestic firms and governments in host countries have an interest in building up an independent technological capability, at the same time raising the quality of their human capital stock as a prerequisite for the former. Moreover, they need to upgrade local technology levels by absorbing more sophisticated technologies from foreign investors through a number of means ranging from reverse engineering to shared ownership. Other sources of conflicts between MNCs and partner firms include choices in input levels and profit shares, decisions on company names, composition of the board of directors, locations of headquarters, and so on.

The model of incomplete technology transfer channelled to LDCs by globalized FDI flows does not allow the bridging of the technology divide. Technological convergence cannot occur owing to the overwhelming role played by MNCs, which hamper the building up of an autonomous technological base in LDCs and hinder their process of learning-by-doing. Also, without independent technological choices and skills the absorptive capability remains low and so too is the effective technology transfer. In a model where LDCs are condemned to imitate MNC technologies without being able to innovate them, the catching up will never end, as the latter will be always at least a stage ahead on the technology frontier. It is generally conceded that the question of technology is enmeshed with the issue of trade, and in this context, the role of WTO seems to be relevant.

The negative role of the World Trade Organization (WTO) is analysed by Raj Kumar Sen. The WTO is planning for an international order in which there would be more freedom for the MNCs and the intervention by the developing countries would be gradually minimized. The powerful trading nations are more likely to influence the policies of the WTO in their favour. Such countries have already started using trade sanctions and other retaliatory measures in the settlement of trade disputes. The attempt to introduce international labour standards for poor countries is by itself a deliberate policy to reduce the comparative advantages of these LDCs. The WTO is being used by the DCs as a powerful instrument to further the cause of MNC-led globalization by making a formal explicit agreement among the member countries to the effect that transnational corporations will have the power to enter and establish themselves in any sector of any member country, and that they should be treated on a par with national companies without any discrimination. Thus, in its new role to regulate and guide the investment policy of MNCs, the WTO will help the DCs not only in the matter of trade but also in locating and dislocating investment in LDCs. The new investment policy is a reflection of the fact that globalization will make the domestic state weaker and helpless in controlling many critical macro variables.

The proposed policy of tariff-free trade by the WTO will also jeopardize the agricultural and industrial sectors of many LDCs that are much less efficient than their DC trade partners. The WTO aims at accelerating globalization that will favour the strong, if left completely dependent on the market mechanism. The gains from trade have been distributed unevenly and primarily in favour of the rich, adversely affecting the poor. All these have led to conflicts of interests both among and within the countries urgently calling for a reform of the WTO rules, which were initially framed by the rich countries and which contained many clauses and provisions not favourable to the low-income economies. The basic objectives of Sen's analysis are to : (a) trace the origin of trade-related conflicts observed in some selected countries during the last decade; (b) identify the clauses of the WTO which are specially unfavourable to the interests of developing countries; and (c) suggest a set of reforms for the WTO in the coming decades that can ensure a true level playing-field for all countries of the world according to their relative economic strengths and weaknesses.

One of the agendas of the WTO is to liberalize further the speed of trade between developed and developing countries. However, such a line of action, as A.K. Dutt explains, may exacerbate the conflicts between the North and the South. Over the last several decades the world has experienced what many have called a process of globalization, reflected in economic terms in increased trade, capital flows and technology transfers. It was hoped by many that all these would shower benefits on all countries, especially developing countries, by allowing them to increase economic efficiency and growth, and also especially by promoting labour-intensive export growth to create employment to reduce poverty. Despite these hopes, however, globalization has given rise to many problems that have resulted in actual and potential conflicts between rich and poor countries.

Chapter 13 examines such problems and conflicts by focusing mainly on the developing countries. It discusses theoretical models of poor countries and the global economy to show how trade liberalization can contribute to development problems in developing countries, and increase the development gap between rich and poor countries. It discusses the empirical evidence of the effects of trade liberalization for poor countries and for international inequality. It reviews historical patterns in trade policy to examine the forces behind trade liberalization in the past. Finally, it explores the institutional aspects of international trading arrangements to examine how trade liberalization in practice creates biases against poor countries.

Globalization leads to higher income elasticity of import of the South from the North due to trade liberalization. Capital inflows that follow an open trade regime may lead to a number of unwanted consequences likely to adversely affect wages and employment in LDCs. If capital inflow increases the production of exportables in the South, the terms of trade may go against these countries. Dutt analyses the reasons why trade has not been serving as the engine of growth in the LDCs during the period of globalization and why such countries are becoming losers, pinpointing the areas of present and future conflicts between DCs and LDCs in the realm of trade interactions.

The disadvantage faced by developing countries in international trade agreements has been characterized as an over-emphasis on industrial trade and a failure of market access arrangements for agricultural produce. An Agreement on Agriculture in the final round of the GATT and a new emphasis on agricultural 'market access' in the WTO's 'Doha Round' were said to be important means of addressing this disadvantage. These arguments were made most strongly by the grain-exporting member countries of the Cairns Group, such as Australia. However tensions within the 18-member Cairns Group have drawn attention to two major problems with this approach. Tim Anderson's analysis is basically concerned with those problems.

First, the 'market access' negotiations have confronted an intransigent, practical barrier. The agricultural protection of the wealthy countries (especially the EU and the USA) has switched into subsidy instruments that are immune to bilateral agreements and effectively quarantined in multilateral negotiations. In contrast, tariffs, the major 'currency' of all 'free trade' agreements, are still heavily relied upon by the developing countries both for revenue and the protection of domestic production. Wealthy states have had the capacity to remain two steps ahead in the game of international trade regulation. Weaker states cannot afford to compete. Secondly, the globalization of agricultural markets has raised new food security dilemmas for developing countries. If domestic food production is smashed by a flood of cheap imports from large scale and heavily subsidized agribusiness, large amounts of foreign exchange will be required simply to replace subsistence food production. Most wealthy and poor countries want to stabilize domestic production as the central component of a food security strategy. However, few possess the capacity for expensive policies of subsidy and infrastructure, which can circumvent the new global trade regulation.

These twin dilemmas of the globalization of agricultural trade – the differential impact of trade regulation and the intensification of food security concerns – have led to conflicts within the Cairns Group (e.g. between Indonesia and Australia) and recriminations within trade blocs (e.g. between Mexico and the USA). Developing countries want to pursue 'market access' opportunities, but not surrender the right to stabilize domestic food production. Agricultural liberalization seems to have stalled at the WTO and new clarion calls for 'food sovereignty' threaten to reconstitute presumptions about the globalization of agricultural trade.

Part I

Clashes, Conflicts and Contradictory Dynamics

1
The Contradictory Dynamics of Globalization

Phillip Anthony O'Hara

Recent decades have seen a greater globalization of economic affairs throughout most of the world. More and more people are going overseas for holidays or work commitments. Businesses can more easily trade goods, while services such as education are increasingly being bought and sold internationally. Capital controls have been mostly demolished and banks more footloose. Businesses are being integrated through transnational commodity chains and production networks. National tax rates are coming into line with the global average as governments encourage firms to move into local areas. Even governance has been taking a global twist through the recent advent of the World Trade Organization, the World Economic Forum and the G-8 power system. The Internet has made these global activities easier through cheap and easy communication and information.

This globalization trend is not universal, though, as many things are still decidedly national, regional and local. While people may holiday and work overseas, much less often do they migrate to a distant location. Many national governments make it difficult for them to immigrate for fear of foreigners, declining GDP per capita, and diminishing quality of life. There are also considerable spatial limits to globalization, since many services – such as haircuts and restaurant meals – are done almost entirely with local content. In many countries there are denser communication and travel linkages locally and nationally than globally, mainly due to cultural, habitual and spatial factors. Indeed, in many nations and areas cultural, local and national relationships are still strong.

Nevertheless, the global trend is a reality and continuing on many fronts. In numerous ways, globalization is not a bad thing. Being able to visit a relative or friend overseas can be a good experience. Being able to buy a better and cheaper commodity overseas reduces the budget constraint and improves overall utility. Operating through a foreign bank may make our global purchases and sales easier and less complex. Having global business networks make the sourcing of production inputs and markets more reliable and long-lasting. Creating global governance institutions can improve the flow of goods and money, but also lessen conflict and poverty. Indeed, isn't a global world working in harmony and peace, with few ethnic or racial tensions, and better communication with all cultures, an ideal that we should all work towards?

This is no doubt true. But to see globalization as a purely positive experience for all may be utopian rather than realistic. After all, there are different ways of propelling globalization and some may be better than others. Since the 1970s, globalization has especially taken a decidedly neo-liberal turn, meaning that it has been undertaken with a view to enhancing the power of capital vis-à-vis labor; promoting the power of business rather than domestic culture; stimulating finance more than workmanship; accelerating production rather than protecting the environment; advancing the interests of the US and its allies rather than the Middle East, Africa and Latin America; stimulating competition more than demand and markets; and propagating unproductive rather than productive government activities. In short, the way in which globalization has been undertaken is not neutral, but often seeks to advance certain vested interests at the expense of the common good. The dominant institutions advancing neo-liberal globalization are thus imbued with internal contradictions that variously promote and inhibit socio-economic and politico-cultural progress. This chapter seeks to demystify these contradictions, and illustrate how it is possible to see either the positives (as many do) or negatives (as their opponents do), when one should recognize that these positives and negatives are inextricably linked.

The dominant contradictions

In political economy contradictions are institutional processes imbued with both positive and negative outcomes. They are contradictory because the positive and negatives are endogenously fused into the fabric of the system. Reducing the extent of the negatives may also reduce the extent of the positives, under certain conditions. In the global economy, rapid levels of innovation are generally regarded as a positive aspect of neo-liberal globalization. Deregulating the system and reducing spatial limits to the expansion of capital may enable the revolutionary dynamic of the system to march forward through new processes, products, markets, sources of raw material and competitive forms (Schumpeter 1911: 35). We are thus able to potentially benefit from the Internet, mobile phones, more complex computers, and complex accounting systems that may make life easier and more pleasurable for hundreds of millions of people.

Greater innovation may also enable prices to decline, inflation to moderate, interest rates to fall and world trade to grow. Indeed, those who sing the praises of neo-liberal globalization show evidence for precisely this pattern of growth and development in the world economy (e.g., Weede 2004, Grennes 2003). Typical data supporting this argument are shown in Table 1.1 from well-known sources.

Adherents of the globalized free market believe that progress has been enhanced by enabling the process of creative destruction to work unhindered. Penetrating the global economy through declining tariffs and subsidies has enabled world trade to expand. Keeping a tight rein on government activities and money supply has supposedly lowered inflation from the high rates of the 1970s to very moderate rates in the 2000s. Declining inflation has enabled interest rates to fall from the highs of the 1980s to very low rates in the 2000s. Adjusting the policy parameters to support intellectual property rights in a global economy has stimulated innovation in the communications industry (e.g., Internet services,

Table 1.1   Positive performance indicators, global economy, 1970s–2000s

	1970s	1980s	1990s	2000s
Internet users (millions)[a]	0.00	0.00	0.07 (1990)	501 (2001)
Cell phone users (per 1000 population)[a]	0.00	0.00	6.00 (1992)	157 (2001)
Global inflation (Consumer Price Index; annual average; weighted)[b]	10.4 (1975)	5.21 (1985)	2.51 (1995)	2.32 (2004)
World real interest rate[b]	−1.3 (1975)	5.72 (1985)	4.32 (1995)	2.70 (2004)
World trade volume trend growth (average annual)[b]		6.0 (1970–9)	6.32 (1980–9)	6.81 (1990–9) 7.42 (2000–03)

Source: Adapted from (a) World Bank (2005); (b) IMF (2004: 6).

cell phones and entertainment). More favorable trade, inflation, interest rates and innovation are thus natural results of neo-liberal globalization, according to most free market adherents.

Neo-liberal economists and policy-makers do tend, however, to ignore the destructive elements of creative destruction. Promoting neo-liberal globalization may well stimulate innovation, help to reduce prices and inflation plus enhance global trade and innovation. Innovation by its very nature, however, creates redundant skills, requires that people move to other areas and nations in search of employment and business, and provides those better at competing in the global market place with greater income, wealth and power. Innovation has a tendency to increase the need for people to upgrade their skills, reorganize their business, change to another industry or area, and follow market trends wherever possible.

Through creative destruction neo-liberal globalization not only promotes positives, but also leads to many negatives that are the natural outcome of the positive growth trends. It is very difficult to instigate changes that support all interests, since every change is usually a cost to some party. And when the dominant powers put forward changes usually the parties not advantaged have neither the knowledge nor the power to argue their case. Typically, neo-liberal theories of globalization do not take into account the lags between destruction of jobs and skills and the creation of new ones for those who lose out. They tend to assume that the world is fairly symmetrical and that the positives will benefit people in a balanced fashion.

More seriously, though, the creation of markets and new products often occur through the destruction of non-market relations. Global capitalism typically works through creating goods and services that used to be produced in the home, so that the decline in family function is not included in the statistics. Household or informal workers moving into the official work-place create a substitute value to those goods and services that previously were produced informally. Rural workers who move to the city buy things in the market that they used to produce outside the market. Creating goods and services in industry promotes more concentrated forms of pollution that previously were either absent or diffuse. People who used to communicate and socialize locally now often work in far away markets, leading to a destruction of local networks and relationships.

All of these destructive elements are typically not included in the analysis of those who support neo-liberal globalization (Fukuda-Parr 2003). Historically they have been the concern of sociologists, political economists, ecologists and psychologists who are left to analyse the resulting disjointed communities, alienated and disturbed individuals and polluted environments. There are very few traditions that specialize in comprehending these positive *and* negative elements, in order to gain a holistic vision of how the global system operates. Political economy is the main such tradition, for it has been able to develop theories about such contradictory processes.

From a political economy perspective the dominant contradictions of neo-liberal globalization are illustrated in Figure 1.1. Eight contradictions are displayed that emanate from the primary one of heavily deregulated markets failing to fulfill the conditions necessary for long-term survival of social economies. This is none other than Karl Polanyi's (1944) hypothesis of the disembedded economy, which states that a society *dominated* by relations of buying and selling commodities in 'free markets' is unable to suitably reproduce itself through long historical time. This is due to insufficient reciprocity and redistribution, or to put it in modern parlance, inadequate social and public capital to support the

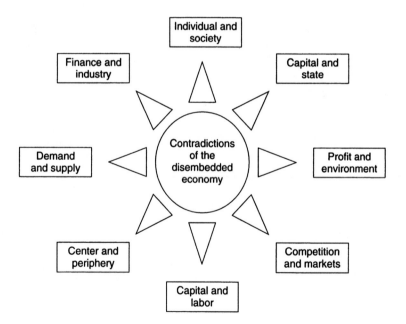

Figure 1.1 Dominant contradictions of neo-liberal globalization

various public goods or system functions of stability, conflict resolution and social infrastructure. When a society is dominated by commodity markets it tends to lack public goods such as lender of last resort facilities, demand management tools, aggregate demand, prudential functions, job security, financial stability, conflict resolution, work-injury compensation, trust and association, environmental sustainability, and ethics and values.

Polanyi argued that market capitalism experiences a contradictory 'dual movement': it undergoes periodic waves of free markets, followed by attempts at social protection, followed by deregulation, and so on ad infinitum. The dominant trend for free market capitalism is to create markets and expand its sphere of influence. However, there is no automatic mechanism protecting the system from the ravages of stimulating anonymous purchase and sale relationships. Various 'protective responses' are required to ensure long-term relationships of trust and association that are not automatically created through market processes. If Polanyi is right, then this would help explain the evolutionary movements from the version of free market capitalism typical of the 1920s and 1930s to the more protected Keynesian welfare state of the 1950s, 1960s and early 1970s, through to the phase of neo-liberal globalization into the 1980s, 1990s and 2000s.

Human society is thus likely to see historical waves of free markets followed by social protection as the market tendency is periodically countered by embedded institutions. Such institutions vary according to the situation, but typically include organizational arrangements to create barriers to free markets destroying networks, relationships and associations. Polanyi's perspective is a powerful tool for comprehending the historical contradictions of market society. It enables one to see neo-liberal globalization as a free market response to what was perceived as the over-regulated system of the early 1970s throughout much of the world. The dominance of the free market ideology since then has reduced protective responses to such an extent as to endanger the long-term reproduction of market capitalism. Hence the emergence in the 1990s and early 2000s throughout the world-system of major financial crises, deep recessions, corporate accounting crises, accelerated global tension, and potential environmental catastrophe. The disembedded economy is well in place, although challenges are emerging to its form of governance, including its theoretical edifice such as neo-liberal and neo-classical perspectives.

The notion of the disembedded economy is central to an understanding of the contradictions of global capitalism and links to various problems in all areas of the social economy. Figure 1.1 illustrates how the disembedded economy links to anomalies such as the contradictions between core and periphery, demand and supply, competition and markets, capital and labor, capital and the state, finance and industry, profit and environment, plus individual and society. The next section details many of these specific contradictions and presents empirical material to illustrate how they are impacting on the world.

Specific contradictions of neo-liberal globalization

Perhaps the best way to illustrate how the contradictions have impacted on the socio-economic performance of the regions and continents of the world is to start with some general problems and then introduce more specific and sectoral limitations of neo-liberal globalization. The first very apparent general problem relates to the inability of recent trends of neo-liberal globalization to re-establish anything like the performance record of the 1950s and 1960s. It needs to be recognized that the neo-liberal global trend was introduced and deepened in order to make an impact on the critical variables of growth and development. Starting in Table 1.2 with the growth rate of GDP per capita, this trend has to be seen as a failure. The pattern here is fairly obvious. Global growth per capita has been cut in half from the long-wave upswing of 1950–1973 through to the downswing of 1973-2001. Furthermore, the record for 1990–2001 was significantly worse than 1980–1990. This trend of deteriorating performance is apparent for the advanced capitalist nations of Europe, North America and Japan. The pattern of growth is far worse in Africa and Eastern Europe, where growth rates have dropped during the downswing to negative figures compared with much better growth

Table 1.2 Growth of real GDP per capita in the global economy

	World	Advanced capitalist nations	Latin America	Africa	Eastern Europe	Asia (excluding Japan)
1950–73	2.93	3.72	2.52	2.07	3.49	2.92
1973–2001	1.43	1.98[a]	1.08	−0.38	−1.10[a]	3.54[a]
1980–90	1.43	2.67	−0.77	−1.09	1.60	6.8[b]
1990–2001	1.13	1.77[a]	1.64	−0.24	−2.26[a]	4.2[b]

Note: (a) 1973–2000 or 1990–2000; (b) Newly industrialized Asian nations only.
Sources: Adapted from Maddison (2000: 126, 129); World Bank (2005).

in the upswing. Latin American growth during 1973–2001 is about one-third the record of 1950–1973, although the 1990–2001 record – mostly *before* the crises of 2001–04 – was better than the 1980s. Looking at most of the regions of the world, then, the current free market, global tendency has either failed to sustain performance or more likely had a negative impact since for most areas things have actually gotten worse. A deeper investigation of the economic performance of global capitalism reinforces the point that, even in areas where neo-liberalism prides itself as a progressive force, it has failed as a governance system. The reasons for growth failing to improve are simply that there have been deteriorating levels of productivity, investment and profit. Table 1.3, reveals the across-the-board inability of the major variables to improve in recent years. The data reveal that global business investment demand growth has deteriorated over successive recent decades from the highs of the long-wave upswing of the 1950s and 1960s. Productivity has also moved downwards over this period as the innovations of recent decades have failed to enhance macro and global value added growth. Not surprisingly, the rate of profit for the largest 500 US corporations has been declining at a similar rate to investment and productivity. Global GDP growth has thus deteriorated due to the inability to propel sufficient investment, productivity and profit in most regions and continents.

To comprehend this performance failure it helps to investigate the matter within a Kaldorian framework of circular and cumulative causation. A stylized view of this is illustrated in Figure 1.2. The Kaldorian framework is one of circular and cumulative causation, in the sense that all the variables are endogenously interrelated and thereby co-determine

Table 1.3 Global investment, productivity, profit and GDP, 1950s–2000s (decade annual averages)

	1950s	1960s	1970s	1980s	1990s	2000–02
Real global investment growth rate[a]	n.a.	7.78	3.97	3.24	2.24	2.1
Global industry value added growth[a]	n.a.	n.a.	3.36	2.59	1.92	n.a.
US largest 500 TNCs profit rate[b]	7.71	7.15	6.30	5.30	4.02	3.30
Real per capita global GDP growth[b]	n.a.	3.19	2.11	1.27	1.05	1.00

Source: Adapted from (a) World Bank (2005), (b) *Fortune* Magazine (1955–2005).

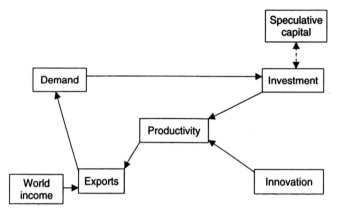

Figure 1.2 SPD and Kaldorian dyamics of cumulative causation

each other. Demand and supply are not independent but interdependent. Nevertheless, there are some causal processes involved, the critical one being the *institutional environment* underlying investment demand, since the prevailing business climate is the main factor determining long-term aggregate demand (and hence supply). Uncertainty as to the future of prospective yield relative to supply price is the main factor (negatively) determining investment demand. It is thus an institutional demand-oriented model. Yet it perfectly explains the current global environment where global demand is inhibited by the uncertainties that pervade the neo-liberal governance system. A high level of uncertainty about profit levels in multiple markets leads to low rates of investment, including a misallocation of resources to unproductive speculation, even as the proportion of investment directed to innovation is historically higher than average. This inhibits endogenous productivity, and thereby lowers export and world demand, leading to further rounds of low aggregate demand and investment.

This is simply another way of saying that prospective global markets are relatively thin, which leads to a bearish business environment. For instance, globally, markets are not opening up fast enough. Currently the major new markets are East Asia (especially China), and Central Europe. Latin America, sub-Saharan Africa, the Middle East, Eastern Europe (especially Russia and the Ukraine), Europe and North America are not opening or growing fast enough to sustain the system. Globally there are insufficient new markets for long-wave upswing. Most of the major markets of the world depend on penetrating the global economy, but not every market can succeed in a global system when national and regional conditions of demand are faltering. Global neo-liberalism is relying on supply conditions to enhance markets, including the cost of labor, raw materials, and technological conditions. This, however, is a recipe for stagnation when internal demand is faltering (and some supply conditions are tightening, such as oil). Hence the contradiction of insufficient global aggregate demand and over-supply, which in a circular and cumulative fashion have been inhibiting global performance for several decades now.

This general contradiction between demand and supply manifests in various forms through the world economy. For instance, it variously establishes certain asymmetric power and accumulation dynamics between center and periphery. This is currently manifesting in the global economy through deteriorating relative conditions in Africa, the Middle East, Eastern Europe and to some degree Latin America. Peripheral nations that institutionalized neo-liberal globalization have been unable to establish strong connections to the dominant production networks and commodity chains. The advanced capitalist nations have generally also seen a relative deterioration in their economic power in the world economy as East Asian nations have taken the initiative. This East Asian initiative has taken the form of a balance between markets and industry-social policy that recognizes the potential problems of the disembedded economy.

There is also the contradiction between *innovation and competition*. The neo-Schumpeterian process in favor of competition and innovation says that the capitalist system will tend to be dynamic and forward-looking since competition and innovation are inherent aspects of its motion. Innovation will generally follow high levels of competition, leading to high growth and accumulation. The establishment of few barriers to the advancement of capital will lead to dynamically competitive markets, and this competition will create high levels of innovation, out of sheer necessity for firm survival. Firms that cannot create new products, processes, markets, reorganizations and sources of raw materials will be driven out of the market, whereas firms that are able to lead the pack will generate high profits and investment. The theory says that this dialectic of competition → innovation → competition will enable profits to be high enough to sustain the system in the long term.

There are, though, sharp limits to the extent that this competition-innovation dialectic sustains profitability and growth in the current neo-liberal system of globalization. We scrutinize this through the rate of profit: more precisely the after-tax profit divided by the value of tangible corporate assets (times 100). According to Dennis Mueller (1990), the rate of profit (π_{it}) is equal to a competitive rate of return (πc_{it}) plus a permanent rent for specific firms (πr_{it}) and a short-run rent (πs_{it}):

$$\pi_{it} = \pi c_{it} + \pi r_{it} + \pi s_{it}$$

where the competitive rate of return (πc_{it}) may be approximated by the yield on long-term government bonds (γg_t) (Kessides 1990). The rate of profit for the largest 500 US transnational (TN) corporations is now compared with the yield on 10-year US Treasury Bonds for the period 1954–2002 in Table 1.4.[1] This data shows the degree to which monopoly profits – above-normal competitive rents – are generated to sustain profit and growth among the major US transnational corporations. Here the evidence is clear that monopoly profits were high during the 1950s and 1960s but declined markedly during the 1970s–2000s. A slight improvement is evident for the 1990s and 2000s, but this is due entirely to the declining rate of inflation. Generally, the profit rate is poor because of a combination of excess competition, lack of markets, and deep recessions. (Similar profit results are shown during the 1980s–2000s for the 500 largest global corporations; see O'Hara 2006.)

Global competition has thus been inhibiting profit and growth since industry needs some degree of dynamic monopoly profit to promote investment. The myth that competition itself will promote innovation and (especially) profit does not seem to be happening in the current

Table 1.4 After tax rate of profit of the largest 500 US (TN) corporations, annual averages (decade by decade) 1954–2002

Years	Raw profit rate figures[a]	Profit rate adjusted for data revision (π)	Yield on 10-year US Treasury Bonds[b] (γg)	Above normal competitive rents $(\pi - \gamma g)$ (monopoly profit rate)
2000–02	1.32	3.30	5.22	−1.92
1990–99	2.29	4.02	6.66	−2.64
1980–89	5.30	5.30	10.60	−5.30
1970–79	6.30	6.30	7.49	−1.19
1960–69	7.15	7.15	5.11	+2.04
1954–59	7.71	7.71	3.01	+4.70

Note: This table shows profit after taxes, after extraordinary credits, and after cumulative effects of accounting changes, divided by corporate assets.
Source: Adapted from (a) Fortune Magazine (1955–2003); (b) Federal Reserve System (2000, 2003, 2005).

global environment. At least a limited degree of monopoly power is needed for firms to protect themselves from the market. Over-supply of commodities due to competition and inadequate demand are the principal corporate anomalies inhibiting performance in the global economy. Linked to this equation is the *contradiction between capital and the state*. Business seldom trusts a strong state, since it sometimes fails to entirely support business interests narrowly defined, and often looks after the general interests of business, or even workers and society. During the 1950s and 1960s state finances expanded three-fold through most advanced nations of the world. Changes during the Second World War increased the taxing power of governments, and during the postwar (1950s-early 1970s) long boom it increased responsibility for social security, education, utilities, infrastructure, health and macro-stabilization. Initially this seemed to benefit both business and labor, but with the global problems of the 1970s, business and governments began to reverse the tide of state power. Initially advanced nations but gradually virtually all nations began to take steps to privatize state enterprises, reduce welfare payments, lessen red-tape, and expand corporate self-regulation or no regulation. Similarly most controls in factor markets were dismantled and capital was given a free rein mostly devoid of hindrance.

This has had a major impact on international performance. Globally, neo-liberalism has seen an expansion of unproductive state spending on military industries plus subsides and transfer payments. The productive areas of education, health, infrastructure and communications have collectively declined relative to GDP. According to Christian Weber (2000), this has *more* than explained the low-growth experience of the US since the 1970s, while other studies draw similar conclusions from developed and developing nations. The empirical evidence drawn from a study of 74–95 nations, for instance, shows that 'Government investment does indeed appear as an important factor in growth, with a significant estimated coefficient in most specifications' while 'Government investment has been severely suboptimal in [the] recent international experience and ... scope remains for greater productive expenditures by the government sector' (Miller and Tsoukis 2001: 1125). This decline in productive public capital is a major problem and needs to be reversed to promote long-term progress in the global economy.

The *contradiction between finance and industry* is especially important in this neo-liberal context. Historically there has been a tension between the workings of stockmarkets/financial systems and production/growth.

As Karl Marx, Thorstein Veblen, Joseph Schumpeter and John Maynard Keynes all recognized, industry and workmanship are the productive activities that require *support* from the relatively unproductive activities of finance. If industry slightly dominates finance, systemic growth and accumulation is strong, but if finance dominates industry then major problems emerge, such as speculative bubbles, excess speculation, and deep recession or depression.

However, with the onset of economic problems into the 1970s, relative industrial dominance diminished through financial deregulation in the advanced nations through to the 1980s; then in less developed ones in the late-1980s and 1990s. Finance had come to dominate industry, leading to successive speculative bubbles and deep recession – first in the late 1980s/early 1990s in the advanced nations; secondly in Asia and some emerging/transitional economies in the mid–late 1990s; and thirdly in many advanced and developing nations in the early 2000s. (Notable cases of public violence and revolt emerged in some developing nations as a result.) Financial instability has thus become institutionalized, as Table 1.5 indicates. This illustrates that banking crises have become more frequent during the 1980s and 1990s. The first period of deregulation in the advanced nations led to greater instability in the 1980s, while the 1980s deregulation in developing and transitional nations led to further instability in the 1990s. Finance currently dominates industry and the social economy has become disembedded through an inability to generate sufficient productive industry and workmanship. Financial incentives are stronger than industrial pursuits through the deregulation process. Binswanger (2000), Arestis et al. (2001) and Stockhammer (2004) are unable to identify speculative finance as a

Table 1.5 Domestic banking crises in the world: 1970s, 1980s, 1990s: percentage of all crises during 1970–1999

	1970s–1990s	1970s	1980s	1990s
Industrial nations	26	4	11	11
Developing nations	55	2	25	28
Transitional nations	20	0	0	20
Percentage	100	6	35	59

Note: Figures may not add up to whole numbers due to rounding.
Source: Adapted from the data in Herrero and Rio (2003).

positive influence on business investment as there is little relationship between financial and industrial activity during the 1980s and 1990s (compared with the 1950s and 1960s) in many nations. A prime contradiction of neo-liberal globalization is that between *profit and the environment*. Neo-liberalism has led to fewer controls on capital, including fewer safeguards against pollution, especially in the major polluting nations such as the US, Russia and parts of Asia. Globalization has seen an expansion of capital and its polluting industries and products to new regions such as China and Russia, which has led to more motor vehicle pollution, deforestation and wetland destruction. The major polluting country, the US, refuses to sign the Kyoto Protocol and seeks to expand oil, gas and mineral production in formerly protected areas as the neo-conservatives take hold in Washington. The process of creating new products and innovations along established lines of energy create the *potential* for greater profit and accumulation at the expense of environmental protection. Under neo-liberal rule environmental protection is minimal. There is thus a trade-off between profit and the environment, and in the current environment the emphasis is on attempting to re-establish levels of profit and accumulation at the expense of the environment.

Table 1.6 illustrates the major global environmental trends over recent decades. Global atmospheric concentrations of carbon dioxide have expanded progressively especially through the 1980s, 1990s and 2000s; global warming has become a more serious concern; and ozone levels have decreased at an alarming rate. The contradiction between environmental protection and profit/business is thus a critical problem as the public goods of a clean climate, species survival and relative climate stability have deteriorated in the pro-business global economy. Greenhouse gases are likely to get worse, global warming to expand, species habitat and biodiversity to decline even further. A major problem is the ideology of weak sustainability, where it is acceptable to trade off lower levels of ecological capital for higher levels of physical and human capital. This leads in the long run to lower levels of well-being as the declining stock of ecological capital leads to fewer species, more overcrowding, greater levels of stress and inferior quality of life (Brown 2002). The long-term viability of ecological capital thus requires that we transcend deregulated markets.

Lastly, a central aspect of the disembedded economy is the *contradiction between individual and society*. When individualism becomes dominant, society is adversely affected. Neo-liberal globalization sings the praises of individualism – that we should look at the material and

Table 1.6 Global environmental decline: carbon dioxide concentration, temperature, and ozone concentration, 1960–2000

	1960	*1970*	*1980*	*1990*	*2000*
Atmospheric concentration of CO_2[a] (ppm; Mauna Loa Observatory data)	317	326	339	354	369
Global temperature change[b] (compared with 1961–90 average)	0 (1960)	−0.05 (1970)	+0.12 (1980)	+0.26 (1990)	+0.38 (2000)
Ozone concentration in Antarctica[b] (Dobson units; October)	293 (1960)	276 (1970)	227 (1980)	172 (1990)	135 (2000)

Source: Adapted from (a) EarthTrends (2002); (b) Meadows et al. (2005).

economic benefits for ourselves, and that this will promote economic performance via the invisible hand. Completely ignored in this ideology are the adverse effects of strong individualism, including a breakdown in society, the inability of people to trust one another, and a decline in nurturance and love (Stanfield and Stanfield 1997). It is essential for a dynamic balance to exist between individualism and concern for others, where people have a moderate level of sociality and trust in their dominant institutions and practices.

Table 1.7 illustrates the degree to which the global society has been in disarray through low declining levels of trust over the past two decades. This shows the results of the World Values Survey for the 'four

Table 1.7 Levels of trust: the world and various nations, percentage that thinks 'people can be trusted', 1981–82, 1990–91, 1995–96, 1999–2001

	World	*UK*	*US*	*Argentina*	*Brazil*	*South Africa*	*Russia*	*Poland*
1981–82	38.4	43.3	40.5	26.1	n.a.	29.0	n.a.	n.a.
1990–91	34.6	43.7	51.1	23.3	6.5	29.1	37.5	34.5
1995–96	24.3	29.1	35.9	17.6	2.8	15.4	23.2	16.9
1999–2001	27.5	28.9	36.3	15.9	n.a.	13.2	24.0	18.4

Source: Adapted from the ISR (2000, 2004).

waves' (interview periods) of 1981–82, 1990–91, 1995–96 and 1999–2001. People from approximately 60 nations were asked to respond whether 'most people can be trusted?' or alternatively whether 'you need to be very careful' with people.[2] The international results for the four periods show that the percentage replying that people can be trusted declined from 38 percent to 25 percent to 24 percent, with a slight increase to 28 percent. People tend not to trust others, in general terms, since there are fewer linkages between people locally; individualism has strengthened, markets and work have replaced sociality and family, while more and more people are not marrying and prefer to live alone. More detailed results show that levels of trust have declined more in neo-liberal nations that have reduced the role of government and sociality more than others (see O'Hara 2006: ch 3). Trust is the critical social cement that binds people together, and without which various path-dependent anomalies concerning lack of information, inadequate interpersonal communication and asymmetric networks and relationships are generated. This tends to result in lower investment and social well-being.

Conclusion

The purpose of this chapter has been to demystify the dominant contradictions of neo-liberal globalization. We began by outlining some of the positive tendencies of the system linked to innovation, inflation, interest rates and world trade. Then it was shown how these positives are endogenously connected to the negatives of obsolete skills, businesses bankruptcy, and the destruction of non-market relations. The central contradiction of neo-liberal globalization was then explained through the concept of the disembedded economy, where dominant free market relations tend to question the very reproduction of social systems through inadequate attention given to public goods and system functions. A dual movement is thus inherent in global capitalism from free markets to social protection and when protection gets too great back to free markets, and eventually the return to more social protection, and so forth.

We then centered on general performance indicators and specific data for some of the critical contradictions; starting with unequal development tendencies associated with inadequate markets, followed by circular and cumulative problems of inadequate demand creating low productivity, investment, profit and growth. Further specific problems were then isolated through the contradictions between competition and markets; capital and labor; capital and the state; finance and industry; profit and environment; plus individualism and society. On balance, neo-liberal globalization has created low performance, uneven development, unproductive state spending, financial instability, pollution and low levels of trust. A critical view of these contradictory dynamics enables one to gain a holistic and practical view of the system, an essential ingredient of attempts to moderate the problems of the global political economy. The only region to advance significantly is East Asia, including China and its archipelago. The contradictions of neo-liberal globalization are thus considerable.

However, there are signs in many quarters of a change to a post-Washington governance system, which seeks to transcend the limits of extreme neo-liberal globalization in pursuit of an embedded market system (Stiglitz 2003). Major changes such as these are required before a more embedded system can emerge devoid of the extreme contradictions of the current system.

Notes

1. The data revision is related to the fact that in 1994 the Fortune 500 largest US industrial corporate list was merged with the 500 largest US service corporate list, resulting in a relative diminution of the rate of profit because service companies (especially financial institutions) typically achieve a very low rate of profit. Generally, the industrial company list is about two and a half times the service list, and the combined list was about 40 percent below the usual (industrial) list. A modification to the industrial list was made by multiplying the 1994–2002 rate of profit by 2.5 to get the 'adjusted' rate of profit for the largest 500 companies.
2. The World Values Survey included adults 18 and over for 22 nations (1981–82), 42 nations (1990–91), 54 nations (1995–96) and 60 nations (1999–2001). In 1999–2001 this included 85 percent of the world's population. While technically the years are not comparable when including all nations surveyed in the respective years, in fact there was not a major change between the results for trust for the original 22 nations over the different periods and the nations that were actually surveyed in the respective years.

References

Arestis, Phillip, P. Demetriades and K. Luintel (2001), 'Financial Development and Economic Growth: The Role of Stock Markets', *Journal of Money, Credit, and Banking*, 107(442), 16–41.

Binswager, Mathias (2000), 'Stock Returns and Real Activity: Is There Still a Connection?' *Applied Financial Economics*, 10, August, 379–88.

Brown, Doug (2002), *Insatiable is Not Sustainable*, Westport, Connecticut: Praeger.
EarthTrends (2002), *Concentrations of Greenhouse and Ozone-Depleting Gases in the Atmosphere, 1744–2001*, World Resources Institute.
Federal Reserve System (Board of Governors) (2000), *Long-Term U.S. Government Securities: 1925-2000* (discontinued series), available from: <http://www.forecastes.org/data/data/LTGOVTBD.htm>.
Federal Reserve System (Board of Governors) (2003). *Flow of Funds Accounts for the United States: Annual Flows and Outstandings, 1945–2002*, Washington D.C., FRS, September.
Federal Reserve System (Board of Governors) (2005), *Rate of Interest: Long term or Capital Market: Government Securities: Ten Year*, available at: <http://www.federalreserve.gov/h15/data/a/tcn10y.txt>.
Fortune Magazine (1955–2005) (various issues), 'Assets' and 'Profit' Data.
Fukuda-Parr, S. (2003), 'New Threats to Human Security in the Era of Globalization', *Journal of Human Development*, 4(2), 167–79.
Grennes, T. (2003) 'Creative Destruction and Globalization', *Cato Journal*, 22, 543–58.
Herrero, Alicia Garcia and Pedro del Rio (2003), *Financial Stability and the Design of Monetary Policy*, Servicio De Estudios. Working Paper No. 0315, Madrid: Banco de Espana.
IMF (International Monetary Fund) (2004), *World Economic Outlook: The Global Demographic Transition*, Washington D.C., IMF.
ISR (Institute for Social Research) (2000), *World Value Surveys, 1981, 1990, 1995–97*, Ann Arbor: University of Michigan. (Purchased from Australian National University, Research School of Social Sciences.)
ISR (Institute for Social Research) (2004), *World Value Surveys, 1999–2001*, Ann Arbor: University of Michigan. (Purchased from Australian National University, Research School of Social Sciences.)
Kessides, Ioannis N. (1990) 'The Persistence of Profits in the U.S. Manufacturing Industries', in Dennis C. Mueller (ed.), *The Dynamics of Company Profits: An International Comparison*, Cambridge: Cambridge University Press, 59–75.
Maddison, Angus (2000), *The World Economy: A Millennial Perspective*, Paris: OECD.
Meadows, D., J. Randers, and D. Meadows (2005), *Limits to Growth: The 30 Year Update*, London, Earthscan.
Miller, Nigel James and Christopher Tsoukis (2001), 'On the Optimality of Public Capital for Long-Run Economic Growth: Evidence from Panel Data', *Applied Economics*, 33, 1117–29.
Mueller, Dennis C. (1990), 'The Persistence of Profits in the United States', in Dennis C. Mueller (ed.), *The Dynamics of Company Profits: An International Comparison*, Cambridge: Cambridge University Press, 35–57.
O'Hara, Phillip Anthony (2006), *Growth and Development in the Global Political Economy: Social Structures of Accumulation and Modes of Regulation*, Oxford and New York: Routledge.
Polanyi, Karl (1944), *The Great Transformation*, Boston: Beacon Press, 1957.
Schumpeter, Joseph Alois (1911), *The Theory of Economic Development*, Cambridge: Cambridge University Press, 1961.
Stanfield, James Ronald and Jacqueline Bloom Stanfield (1997), 'Where Has Love Gone? Reciprocity, Redistribution, and the Nurturance Gap', *Journal of Socio-Economics*, 26(2), 111–26.

Stiglitz, J. (2003), 'Globalization and the Economic Role of the State in the New Millennium', *Industrial and Corporate Change*, **12**(1), 3–26.

Stockhammer, Engelbert (2004), 'Financialisation and the Slowdown of Accumulation', *Cambridge Journal of Economics*, **28**(5), 719–41.

Weber, Christian E. (2000), 'Government Purchases, Government Transfers, and the Post-1970 Slowdown in U.S. Economic Growth', *Contemporary Economic Policy*, **18**(1), 107–23.

Weede, E. (2004), 'The Diffusion of Prosperity and Peace by Globalization', *The Independent Review: A Journal of Political Economy*, **IX**(2), 165–86.

World Bank (2005), *World Development Index Database*, Washington D.C.: World Bank. (Access limited by subscription.)

2
Globalization, Cultural Conflicts, and Islamic Resurgence

Mustapha Kamal Pasha

The ascendancy of market fundamentalism[1] on a world scale and Islamic religious resurgence[2] appear to follow opposite structural trajectories informed by competing logics of openness and closure. On this popular construction, unabashedly drawn from earlier modernization claims, globalization is future directed, promising a brave new world of freedom and wealth, of porous boundaries and inclusiveness. Fulfilling the evolutionary, teleological promise of progress and the Enlightenment, globalization underscores the last phase of the unfinished project of modernity (Beck 2000), an irreversible march towards a universal civilization, the world-wide embrace of liberal economic and political rationality (Fukuyama 1992), and the emergence of a 'flat' world (Friedman 2005). By contrast, Islamic resurgence is backward looking, a retrograde ideological obstacle to emancipatory movement, more in the nature of a social pathology than a self-subsistent social phenomenon (Lewis 2001), a reaction to Western modernity and its global diffusion (Lewis 1976).

Echoing orientalist cartographies (Said 1978) and familiar tradition–modern dichotomies (Parsons 1951; Eisenstadt 1966), this hegemonic view, with pervasive appeal in the corridors of global power and policy, takes Islamic religious resurgence as a repudiation of modernity, a rejection of cosmopolitan impulses unleashed by time–space compression and increased social interconnectedness, or merely regards it as a moralizing lament against the rationalizing force of capitalism and individualism.

Accordingly, Islamic resurgence is seen fixated on the past, an atavistic residue of a dying civilization, yielding bigotry and barriers (Lewis 2001; 2002). Against the liberating force of West-centred globalization (Friedman 2005), social movements inspired by Islam reveal the stubbornness of traditional culture (Tibi 1990). Ascriptive attachments of faith and family, tribe and community collide with volitional drives for individual selfhood and autonomy. Hence, conventional wisdom views globalization and Islamic resurgence as completely contrary phenomena. If, indeed, there is a nexus between the two, it can only replicate a universal-particular hierarchy and a stimulus-response modality. In the first instance, globalization represents a universal and univeralizing phenomenon; Islamic resurgence manifests the distempers of particularism and exclusivity. In the second instance, there is a recognizable temporal sequence – first globalization, *then* resurgence, mirroring active (Westernizing) and passive (Islamic) cognitive and experiential registers. Globalization congeals flow and fluidity (Appadurai 1996; Castells 1996), Islamic resurgence stasis and rigidity (Lewis 2002). Merely reactive, the latter can only respond, not initiate; 'outside' modernity, Islam-inspired social movements lack agency or originality (Lewis 1976; 2001; 2002).

An integral part of hegemonic consciousness, these representations circulate as common sense,[3] fully backed by the institutional power of global capital in the public domain. 'Common sense' sees neoliberal globalization and religious resurgence to reside in separate worlds, unbridgeable and incommensurate.

If Islamic resurgence is considered as a variant of world-wide religious resurgence (Marty and Appleby 1991); a wider process of global desecularization (Berger et al. 1999); or a challenge to teleological understanding of historical movement (Beyer 1992), contemporaneous with globalizing modernity, and in fact the latter's instantiation, then these claims can potentially raise serious disquiet and tension in hegemonic thinking. However, in an environment of binary opposites, a global State of Emergency, and renewed orientalist mapping of the world, the Islamic Cultural Zones (ICZs)[4] assume a naturalized otherness (Pasha 2003), removed from the general flow of history, politics, or political economy. The particularity of these areas metamorphoses into particularism, uniqueness and 'repellent otherness' (Al-Azmeh 1996). While the distinction between the *different* and the *exceptional* is an important one, in a geo-cultural context of friend and enemy (Schmitt [1932] 1996), Islamic specificity appears as deviance from the global norm.

Mapping Islamic resurgence

Islamic resurgence is an undeniable fact (Esposito 1994; Ayubi 1991; Roy 1994). In generic (and minimal) terms, it is characterized by: (1) an increased assertiveness of Islam in the public and private domains; (2) self-consciousness of Muslims *qua* Muslims combined with a certain self-assuredness in their *Islamic* identity within a diverse field of multiple identities drawn from religion, nationalism or ethnicity; (3) attempts to restructure the moral code and conduct in a secularizing world, especially with regard to the question of gender and sexual relations, on the one hand, and assumed corrosion under conditions of materialism, on the other; (4) politicization of Islam and the Islamization of politics, reflected in increasing participation by Islam-inspired social agents in political discourse and institutions, including political parties, universities, think-tanks, and, in some instances, outside established channels of government and governance; (5) self-help and reliance on Islamicist non-state organizations and associations for economic and social welfare; and (6) reshaping of the terms of political and social discourse in light of assumed religious principles, among others. The relative mix of these elements is varied across regions, localities, and nations, from Jakarta to Algiers – virtually all corners of Muslim heartlands and peripheries, including the majority non-Muslim cultural zones. Moreover, within these cultural spaces there are degrees of commitment to the faith; Islamic resurgence though ubiquitous is not necessarily the most significant phenomenon in the social and life-worlds of Muslims. The crucial distinction between *Islam as culture* and *Islam as politics* can help dispel over-categorization of social reality in the ICZs, a by-product of religion. The first speaks to the wider social milieu, offering no political projects but the assurance of commonality or familiarity. By contrast, the second aims to enter the public and private worlds of Muslims to restructure links to authority and power, morality, and social conduct. Collapsing the two, as in orientalist constructions of Islam, yields a totalized and totalizing view with few analytical spaces to grasp the complex relation between globalization and Islamic resurgence.

Islamic resurgence is primarily linked to processes within civil society, but its principal aim is to restructure the state. The failure of secular-nationalism has dramatically shifted the political discourse towards the question of cultural assertion. With neo-liberal globalization downsizing the welfare (not coercive) functions of the state, civil society has become an arena of contesting the cultural form of globalization and providing an alternative resource for material sustenance. Islamic social movements are, therefore, both avenues of mobilization against perceived cultural corrosion as well as the provider of last resort in an environment of diminished or failed welfare state capacity. With the state receding from its historic Keynesian (and developmental) role, the task now falls upon Muslim schools, clinics and other self-help associations. A close nexus links state retrenchment and its delegitimation in the public domain. Islamic resurgence, on this premise, is not simply a crusading moral order to construct a City of God, but a discursive framework and movement to build or rebuild communities abandoned by the neo-liberal state. The assumed appeal of Islamic institutions among the *lumpen* and middle-class sectors of the population is largely based on their amphibious character as reservoirs of cultural cohesion against materialism and providers increasingly of scarce public goods in a climate of atomistic contentment and social apathy. Those with diminished power and material capacity are most likely to gravitate to Islamic resurgence. Islamicists tend to emerge from the peripheral sectors of political economy.

Islamic resurgence is a highly differentiated, heterodox and contradictory phenomenon. Islamicists demonstrate ambivalence towards modernity, generally embracing its technical-instrumental side, but rejecting its cultural forms. In the arena of politics, for instance, the aspiration to exercise power in the service of social or moral purpose is easily entertained, but the institutional implications of modern political subjectivity receives, at best, a lukewarm reception. In part, this ambivalence emanates from the tortured historical experience of political subordination vis-à-vis the West, the duality of liberal colonial institutions in the subordinated zones producing subjects rather than citizens, and the unending neo-colonial dispensation in the post-colonial period. Needless to say, Islamic resurgence must be placed within an historical context to avoid hasty inferences regarding its character and goals.

Cultural or class conflict?

Conventional wisdom tends to see not only a basic cleavage between Islam and the West (Huntington 1993),[5] and as a corollary, a battle between Islam and modernity (assuming the natural affinity between modernity and the West), but cultural conflicts *within* the Islamic Cultural Zones (ICZs) in isomorphic terms. From this perspective, the fault line in the world of Islam is between traditionalists and modernists, between those who reject Westernization (and modernity) and the 'reformers' seeking to embrace post-Enlightenment West-centred progress. The binary, Manichean world separating the savage and the civilized reappears, now disguised in the language of globalization, particularly in its neo-liberal variant. Huntington's (1993; 1996) cultural cartography sums up this uncomplicated view, and by extension the nature of cultural conflict. The possibility of entanglement between Islam and the West/Modernity (Pasha 2003) or 'intertwined histories' (Said 1993) is not seriously entertained to allow a more complex picture of historical trends. Rather, the surgical economy of irreconcilable difference is summoned to afford analysis, but also to rationalize attitude and policy towards Islam and its diverse cultural instantiations. Alternatively, as subsequent discussion will show, the imbrication of Islam and modernity/West/globalization renders binary classifications and analyses problematic.

Within the broader context of a transformed post-Cold War world order leading public intellectuals with strong links to Western hegemony have either celebrated the triumph of Western liberalism marking the 'end of history' (Fukuyama 1992), permitting no room for alternative projects to structure society, or cautioned that the end of ideological and political conflict has ushered in a more protracted 'clash of civilisations', principally between the West and Islam (Huntington 1993; 1996). 'For the relevant future, there will be no universal civilization', warns Huntington (1993:49); the driving force in history is likely to be cultural conflict. The implicit battle between globalization and resurgence in both triumphalist and alarmist accounts is not hard to detect, informed by a universal-particular distinction. Given the normative hierarchy of civilizations, an understanding of cultural conflicts is already transparent, premised on the assumption of a totalizing Islam feeding the ICZs against a liberal West. This hegemonic image presents an assumed clash between Islam and the West as more pivotal than conflicts *within* the ICZs.

In the post 9/11 Manichean climate of the saved and the damned especially, complex cultural dynamics have readily succumbed to orderly classifications. Islamic resurgence appears uniform, indistinguishable from militancy, rage or terrorism (Lewis 1976; 2002). The twin pillars of market fundamentalism and secularism provide the promised frontier; any deviance from pathways leading up to that destination is condemned as heresy. Consequently, the demonization of any recognizably self-subsistent Islamic current untamed by capitalist rationality or secular leanings appears as a sinister global presence. The drive to secularize the Muslim world through public diplomacy or conquest becomes explicable on this view.

A favourite corollary to hegemonic mappings of the nexus between globalization and Islamic resurgence is an allusion to political contingencies, either the Arab defeat in 1967 and the 1973 oil crisis (Lubeck 2000), or the decline of communism (Mazrui 1991). On this reading, Islamic social movements are *responses* to dramatic events. Stressing the changing regional or global environment in the ICZs, these claims situate the rise of political Islam basically to shifts in the political field. Absent in these accounts, however, is an *extended* historical understanding of globalizing processes working both within the ICZs, *and* providing the wider context of their constitution. Eschewing presentist accounts of globalization that typically reduce this complex phenomenon to structural changes in the global political economy during the 1970s (Cox 1987), or new international division of labour (Mittelman 1996) or the advent of the cyber revolution (Castells 1996), an historical map of globalization would decidedly capture neo-liberal globalization only as a more recent 'moment' of an otherwise extended process.

The central claim in this chapter hinges on a serious reappraisal of globalization as an extended historical process implicating inter-civilizational exchange, cultural borrowing and the agonizing experience of domination/subordination. If the ICZs are regarded as an *integral* part of historical processes of globalization or increased social connectedness on a global scale (Held et al. 1999), the relation between globalization and resurgence acquires a different trajectory and substance. The two phenomena appear contemporaneous on a single temporal scale and distempers in the ICZs materialize fault lines within historical structures. Neo-liberal globalization has *deepened* extant socio-economic, political and cultural fractures. A key implication here is the repudiation of the tradition-modern dichotomy. The analytical task then is one of deciphering *internal* movement and connectivity, not correlation. In this sense, cultural conflicts within the ICZs mirror the polarizing logic of globalization; social agents within the ICZs embody that logic.

In recent years, a variety of sociological approaches to understanding Islamic resurgence have also added to the fast growing cottage industry of Islamic Studies, particularly those that take 'political' Islam as a geopolitical threat requiring policing and surveillance. More sober, mostly pre-9/11, accounts identify important determinants of Islamic resurgence in varied settings: demographic changes and the swelling *lumpen* populations (Richards and Waterbury 1996), urbanization and changes in social interaction (Ayubi 1991), and general economic malaise (Roy 1994). Unlike accounts that privilege the global over the local, analyses premised on contingent factors tend to over-specify rupture at the expense of continuity and transcendence. These lacunae are largely filled by scholars, who find in Islamic resurgence a search for 'alternative' modernity (Göle 2000), a realization of identity politics.

Islamic resurgence in these 'alternative' formulations is treated in non-essentialized terms recognizing variance and contingency. However, the quest for authenticity and cultural autonomy captured in 'alternative modernities' appears *particularistic*, but not as a *particular* feature of generalized modernity. Missing in this formulation also is an appreciation of co-construction of modernity. Rather, the West continues to serve as the norm against which 'alternative' (non-Western) variants are assessed.

The failure to recognize co-construction and contemporariness produces a dualistic model of cultural conflicts sparked by globalization in the ICZs, best expressed in treating Islamic resurgence as a reaction. According to Lubeck, for instance, 'Islamic movements have now largely displaced secular nationalist and leftist movements as the *primary mobilizing force of resistance* against real and imagined Western political, economic and cultural domination.' (2000: 149; emphasis added). This recurrent image of Islamic *resurgence as resistance* fails to recognize the mutually constitutive nature of globalization and religious resurgence. Though a considerably more charitable view than the established tradition-modern frame, the characterization of resurgence either as resistance or a reaction is ahistorical and reductionist. The notion of Islamic resurgence challenging West-centred globalization, or as a struggle against the corrosive effects of 'savage capitalism', fails to consider the historical wellsprings of Islamic social movements (Butterworth 1992; Keddie 1994; 1998). It also fails to recognize their multiple forms, antecedents and aims. Resistance to globalization is but *one* expression among many, though this expression appears hegemonic. For the most part, Islamic social movements are inwardly directed, seeking to transform state and civil society within the ICZs, notwithstanding the rhetorical content of their discourses (Esposito 1994). In other instances, resistance to globalization becomes indistinguishable from struggle against an unjust political and social order. Upon closer scrutiny, the terms of Islamic political discourse share 'functional equivalence' with familiar terms drawn from the Western experience. The context may be different, but they typically address questions of legitimate authority, the ends of government, the balance between acquisition and social cohesion or the relation between private acts and public consequences. Summary repudiation of Islamic discourses obfuscates the experiential and ideational dynamics of alternative settings and, therefore, misguides an appraisal of deeper motivations undergirding social action.

Despite demographic and sociological variance in local conditions, in all the ICZs class tensions show elective affinities with cultural contestation between globalizing elites and the bulging ranks of the disenfranchised. However, this contestation is often mistaken as a struggle between reformers and traditionalists, (or in the present vocabulary between reformers and extremists). Given the tradition–modern frame of reference, cultural conflict appears autonomous, divorced from questions of power/powerlessness or domination/subordination. The intrinsically class dimension of this conflict recedes from the analytical field of vision. Conversely, the struggle between modernizers and traditionalists (or 'extremists') is presented without an accounting of overlapping discursive and non-discursive elements. Intersubjective commonalities usually blunt the intensity of cultural and class conflict. Given shared historical memories, symbols and lived experience, conflict can be mitigated, but not always. As the Algerian civil war demonstrated, for instance, a breakdown of the discursive and cultural fields is also possible. On the other hand, the ICZs typically appear as monolithic entities, especially those designated as 'rogue' states by hegemonic Western powers, Iran being a case in point. Typically, these states are said to harbour rabidly anti-Western fervour, without internal fractures except those drawn by a tradition/modern vector. Totalizing views such as this can lend credence to the thesis of a 'clash of civilizations' (Huntington), legitimizing policies of destabilization and 'regime change'. An understanding of the role of Islam in generating the terms of political discourse in the ICZs is easily subordinated to Western anxieties.

Antecedents

From an ideal typical Islamic civilizational perspective, the current phase of globalization is superimposed on earlier Christian–Muslim encounters and subsequent European ascendance. In the first instance, opposing civilizations drawn from a common monotheistic tradition faced each other, discovering commonality and difference in their respective cosmologies and social order. The inter-civilizational encounter contained misgiving and respect, recognition and denial, complex motives separating two communities of faith, conscience and political power. Both commerce and cultural exchange impacted the exchange. Both eastern and western Christendom acknowledged Islam as a superior civilization for over five centuries. During the eighth and twelfth centuries, the Islamic civilization demonstrated unprecedented achievement in philosophy and science, literature and the arts.

The second great encounter between Islam and the West occurred in a radically transformed political environment with an increasing sense of Muslim weakness in the face of rising Western military, technological, economic and political might (Keddie 1994; 1998). As a consequence, new pressures were introduced into the fabric of Muslim social life, but also self-doubt and subsequent humiliation. The colonization of large areas of Muslim empires through direct, mediated, or indirect control undermined Muslim self-confidence and collective identity. During this phase inter-civilizational dialogue was replaced by confrontation, re-territorialization and consolidation of fixed attitudes of cultural particularism. A key impact of colonialism was not only the break-up of Muslim empires, but forms of principal identity inclined towards nationalism. The post-colonial period witnessed a growing wedge between secular-nationalist leadership in the ICZs and the vast majority of *Muslim* masses, whose faith remained important to them, particularly in the face of alienating political and social processes.

To a large degree, the sources of Islamic resurgence lie at the fault-line between the different forms of political and cultural identity imported to the ICZs. However, there is also considerable overlap and fusion between the social agents located at the interstices of fractured identities. A binary classification of fractures in the ICZs evades the complexity of living Islam. Hence, the struggle for decolonization contained elements of nationalist fervour, religious identity, and cultural autonomy. The picture of a bifurcated post-colonial world of 'westernizing' reformers and traditionalists also misguides analysis. The social field in the ICZs is characterized by overlapping identities, 'religious' and 'secular', political and non-political. A more accurate depiction would show the presence of heterogeneity, if not hybridity.[6]

Historically, Western domination produced two distinct temporal structures in the Islamic World, one linked to the past, the other denying the past. Under globalizing conditions, an externally driven modernization project sought to erase the Muslim past. Initiated first by secular-modernists in the opening phase of the post-colonial era, this largely failed project has now acquired a totally new character, compromising 'national' autonomy in favour of a transnational order of global capitalism. Despite historical constrictions, the spirit of decolonization minimally ensured respect for cultural autonomy and independence, albeit of an 'imagined' kind under nationalism, subordinating internal differentiation. The zealousness to the aims of modernization under a secular-nationalist banner reflected the constriction of nationalism in complex cultural environments. Secular-nationalism failed either to articulate deeper cultural moorings of subordinated and colonized populations or realize the false promise of economic development. Rather the post-colonial state in ICZs in many instances appeared even more intrusive than its colonial predecessor, yet inadequate in delivering material progress. The suppressed temporal structure of cultural meaning and identity has managed to rework post-colonial institutions simultaneously repudiating secular-nationalism and its more aggressive neoliberal successor.

Falk's (1992) distinction between two variants of globalization offers a useful point of entry into an account of the contradictory dimensions of the neo-liberal 'phase' of globalization. 'Globalization-from-above' mirrors 'the collaboration between leading states and the main agents of capital formation' (Falk 1992). A key aspect of this type of globalization is a ceaseless quest for accumulation driven by a culture of consumption. The principal agents in this process are transnational capital and transnational political elites. Homogenizing in scope and content, neoliberal globalization equates material culture with civilization, making consumption the centerpiece of human self-expression. Ensconced in this framework is the implicit recognition of exchange as the ordering principle of social life and atomistic self-seeking a natural human tendency. Social action designed to pursue alternative ends appears irrational or savage. Affinities drawn from non-material principles become fetters to progress and prosperity. Hence, social limits to the logic of unfettered consumption placed by the state or community must be removed. Paradoxically, proponents of neoliberal globalisation deny historicity to its tall claims, preferring a naturalized view of societal phenomenon. The cultural underpinnings of this project seem opaque.

By contrast, 'globalisation-from-below' addresses the corrosive elements of neo-liberal globalization, including a collapse of community, individual autonomy, social capacity, an ecological crisis and cultural coherence. The self-organization of 'global civil society' imbued with a new consciousness seeks to reverse these negative trends, contesting cultural, social and ecological breakdown. 'Globalization-from-below' is a cry of the disinherited, a call for reversing the onslaught of neo-liberalism on society and nature, and resistance to its predatory logic. Global social movements of various hues – human rights, feminism, labour, peace, the environment seek a common two-fold end: to tame neo-liberal globalization and envision an alternative social order. On this terrain, religious social movements are also regarded as a part of 'globalisation-from-below'.

Revisiting cultural conflict

To reduce Islamic social movements to the *effects* of globalization, however, misreads its instantiation in the ICZs in both form and content. As noted, in its neo-liberal variant, globalization tends to deepen the fractures and tensions between state and civil society, on the one hand, and between various strata of society within the ICZs. On this alternative reading, the divide between state and civil society is not simply a product of neo-liberal globalization but a structural legacy of colonial and post-colonial arrangements within political economy; the state increasingly diverging from civil society in areas of legitimacy, political orientation, and cultural policy. Recent statist attempts congealed in 'Islamization' drives to bridge the divide have either come too late or lacked substance. They have merely exposed the political fragility of state managers in the face of a revolution of rising frustrations in the context of faltering accumulation and legitimation process, on the one hand, and demands for religious assertion within a wider process of cultural decolonization, on the other.

Indeed, the chasm between privilege and misery, domination and powerlessness takes on the appearance of cultural conflicts given recognizable distinctions drawn from the degree of proximity to state power and capital; spatial apartheid and forms of internal othering; life-style and patterns of consumption; degrees of Westernization and access to global symbolic and cultural capital, often congealed in foreign (usually English) language proficiency; and varied scales of religious commitment in quotidian practices encompassing public or private realms. The hold of globalizing elites over political and economic power has only increased with the advent of neo-liberal dispensation. In virtually all the ICZs, the lines between plenty and want are visible on the spatial landscape (patterns of housing), but also new lines of distinction between the few 'gated' communities guarded by private security personnel and the masses without adequate access to material sustenance. But there is also a psychological chasm that has grown between the privileged and the dispossessed with the intensification of atomistic self-seeking, the decline in state welfare and a diminutive culture of sharing. Distinct patterns of consumption and life-style further this divide, enhancing the process of 'internal othering' or the stereotypical negative attribution of 'the poor' – the undeserving, indolent, or unclean – by the rich or conversely of 'the rich' as immoral, Westernized and unkind by the poor. The picture is obviously complicated, but 'internal othering' combines class with cultural distinctions, widening the gulf between the haves and the have-nots. In this wider framework, unequal access to 'global' culture (foreign language proficiency, products or travel) plays an equally divisive role. The form of access can usually translate life-chances into guarantees of a 'good life' or relegation to a lifetime of unending struggle without discernible improvement. Neo-liberal globalization has fostered these varied distinctions, sharpening the historical partition between the privileged and the under-privileged. Hence, Islamic movements do not lie *outside* globalization, but within its polarizing cultural (not merely economic) logic, seeking to redress social wrongs within a religiously-inspired ethical order. The temptation to separate an economic logic (neo-liberal globalization) from a cultural logic (religious resurgence) mischaracterizes the mutuality and complexity of the societal make-up of globalization processes.

Cultural contestation within the ICZs also defies assumed patterns including, for instance, the alignment of Islamic assertiveness to 'traditional' sectors of society. The apparent concentration of self-proclaimed Islamicists in the urban sectors of Muslim society, modern institutions of state and civil society (including the bureaucracy, universities and schools), and technical and scientific competence seems paradoxical. However, the source of this 'paradox' lies both in the flawed equation of modernity and the West (and by default the designation of Islamicists as anti- or pre-modern) as well as the anticipation of an isomorphic link between religiosity and tradition. To the degree that living Islam in the ICZs is modern, not traditional, the assumed anomalies suggested in extant analyses (for instance, Lubeck 2000) evaporate.

The suggestion that living Islam is *modern* denotes an important corrective to established readings of Islamic resurgence within a tradition–modern frame. There is no outside to modernity, particularly in its globalizing expression. As previously suggested, the idea of co-construction eliminates the fiction of an untouched traditional zone in the ICZs. This is not to propose the obverse fiction of homogeneity and uniformity now produced by modernity, but the difficulty of sustaining the notion of duality, a traditional–modern bifurcation. Clearly, modernity materializes unevenly in institutional, ideational, and experiential terms, but it can radically redraw the social and political landscape.

This uneven pattern is reflected in the emergence of the (modern) nation-state, the principle of sovereignty, and the ubiquitous presence of exchange as the ordering arrangement for material provisioning. These elements have not remained unchallenged, especially in subordinated environments, including the ICZs. Alternative commitments to religious community, ethnic or tribal affiliation or pan-national awareness have helped dilute the potential hold of nationalism or diminish the state's monopoly over the symbolic economy. The (secular) principle of sovereignty has also encountered strain and challenge from an alternative understanding of (divine) sovereignty, often placed in contention with claims for legitimate authority and governance. Cries for a City of God have been inextricably bound up with ideals of justice and fairness lacking in actually existing polities, perhaps a displacement of sentiments against illegitimate government. Invariably, modernity bears a local stamp, conditioned by available material and symbolic resources.

Yet, the arrival of capitalist exchange has radically transformed the system of needs, expanded and transformed the social division of labour, redirected social provisioning from 'subsistence' to 'exchange' and produced conditions for the emergence of new subjectivities and sentiments. Erstwhile family structures have changed under new conditions of work and the balance between labour and leisure. Despite compulsory indictment of materialism in the discourse of the Islamicists (see Esposito 1994), the pervasiveness of capitalist exchange remains undeniable and irreversible. The social and life-worlds of Muslims have been profoundly conditioned by a modern world. Perhaps, a decoupling of the institutional structure of modernity from Westernization permits a less opaque picture of the ICZs.

Conclusion

The sources of Islamic resurgence run deep, but under globalizing conditions the character of Islamic resurgence acquires a distinctive tenor. Neo-liberal globalization makes fractures within Muslim society appear as a cultural contestation between tradition and modernity or Islam and the West. Islamic resurgence is both a moment of, and a reaction to, neo-liberal globalization, but not reducible to its imposing presence and impact. Highly heterodox in its social and political make-up, Islamic resurgence congeals multiple currents conditioned by local conditions. Resurgence is neither new nor a monolithic phenomenon. There are historical antecedents to Muslim self-assertion. Furthermore, resurgence scarcely exhausts the spatial or symbolic spheres of Islamic cultures and civilization. It is simply one expression, albeit a significant one. Invariably, it is the political idiom of Islamic resurgence that attracts notice. Political Islam is not the solo realization of Islamic resurgence, the latter ranging from quietist attempts to redefine Muslim social and life-worlds to seeking political power within established institutions of party, civil society and the state to militancy that typically operates outside the zone of politics.

The unifying thread in Islamic resurgence is a sense of rupture in the social and life-world of Muslims traceable to the collapse of Muslim empires in the eighteenth and nineteenth centuries and the consolidation of Western power. Muslim society has been in a state of reconstitution and self-examination, a process exacerbated by a growing internal cultural conflict over questions of legitimacy, identity, and an ideal Islamic political community. In this historical trajectory, several social movements can be situated, bearing reformist, revivalist, or fundamentalist (or scripturalist) proclivities. Often these movements supplied symbolic and material resources to anti-colonial movements, only to be abandoned by the nationalists in the post-colonial era.

Alternatively, the assumed paradox between globalization and Islamic resurgence embodies the materialization of a clash of civilizations between large liberal and illiberal cultural entities seeking domination, a spatial contestation reminiscent of imperial rivalry and civilizational conflict. This cultural cartography takes essentialized difference as the marker and arbiter of international relations in the post-Cold War era. Missing in extant analyses is an appreciation of the *modernity* of Islamic resurgence as a here-and-now social phenomenon, the divisive cultural logic of globalization, and the decoupling of identity and territory that provides Islamism its transnational appeal despite the nationalization of religion in the ICZs.

Since 9/11 Islamic resurgence appears coterminous with global terrorism, a view naturalized in the Western media and mainstream scholarship. Conversely, the militant tendency within political Islam is readily rebuked in apologetic accounts as Western hubris. Neither view is sustainable. Despite popular representations, the violent expression within Islamic resurgence remains in the margins of both faith and politics although, in the symbolic economy of domination/subordination, it has acquired an exaggerated presence. Militant Islam overlaps with nihilism, the death of politics; it is an acknowledgement of the impossibility of producing alternatives within the received worlds of modernity or the West. The anti-Western or anti-modern garb it adorns disguises how patently 'Western' and 'modern' militant Islam is both in embracing a rationalized vision of governmentality and abandoning divine interlocution in human affairs in favour of technical materiality of Western civilisation. The world it seeks is neither the City of God nor a City of Man, but the destruction of all that exists. To the extent that a death wish inspires militant Islam, it stands in the centre of modernist currents that have punctuated Counter-Enlightenment musings on nihilism and civilizational death. It also speaks to the weakness, indeed the impossibility, of creating a City of God, not strength within the cultural or civilizational boundaries of Islam.

Notes

1. As Seabrook (2001) puts it: 'The industrialized world has for 200 years subjected its own peoples to a long and persistent development that has taken a single direction: the extirpation of all previous ways of answering need and its supersession by the market. It is no wonder that we invest in the market with a veneration bordering on idolatry, and see it as vehicle of salvation, arbiter of destiny and embodiment of morality. Not for the first time, human beings make a cult of that which is destroying them, even as the wealth accumulates around us, and the iconography of luxury and ease bid us assent to the endless expropriations to which our daily life is witness.'

2. Throughout this chapter, the term 'resurgence' is used in place of the politically charged language of 'fundamentalism'. Resurgence underlines the *political* nature of Islamic social movements seeking to restructure state and civil society, not simply conform to some 'fundamentals'. Fundamentalism also carries an implicit liberal preference of relegating religion to the private realm.

3. For Gramsci, common sense covers the 'diffuse, unco-ordinated features of a general form of thought common to a particular period and a particular popular environment' (Gramsci 1971: 330n).

4. The term 'Islamic Cultural Zones' (ICZs) connotes the plurality of the institutional and cultural experience of Muslims rejecting essentialist readings of Islam as a totalizing, monolithic entity.

5. 'The fault lines between civilizations are replacing the political and ideological boundaries of the Cold War as the flash points of crisis and bloodshed. The Cold War began when the Iron Curtain divided Europe politically and ideologically. As then ideological division of Europe has disappeared, the cultural division of Europe between Western Christianity, on the one hand, and Orthodox Christianity and Islam has remerged' (Huntington 1993: 29–30).

6. The term 'hybridity' can deflect analysis in the wrong direction given the prior assumption of 'purity' but also given the inability of hybrids to mutate. Neither form can be sustained. Analogy can be a useful tool for edification, but examples drawn from the natural sciences to illuminate social processes often fail to capture the reflexive character of human, and therefore, societal action.

References

Al-Azmeh, Aziz (1996), *Islams and Modernities*, 2nd edition, London and New York: Verso.

Appadurai, Arjun (1996), *Modernity at Large: Cultural Dimensions of Globalization*, Minneapolis: University of Minneapolis.

Ayubi, Nazih (1991), *Political Islam: Religion and Politics in the Arab World*, London and New York: Routledge.

Beck, Ulrich (2000), *What is Globalisation?* Translated by Patrick Camiller, Cambridge: Polity Press, 2000.

Berger, Peter L. et al. (eds) (1999), *The Desecularization of the World: Resurgent Religion and World Politics*, Washington, D.C.: Ethics and Public Policy Center.

Beyer, Peter (1992), 'The Global Environment as a Religious Issue: A Sociological Analysis', *Religion*, 2(1), 1–19.

Butterworth, Charles E. (1992) 'Political Islam: The Origins', ANNALS, *AAPSS*, 524, November, pp. 26–37.

Castells, Manuel (1996), *The Rise of the Network Society*, Oxford and Malden, MA: Blackwell.

Cox, Robert W. (1987) *Production, Power and World Order: Social Forces in the Making of History*, New York: Columbia University Press.

Eisenstadt, S.N. (1966), *Modernization: Protest and Change*, Englewood Cliffs, N.J.: Prentice-Hall.

Esposito, John L. (ed.) (1994), *Voices of Resurgent Islam*, Oxford: Oxford University Press.

Falk, Richard (1992), 'The Making of Global Citizenship', in *Global Visions: Beyond the New World Order*, Jeremy Brecher et al. (eds) Boston: South End Press.

Friedman, Thomas (2005), *The World is Flat: A Brief History of the Twenty-First Century*, New York: Farrar, Strauss and Giroux.

Fukuyama, Francis (1992), *The End of History and the Last Man*, New York: Free Press.

Gole, Nilufer (2000) 'Snapshots of Islamic Modernities', *Daedalus* 129(1), 91–118.

Gramsci, Antonio (1971), *Selections from the Prison Notebooks*, Quintin Hoare and Geoffrey Nowell Smith (eds), New York: International Publishers.

Held, David, et al. (1999), *Global Transformations: Politics, Economics and Culture*, Cambridge: Polity Press.

Huntington, Samuel P. (1993), 'The Clash of Civilizations', *Foreign Affairs*, 72 (3) (summer), 22–49.

Huntington, Samuel P. (1996), *The Clash of Civilizations and the Remaking of World Order*, New York: Simon and Schuster.

Keddie, Nickki R. (1994), 'The Revolt of Islam, 1700 to 1993: Comparative Considerations and Relations to Imperialism', *Comparative Studies in Society and History*, 36(3) (July), 463–87.

Keddie, Nikki R. (1998), 'The New Religious Politics: Where, When, and Why Do "Fundamentalisms" Appear?' *Comparative Studies in Society and History*, 40(4) (October), 696–723.

Lewis, Bernard (1976), 'The Return of Islam', *Commentary*, 61 (January), 39–49.

Lewis, Bernard (2001), 'The Revolt of Islam', *The New Yorker* (November 19), 50–63.

Lewis, Bernard (2002), *What Went Wrong? The Clash Between Islam and Modernity in the Middle East*, New York: Oxford University Press.

Lubeck, Paul M. (2000), 'The Islamic Revival: Antinomies of Islamic Movements Under Globalization', in *Global Social Movements*, Robin Cohen and Shirin M. Rai (eds), London and New Brunswick, NJ: Athlone Press, 2000.

Marty, Martin E. and R. Scott Appleby (eds) (1991), *Fundamentalism Observed*, Chicago: University of Chicago Press.

Mazrui, Ali A. (1991), 'The Resurgence of Islam and the Decline of Communism', *Futures*, 23(3) (April), 273.

Mittelman, James H. (ed.) (1996), *Globalization: Critical Reflections*, Boulder and London: Lynne Rienner Publishers.

Parsons, Talcott (1951), *The Social System*, Glencoe: Free Press.

Pasha, Mustapha Kamal (2003) 'Fractured Worlds: Islam, Identity, and International Relations', *Global Society*, 17, 47–54.

Richards, Alan and John Waterbury (1996), *A Political Economy of the Middle East*, Boulder: Westview.

Roy, Olivier (1994), *The Failure of Political Islam*, Cambridge, MA: Harvard University Press.

Said, Edward W. (1978), *Orientalism*, New York: Vintage.

Said, Edward W. (1993), *Culture and Imperialism*, New York: Knopf.

Schmitt, Carl [1932] (1996), *The Concept of the Political*, translated by George Schwab, Chicago: University of Chicago Press.

Seabrook, Jeremy (2001), 'The Metamorphosis of Colonialism', *Globalization* (2001) ISSN: 1935–9794. <http://globalization.icaap.org/content/v1.1/jeremyseabrook.html> Accessed on 5/5/04.

Tibi, Bassam (1990), *Islam and Cultural Accommodation of Social Change*, translated by Clare Krojzl, Boulder: Westview Press.

3
Globalization and the Clash of Civilizations

*Halil M. Guven**

In less than 150 years the world has gone from a global population of one billion to one that is now about six billion, and more than three-quarters of these people live in developing countries. As the number of countries registered with the UN rose, a troubling tendency emerged in the 1990s that looked at the world as *'us versus them'* and defines and redefines the 'other'. Certainly, Huntington's 'west and the rest' segregation is one such unfortunate example. On a wider scale, a number of countries (or whole civilizations) were lumped into a group to be termed as the 'other', or targeted as the enemy (Huntington 1993). For instance, the 'Moslem world', or the poorer developing countries (once called the *Third World*) were readily molded into the 'other' in the eyes of the richer 'west'.

Whether the definition of the *'other'* is based on differences in civilization, culture, religion, or simply 'economic interests' is an open debate. In recent decades cultural differences and differences in civilization have been cited as the root cause of the problem and Huntington's 'clash of civilizations'[1] received much publicity (Huntington 1996). However, it is safe to assume that economic interests play a substantial role and act as the main driving force in such segregation. Highlighting differences will obviously, in time, pave the way for *conflicts*.

Globalization is looked upon by many as the ultimate solution in avoiding conflicts. Globalization should lead to more competition and hence more interdependence and harmony among countries. Although the word may not have been always in use, 'globalization', in one form or another, has always been there, all the way back to the beginning of civilizations and religions. Though nineteenth-century globalization was mostly concerned with the economic dimension, nowadays 'modern' globalization spans the whole range: from economic, political, military, to cultural globalization (Sözen 2002). Dynamics of globalization seek harmonization in all areas.

With the help of communication and information technology, globalization aspires to bring about universal values, unity, interdependence, understanding, tolerance, economic growth, and so on, and hence minimize differences and cure the problems of the *'other'*. There will no longer be the 'other' as the world becomes 'one', and harmonizes into one giant economic, cultural and political animal, thinking and acting as 'one'. Globalization will help solve the problems of the developing countries also, as it will bring about rapid development in these countries in all areas (economic, political, cultural, etc.).

However, thus far, globalization has led to another kind of conflict in that it is viewed by many as 'Americanization', 'injustice' and 'degeneration (corruption) of values' (Sözen 2002). It is argued that, under the pretext of economic globalization, industrialized developed countries are getting richer at the expense of the developing and under-developed countries. While the developing countries are increasing their foreign debt at alarming rates, the economic gap between the developed and developing countries is rapidly widening. While the citizens of the industrialized countries enjoy an income of more than $50 a day, half the world population is trying to get by on less than $2 per day.

As pointed out by Sözen, it would be wrong to draw clear lines of separation among economic, political, military and cultural dimensions of globalization (Sözen 2002). However, this chapter will attempt to focus only on the cultural and civilization dimension of globalization and study its implications on civilization harmony. The impact of globalization on civilizations and the root causes of the civilizational conflicts will be studied.

Civilization revisited

In light of the title of this chapter and its essence, here it is appropriate to revisit the concept of 'civilization' itself and analyse it at some length (Guven 2003a). Braudel defines *'civilization'* as 'an "ordered" urban way of living which consists of integrated material, moral, intellectual and psychological components, and which has been set up and conserved by a certain group of people from generation to generation' (Braudel 1995). Every civilization is based on a geographical area or system of areas; presupposes the existence of fully developed cities; is inseparable from its hierarchical society (Levi-Strauss in Charbonnier, 1961); survives through mobility and also mutual impact with other societies; involves challenges and responses (Toynbee 2001 [1946–57]); depends on economic, technological, biological, and demographical circumstances; and presupposes an underlying psychological structure with its own peculiar ritual practices.

In very simple terms, the concept of '*civilization*' can be linked to creation of *order* (laws, rules and regulations), *organization* (political and social), and *efficiency* (least loss of effort due to disorder and disorganization, time savings from good infrastructure and order, mass production, etc.). 'Western' societies have more experience in organized living; so it can be argued that these better-organized societies with greater efficiency in their political and social organizations and a more 'ordered urban way of living' can be regarded as '*more civilized*', or possess '*higher civilization*'. Some other nations, such as Bedouins of the Middle East, Turkic peoples of Central Asia, natives of the North American Continent (red Indians) and African tribes, have tribal beginnings, and have less experience in organized (established) cities and permanent settlements. And so this group of people, and nations with tribal roots, can be regarded as '*lower or lesser civilizations*' (Diamond 1999).

The arguments above are, of course, incorrect. Stage of development and the notion of 'civilization' are somewhat confused. Or is it the case that the notion and definition of 'civilization' needs to be re-examined? Is it the case that the definition of civilization given by Braudel, Toynbee and others suit primarily the purposes of the *West*? It is widely accepted that all civilizations have 'material' and 'social/spiritual' dimensions. However, has something been overlooked? Should there be another approach to defining civilization? Therefore, before looking at globalization and the 'clash of civilizations', this chapter will first search for a new definition of 'civilization'. For the purposes of this study, a bifurcation of the concept of civilization basically in the form of 'material civilization' and 'social civilization' will be attempted.

Material civilization

There is no doubt that a civilization requires a certain degree of organization at its outset. This organization has to have a political and social nature, and should set up the necessary mechanisms for regulating political and social aspects of society. Institutions must be in place for making laws, rules and regulations, the end product of which should amount to the orderly functioning of the society's everyday life, through which its citizens survive, work, produce, reproduce, be entertained, and be properly compensated in harmony. All the needs must be satisfied to such an extent as to create security and a fair environment to allow for the 'pursuit of happiness' for all. This has been the motto of most Western societies that have made enormous progress in setting up advanced democratic institutions resulting in what we refer to as 'Western civilizations' today. These civilizations have succeeded in amassing enormous material wealth, and a tremendous 'material civilization' has resulted. According to Toynbee, throughout history world civilizations have gone through several stages.[2] For Toynbee, abundance (i.e., 'material civilization' and wealth) and individualism are closely related. A smooth-functioning, advanced society, which creates an abundance of material wealth ('things'), invariably gives birth to individualism. Proper functioning of the rules, regulations and laws of a well-lubricated civilization machine necessitates the weakening of the social ties among its constituents. Hence 'individualism' is implicitly promoted. A society with an advanced stage of individualism is expected to have less deviation from its rules – more order, upholding 'rule of law' (i.e., proper implementation and enforcement of laws, rules and regulations), and full organization. This then promotes a rule-driven (dominated) society with a high level of obedience, less uncertainty in the implementation of rules and less uncertainty in social interactions. Then the sought-after civilization, which starts out to provide order, organization and efficiency in pursuit of happiness, results in the creation of citizens who are like '*small islands*' – cut off from each other – leading to a lonely and unhappy existence.

Social civilization

Every civilization presupposes a specific world-view that defines the way members of that civilization perceive and even dream of their own 'world' as the setting for the state and process of their existence and being. This directly shapes the way people of diverse cultures, or civilizations, behave and act. For instance, in most non-Western civilizations and cultures, people live collectively. They can sit together in close proximity or even walk around holding hands. For them '*friendship*' is very important, and the individualism of Western civilization is foreign to them. We can use the term 'social civilization' to describe the 'wealth and depth' a civilization has in its social and spiritual dimension. This can also be regarded as a 'non-material' component of a civilization, or referred to as the 'spiritual capital' of a society (Elaagab and Bruce 2003). In pursuit of happiness, certainly order, organization, efficiency and taming of nature are essential, but not sufficient, conditions. Obviously, the role of religion in social civilizations, and 'spiritual capital' must also be studied and not overlooked.

If human beings live closer together in extended families with more random social interaction, and greater uncertainty in allocation of their time, this creates more uncertainty and disorder. This results in less urban crime, fewer homeless people and gentler (or closer) human beings. However, lack of (or weak) individualism, more social ties, extended family relations, friendships, and so on almost, certainly leads to inefficiencies in implementation and enforcement of rules, regulations and laws. It may also lead to the creation of a lesser 'material civilization'. Societies with high social civilization and less or little 'material civilization' may also be unhappy and live out a pretty miserable existence.

Comparative civilizations

It goes without saying that today there are numerous civilizations around the globe, some larger than others, some more 'advanced' than others, some younger and some not so young. 'Western civilizations', building upon the earlier successes of human development, took humanity to its current pinnacle, the *'techno-global' stage*. Figure 3.1 shows a comparison of different civilizations. For the sake of argument in this treatise, Huntington's classification of civilizations, Western and non-Western, is used. This author argues that in any civilization, both 'social' and 'material' components are equally important and they should be kept in balance. However, the author also believes that these two components of a civilization are mutually exclusive. That is, both material and social civilizations cannot be sustained at very high levels. Development of material civilization requires promotion of Western-type individualism, which in turn leads to a weakening of social civilization. Conversely, maintenance of a high level of social civilization and a lack of advanced individualism concepts leads to less material civilization, less material wealth.

In any society, however, significant discrepancy and deviation between the two components of civilization will create societal problems and discontent. Only a number of 'points of departure', which consist of the conceptions or norms of living peculiar to the two main groups of civilizations, exist. These are listed in Table 3.1 below.

Certain terminology dear to Western civilizations, or the Western world-view, does not even exist in some of the non-Western civilizations in any equivalent form. Some of these are: professionalism;

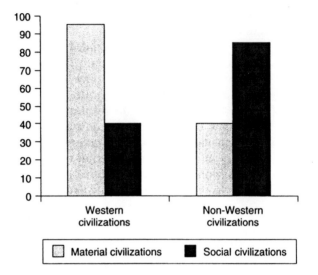

Figure 3.1 Comparison of material vs social civilizations (Western 'vs' non-Western civilization[3])

Table 3.1 Comparison of Western and non-Western civilizations

Western civilizations	Non-Western civilizations
Rule of law	Social duties and responsibilities regarded as sacred laws
Human rights	Inner feeling of justice apart from law itself
Individualism and autonomy	Society or groups being more important than the individual
Secularism	Holistic approach to life, religion, fate, governance
Social contract	Solidarity
Competitiveness	Various forms of tolerance among social groups
Innovation	Linked to individualism, critical, independent thinking
Self-made man	Altruism considering all humanity as one
Change	Traditions
Conflict of interests	Overlapping of interests

planning; challenge; competitiveness; equal opportunity; rule of law; balance of powers; innocent until proven guilty; rules versus freedoms; etc. In Guven , this was described as lack of *'common language'* (Guven 2003b).

Concepts such as these do not have the same meanings in non-Western civilizations. The notions of *'challenge'* and *'competitiveness'* are very important in the West. These, however, are devoid of any real sense in most non-Western civilizations. 'Conflict of Interest' 'Planning' or 'Professionalism' do not ring the 'same bell' (figuratively speaking) in, for example, Turkey. This does not mean that things are not getting done, or that progress is not made. Simply, the case is that these concepts *are not the same* in non-Western civilizations, and the rate of progress and development is not the same. Western mentality finds it difficult to allow for the absence of such concepts that are fundamental to its achievements.

Therefore, it can be argued that individualism, which is a product (or stage) of civilizational progress, is the *key parameter* in the measurement of harmony between Western and non-Western civilizations.[4] For example, in the West, children are raised with the basic understanding that 'they should be self-reliant', with a sense of self-responsibility, and a great deal of individualism and self-confidence. They are taught to grow up with more independence than dependency. The basic *modus operandi* is independence and individualism: kids must be *independent and self-sufficient* as soon as possible, actually starting from the nursery school. On the other hand, in most non-Western civilizations, children are raised under as much protection as possible, at the expense of their individualism. Lack of individualism in the kids and youth may result in more dependency, less freedom, lack of self-confidence, inability to express opinions, fear of saying 'no'. So, the concepts of *'Privacy Circle'*, *'I can do it myself'*, the *'self-made man'* and, of course, *'individualism'*, are somewhat absent in certain non-Western civilizations.

It is obvious that the creation of more 'material civilization' requires progress in 'individualism'. Conversely, a high-level of 'social civilization' may hinder rapid development of 'material civilization'. This is believed to be the root cause of the civilizational disharmony and the potential *social conflict*. Oberschall noted that 'social conflict is one of the ubiquitous events that encompass a broad range of phenomena including class, racial, religious, and community conflict, in addition to riots, rebellions, revolutions, strikes, marches, demonstrations and protest rallies' (Oberschall 1978). The author believes that modern globalization, which is perceived by many as cultural imperialism, is creating social conflicts that may in the short term trigger peaceful or violent protests.

Civilizational disharmony: cultural globalization

As argued above, the industrialized Western civilizations developed advanced material civilizations, amassing enormous amounts of wealth and with it the potential to dominate other civilizations. Globalization, which should lead to more competition and hence more interdependence and harmony among countries, is in reality providing the mechanism for domination. Globalization is perceived as 'exporting of the way of life' or the 'culture' of America ('Americanization') to the rest of the globe.

As Barber points out, cultural globalization in particular is creating universal discomfort and propagating civilizational disharmony (Barber 1995). Cultural globalization from industrialized Western civilizations, carrying the culture and promoting the lifestyle of these countries to developing countries, has been greatly aided by communication technology and the Internet. There is an intense downpour of 'cultural globalization' from satellite TV broadcasts; for example, satellites allow over 150 million households in approximately 212 countries and territories world-wide to subscribe to CNN (Galeota 2004) and American movies and soap operas replace local movies and productions.

These developments are watched with grave concern in most developing countries. The rapid progression of independent life-styles and individualism are not welcomed in Asian and Middle Eastern countries. These countries view the rapid spread of '*individualism*' as a serious threat to their local cultures and as a degenerative disease that will destroy their core culture and values. This is particularly alarming for them. In the 'non-Western civilizations' of the Third World, the superimposing of concepts directly borrowed or imported from Western civilizations into their own traditionally inherited norms can lead to corruption or moral disintegration.

On the other hand, very often globalization is promoted by its advocates as the process bringing about economic development, modernization, prosperity and greater opportunities for the members of the Third World. It is believed that the standard of living can be raised and human development can be accelerated through globalization. What is forgotten though is that, among other things, penetrating globalization requires that a country's internal institutions are 'tuned' to the rules of materialistic factors, that is, rules of 'material civilization'. The challenge presented by globalization, from the standpoint of the institutional adaptation, is most evident in the pre-capitalist traditional societies that try to modernize rapidly. For instance, many republics of the former Soviet Union had experienced sudden shift from the planned economy to open (or partially open) competition. Among other things, this led to a sudden decrease in demand for local goods and products, and rapid decrease in social welfare and health care. On the other hand, demand for foreign investment, and foreign products rapidly increased. Demands on the professional world also experienced shift change. Pressure of these forces on the society has molded new generations of people that are more appreciative of the material component of civilization. Other groups and generations who do not adapt to the new conditions, are destined to live out a largely miserable existence. By generations, not only are age cohorts meant: Region (capital vs. periphery) or family values (conservative vs. liberal) will also play a role in determining the adaptability of a person to the new cultural and institutional requirements in society. This situation could aggravate cleavages among the layers of society promoting conflict among its sectors.

Quite often, modernization, globalization and Westernization are all mixed together or mixed up. Most certainly, internationalization and globalization are confused. However, in the end the economically less-developed societies have either to adapt and assimilate, or fall into the state of rejecting globalization. The inability to accept the realities of globalization and/or total rejection of globalization leads to alienation, Islamic resurgence and many other regional insurrections. Some even suggested that 9/11 was a reaction to this very thing, 'American globalization' (Sardar and Davies 2002). Globalization involves two types of reactionary movement (alienation) for these marginalist groups. First, they are not involved in the process of globalization, and secondly, domestic states break down and cannot protect their interests, or are inimical to them. A large number of countries in Africa today can be regarded as in this marginalized category.

Globalization is also associated with the increased inflow of financial resources, greater exposure to international competition, and demand for effectiveness, in the pure economic meaning of the term. As soon as the internal market of a developing country becomes less protected by the barriers (tariffs and non-tariff barriers – the reduction of which is encouraged by such globalization-promoting organizations as WTO, NAFTA, GATT), local producers of goods and services may experience tremendous pressure from stronger, more technologically and financially advanced, international corporations. In many instances, such corporations have an annual budget many times that of a developing country, making it difficult for the governments of such countries to negotiate protective terms for the local producers.

One of the most vulnerable among those businesses is small local craft shops and artisans who produce their goods on very small scale. Those businesses are often unique and endemic to a particular culture and civilization; though quite pricey, they contribute to the unique face of a city, culture or particular society. Producing goods of a high quality, then are unable to reduce the price below a certain level because of the small scale of production and this makes it impossible for them to compete. Opening the market to competition with MNCs and TNCs could lead to the certain death of these businesses, and along with them the death of unique local traditions and culture. Of course, by and large, the most visible symbols of globalization are still Pepsi and Coca-Cola as popular drinks, and McDonalds, Denny's and Burger King as popular fast-foods. These outfits were rapidly established as franchises in most developing countries. The loss of cultural identity (or the evolution of a hybrid identity) in the cities of developing countries is moving at an alarming rate. The situation is no different in other sectors: for example, in the field of health, MNCs are promoting Western medicines in developing countries, trivializing the culture of traditional arts of healing, folk medicines, and local and complementary systems of health. At the same time some TNCs are trying to commercialize even the local medicines and sell local folk drugs. Although the concern over the Americanization of national cultures is not new, recently many of both established and infant industries in less-developed countries now have to compete with American counterparts. For example, the film industry in many Third World countries is now concerned at the prospect of a free market that would lead to the disintegration of national culture from cheap American films.

Globalization means standardization not only on the level of weights, measurements and potential equalization in salaries, but also on the level of types of goods one can find in different parts of the world. Pressure on local culture will definitely create tension within societies where social and cultural components are dominant, which in turn may give rise to civil and international conflict, causing riots and unrest. For example, fast-food culture inspired a 'slow food movement' in Italy, and the first Kentucky Fried Chicken outlet in India sparked a demonstration involving the burning of chickens outside of the KFC restaurant (Galeota 2004). Modern globalization aimed at developing a uniform global culture, or a Western cultural hegemony, is not based on any normative and moralistic culture. It can be summarized as neo-liberal, not democratic and against any form of religious ideals or traditional culture.

Globalization and the clash of civilization

According to Huntington civilizations can be categorized as 'the west and the rest'. It is safe to assume that Huntington's definition of civilization is quite different from the definitions and approach given above, and his implicit assertion that Western civilization is 'the norm' is not acceptable. Part of the problem may lie in the fact that *'other civilizations'*, or other forms of civilization, are looked down upon as inferior to the 'Western civilization'. According to Huntington the 'rest' does not include just the former *Third World*, but engulfs a whole range of other 'non-Western civilizations'. He divides the world into 'seven or eight major civilizations': Western, containing Western Europe and North America, Confucian, Japanese, Islamic, Hindu, Slav-Orthodox, Latin American and 'possibly an African civilization' (Karlsson 2003). Huntington claims that the 'clash of civilizations' will occur on different levels. At the micro-level various neighboring groups will get into a state of conflict, which can frequently become violent, along cultural 'fault lines', fighting over the control of territories and each other. At the macro-level states with different cultural ties may struggle for military and political dominance, for control over international bodies, and for power over third parties. However, after a decade it is obvious that Huntington's prophesies are not about to come true. He could not think of an international system like globalization that may in fact work for the unification of cultures and even civilizations. The clash that seems to be inevitable may be because of differences in economic factors that globalization engenders, particularly the rise of income inequality and trade wars between the developed and less-developed nations. The possibility of a clash of civilizations simply based on religion does not seem to be realistic in the present world. As discussed above, it is the very process of unification of cultural differences attempted by globalization that may provoke protests and clashes.

Humanity's pursuit of order, organization and efficiency (i.e., 'civilization') produced an unwanted and undesired outcome – a decline in social civilization. Industrialized Western civilizations, who mastered the trades of 'civilization', accumulated enormous amounts of 'material wealth' at the expense of their social civilization, or 'social wealth'. A material civilization that has the ability to accumulate more wealth and control more resources of the world, and hence build more material wealth, may start looking down on the 'other' as 'not as civilized'. With the wealth, and the tools of a techno-global world (e.g., communication technology and the Internet), came the potential and danger of dominating other civilizations and upsetting the 'equilibrium and harmony of other civilizations'. By speeding up 'individualism', globalization is simply accelerating the decline in the social civilization of the 'other' (or the 'rest').

As discussed earlier, according to Toynbee, civilizations develop '... from liberty to abundance, and from abundance to individualism' (Toynbee, 1946–1957). As a result, it can be argued that globalization is introducing and promoting 'individualism' in societies which has not first experienced liberty and abundance. It could also be argued that civilizations may *not* all follow the same path of development or the same developmental stages as Western civilizations. Then it would be wrong to accept 'the West and the rest' segregation of civilizations, which could lead to accumulated civilizational disharmony and clash (see notes 1 and 3). On the other hand, the fact that individualism is promoted in pre-capitalistic traditional societies that have not yet experienced an abundance of material civilization ('things') paves the way to an insurmountable imbalance problem, creating 'needs' and 'wants' beyond the means of these societies. For example, young people aspire to be independent like their counterparts on MTV or in the American movies. As an extreme example, one can look at the case of North Cyprus where the population is around 230 000 and there are 250 000 registered auto vehicles and 180 000 mobile telephones.

There are *limits to growth*. The world does not have the resources to sustain the material greed created from globalization and the resulting 'worldwide-consumerism' (Berry 2003). The natural resources of the world are simply not enough. 'Equilibria' and 'civilizations' established by those societies over centuries have been irreversibly upset. Now, the 'greed' has set-in. Through mass-communication and the Internet these societies and groups of people want TVs, mobile telephones, cars, jeans, 'fast food', and so on. Equilibria can be regarded as 'low-level' or 'high-level' and the reality is that they were equilibria and should not have been destroyed. Actually 'globalization' appears to have resulted in fueling the very principle of consumer economics, which aims at selling more and making more money. So far this is benefiting the Western industrialized countries, and the poorer Third World countries are on the losing end.

Moreover, globalization and consumer economics lead to the corruption of subcultures in the cities of non-Western civilizations, causing the social civilizations of these countries to rot from inside, like an apple. Japan is an interesting example: a non-Western civilization that modernized and prospered in a relatively short period of time. However, Japan is still a very traditional and conservative country with a high-level of 'social civilization' at odds with the cultural invasion of individualism and 'Americanization'. Unfortunately, this is causing Japan to experience the highest level of suicides in the world.

Concluding remarks

It would be wrong to assume that civilizations can be rank ordered, that is, one superior to another. We have to continue living together on this planet. Huntington claimed that non-Western and Western civilizations are bound to clash (Huntington 1996). In light of the analysis of the impact of globalization on civilizations and cultures, and other issues identified in this chapter, the conclusion is that a Huntington clash, along the lines of religious differences, is next to impossible. Instead it is the civilizational disharmony that will continue to create negative energies. This may not lead to open and bloody clashes in all cases, but nevertheless a deep and sustained undercurrent of conflicts. The author believes that such conflicts and clashes can be avoided through:

- Awareness that, in any society, significant discrepancy and deviation between the two components of civilization, 'material' and 'social', will create societal problems and conflict.
- Establishing a better *dialog among civilizations on an equal footing*, as opposed to monologues and dictation from one to another.
- More sharing, understanding, respect, goodwill and empathy.

Globalization cannot be stopped. But as a way of minimizing the disharmony and discomfort resulting from cultural globalization Friedman's suggestions 'to absorb influences that naturally fit into and can enrich local culture; to resist those things that are truly alien; and to compartmentalize those things that, while different, can nevertheless be enjoyed and celebrated as different' are worth noting. Civilizations have a lot to learn from each other, and globalization may be the answer (Friedman 2000).

We need better inter-civilization education, similar to 'interdisciplinary education'. Better models for coexistence, which have elements of both 'non-Western' and 'Western' civilizations (an amalgam of cultures), can be created. This can pave the way for the establishment of *common values, common language*, and *common goals* among countries, cultures and civilizations (Guven 2003b). A possible approach to and the elements of an inter-civilizational education and some initial ideas on creating a 'common language' are presented in (Guven 2003c). In a time-span of say 15–20 years we can do away with the notion of the *'other'* and create an understanding of *'civilizations on equal footing'*. In 2001 UNESCO declared: 'Education is one of the essential foundations of both a culture of peace and a dialogue among civilizations. It advocates for the respect for universal values common to all civilizations...' (UNESCO 2001). Therefore, the forces and powerful tools of globalization (mass media, communication technology, Internet, etc.) should be used to launch an inter-civilizational education campaign, so that globalization can bring true hope to the world and stop being regarded as Western cultural hegemony or domination. It is through education that wild consumerism can be restrained. Unless we stop the current cycle of greed in ourselves, environmental degradation and the effects of global warming will stop it anyway!

Notes

* This book is based on the notion of disembedded nature of equilibrium generated by globalization in LDCs. The point is pursued at length by B.N. Ghosh in his work on *Gandhian political economy*. We have many commonalities of thoughts that configurated the theme of the present book. I offer my sincere thanks to him for inspiring and successfully completing the project. I also thank my wife, Oya Atakan (Olga Atajanova), for her continuing support, love and encouragement.

1. The phrase 'clash of civilizations' is widely accepted and associated with Huntington's work. Using the phrase without quotation marks would have meant that the author is implicitly in agreement with the concept of the 'clash of civilizations' as a reality. This is not the case. The author does not subscribe to Huntington's 'west and the rest' segregation, and the implicit assumption that Western civilization is the norm or is superior to the rest.

2. According to Toynbee , stages of civilizations are: 'From slavery to faith, from faith to courage, from courage to liberty, from liberty to abundance, from abundance to individualism, from individualism to obedience, from obedience to indifference, and from indifference to the loss of liberty. Nineteen of 21 great civilizations collapsed because of internal threats. As we can see, civilizations start with slavery and end with slavery. This period goes on for 200 years and then history repeats itself.'

3. In this chapter, for the sake of clarity, Huntington's 'Western' and 'non-Western' classification is used. However, it should be pointed out that it would be wrong to talk about polarity between and among civilizations: Western 'versus' non-Western. Today, we can easily say that west is in the east, and east is in the west. West became west because of the east and vice versa. Therefore, a clear definition of the Western and non-Western is near impossible. It will therefore be more correct to talk about *hybrid civilizations*.

4. 'Individualism' and 'collectivity' can be looked at as the opposite of each other. At the extreme, they are both damaging to the soul, existence

and happiness of human beings. Individualism is much discussed in the article. Collectivity limits freedom and creativity of individuals and creates suppression.

References

Barber, Benjamin R. (1995), *Jihad vs. McWorld*, Random House, New York.

Berry, Howard (2003), 'Constructing the World Anew: Education, Leadership and Global Realities', *New Paradigms in Leadership*, University of Bahçeşehir Press, Istanbul, Turkey, pp. 80–8.

Braudel, F. (1995), *History of Civilizations*, Penguin/Viking, pp. 10–35.

Diamond, J. (1999), *Guns, Germs, and Steel: The Fates of Human Societies*, W.W. Norton.

Elaagab, Mansour (2003), 'Leadership and Human Rights for Development', *New Paradigms in Leadership*, University of Bahçeşehir Press, Istanbul, Turkey, p. 95 and Lloyd, Bruce, 'Leadership, Globalization and a New Economy: What is different and what is not', *New Paradigms in Leadership*, University of Bahçeşehir Press, Istanbul, Turkey, p. 137.

Friedman, Thomas (2000), *The Lexus and the Olive Tree*, Anchor Books, New York.

Galeota, Julia (2004), 'Cultural Imperialism: An American Tradition,' *Humanist*, May-June.

Guven, H. (2003a), 'Civilizations and Natural Laws: A Positive Sciences Perspective,' *New Paradigms in Leadership*, University of Bahçeşehir Press, Istanbul, Turkey. (This chepter is a revised version of this work.)

Guven, H. (2003b), 'Dialogue of Civilizations: Paradigms on Economic Development and Social Advancement,' *New Paradigms in Leadership*, University of Bahçeşehir Press, Istanbul, Turkey, pp. 306–21.

Guven, H. (2003c), 'Leadership in Education: A Intercultural Model in Progress', *New Paradigms in Leadership*, University of Bahçeşehir Press, Istanbul, Turkey pp. 322–57.

Huntington S. (1993), 'The Clash of Civilizations,' Agenda 1994, *Foreign Affairs*, Summer.

Huntington, S. (1996), *The Clash of Civilizations and the Remaking of World Order*, Simon and Schuster, New York.

Karlsson, Ingmar (2003), 'The Clash of Civilizations – a European Perspective', *New Paradigms in Leadership*, University of Bahçeşehir Press, Istanbul, Turkey, pp. 276–88

Levi-Strauss in G. Charbonnier (1961), *Entretiens avec Claude Lévi-Strauss*, Plon.

Obserchall, Anthony (1978), 'Theories of Social Conflict', *Annual Review of Sociology*, 4, 291–315.

Sardar, Z. and M.W. Davies (2002), *Why Do People Hate America?*, Disinformation Company, New York.

Sözen, Ahmet (2002), 'Küreselleşmenin getirdikleri ve ABD'nin İkilemi'. (Jan-Mar), manuscipt in Turkish, *Karizma*, Istanbul, Turkey.

Toynbee, A.J. (2001), *A Study of History*, abr. by D.C. Somervell, 2 vols., Oxford University Press, 1946-57. Also: A. Polat, *An Accumulation of Three Thousand Years* (in Turkish), Enes Matbaacilik p. 311.

UNESCO (2001) <http://www.unesco.org/dialogue2001/en/education.htm>

4

Globalization, Sub-national Governments and Urban Crises in the Developing World

Partha Gangopadhyay and Shyam Nath

This chapter highlights an inherent and serious contradiction that the gathering momentum of globalization has unleashed for many nations in the developing world. On the one hand, these nations have witnessed significant acceleration in their GDP growth in recent years, which induced rapid increases in the pace of urbanization and urban population growth. On the other hand, governments at regional levels have accumulated huge debts owing to privatization and sales of state-owned enterprises and assets, declining fiscal revenues, unsuccessful reforms, corruption and inappropriate accounting practices. Many regional governments in these countries are finding it difficult to service their debts, which force them to impose austere fiscal measures. This has an adverse impact on the provision of local goods and infrastructure in the urban areas. In most of the developing world there has emerged a widening gap between demand for and supply of local goods and infrastructure in urban areas, e.g., urban water supply, roads, basic public health facilities, primary schooling, housing and so on. This is despite the fact that large cities, which are the focus of globalization, accumulate urban wealth and business infrastructure. Richardson (2004) discusses the implications of globalization for cities at the receiving end. His findings are that large cities, on balance, benefit from globalization even in developing countries, although in some cases at the expense of widening regional disparities.

The special institutional structures of local governments in developing nations were inherited from the colonial rubrics of these nations in which national/state governments offer finances to municipalities (local governments) for supplying local goods and local infrastructure. The urban crises are partly a spin-off from the indebtedness of national/regional governments that forces them to cut back on all local expenditures; more importantly, local governments traditionally levy low tax rates on local residents and businesses. Given the current institutional milieu we develop a simple game to establish that the inadequate supply of local goods and infrastructures in urban areas of developing nations is an equilibrium phenomenon. We argue that the source of urban crises is an incorrect tax scheme that is propelled by the electoral motive of local governments. This chapter, hence, calls for reforms of property taxes, the implementation of property rights and the introduction of Tiebout-type competitive forces in the provision of local goods.

We take the recent experience of India as a test case with the following features. First, GDP growth has been remarkable during the last decade; secondly, reform programs at the national level have been appropriately implemented; thirdly, in terms of the Sachs–Warner index, the economy is moderately globalized; and fourthly, the pace of urbanization is moderate to low, in comparison with other developing nations. We show empirically that economic growth with increased pace of globalization has made most of the Indian states (regional governments) heavily indebted. We establish that local governments have been forced to offer (per capita) expenditure on local goods and social infrastructures below the absolute minimum, or norm, recommended by the Zakaria Committe (1963). This serious problem has not gone unnoticed: the Government of India introduced a series of measures from 1992 to devolve more power to local governments in order to redress this problem (the Eighth and Ninth Five-Year Plans). The World Bank and the Asian Development Bank (ADB) recommended a string of policy measures and introduced a number of projects to improve the quality of local goods and social infrastructure in the urban areas under several schemes. According to the Government of India Infrastructure Report (1996), an annual investment to the order of US$60 billion would be required for ten years in order to close the gap between demand for and supply of the urban water supply, sanitation and road networks. To put it baldly, the Government of India does not have necessary resources to fund these investment projects. The First Urban Development Plan of 1996 recommended a gradual reduction of traditional funding to local governments and a complete withdrawal of traditional funding by 2020 due to endemic budget deficits at the national level. The emphasis by the Government of India is on the commercialization of urban development projects, private partnership/participation in financing and delivery of the infrastructure at the municipal level, external assistance, foreign direct investment in urban development, tax-free municipal bonds, and expanding the local tax powers for local governments.

We argue in this chapter that these recommendations regarding various schemes and the legislative measures of the Indian Government to combat the urban crises may fail because of the equilibrium nature of urban under-development. To our understanding, this equilibrium feature of urban crises is a new finding and we argue that the urban crises cannot be overcome by one-shot closure of the gap between demand for and supply of urban local goods. For sustainable urban development our recommendation is two-fold: first, to introduce serious reforms at local levels so that local governments can raise significant revenues from the local base with appropriate accountability clauses. Secondly, it becomes mandatory to implement the property rights bill that will be a gigantic step towards introducing the forces of 'voting with their feet' in the urban sector. This may lead to some kind of efficient 'zoning' – an optimal tax-service package as predicted by the Tiebout model (1956). More particularly, the role of intergovernmental fiscal transfers is reduced and local governments can become financially more viable.

Globalization and provision of local public goods

The economic consequence of increased integration due to globalization is two-fold: first, nations become more interdependent in economic terms. Secondly, there arises a *perception* that trans-border trade and investment offer tremendous and often unprecedented economic opportunities for a nation. The first transition thus results in an increased integration of the world economy – through a mesh of multinational investment, trade flows and flows of financial capital – with an equally important transition in the *perception* about the importance of trans-border trade and investment as a vehicle of economic progress and prosperity for a nation. The second transition impacts on the realm of *national management* as national governments actively respond to this new perception that trans-border trade and investment offer great benefits to those nations that entertain relevant openness to foreign trade and investment. With the growing dose of competition, policy-makers tend to agree that the main barrier to the access of these spoils stems from the labyrinth of controls that became a by-product of the Keynesian era of lack of globalization. This leads to the third transition that paves the way for homogenization of economic ideologies, convergence of macroeconomic and trade policies and the consequent adoption of measures of domestic liberalization, privatization, decentralization and devolution. For any national government, options are pretty limited. Either it chugs along with the pre-existing regime of economic control with limited global trade as pursued by China and India in the 1960s, or alternatively the nation must ditch the *old-style* economy and substitute it with a functional market mechanism, openness to trans-border trade, liberalization of domestic and external sectors and exchange rates, and privatization of state-owned enterprises. The plan of this chapter is as follows: the next section documents how globalization can cause serious indebtedness to sub-national governments. The section after shows how globalization can be accompanied by serious urban crises in developing nations and in the last sections it is emphasized that simple economic growth calculus may not resolve urban crises.

Adverse impacts of globalization on sub-national governments (a case study of Indian states)

Economic globalization has resulted in a gradual reduction in restrictions on the free movement of capital along with harmonization and increasing standardization of the rules of the game that underpin global trade and investment and the regional dynamics. The driving force behind globalization is the mobility of corporate capital facilitated by the spread of modern technology. This aspect of globalization with a central role for corporate capital is having a profound impact on the functioning of governments in all countries. Large business corporations and multinational enterprises, in their quest for the maximum return on their capital, locate themselves in nations that provide the best environment for their operation such as easy enforcement of contracts, flexible labour laws, relative job insecurity of workers and friendly tax regimes. The most visible outcome has been that governments are obliged to provide public goods and services to corporate capital at taxes (prices) that do not meet the cost of their production and delivery. The citizens are therefore forced to accept fewer (and lower quality) governmentally provided goods and services than before. Not surprisingly globalization is accompanied by a transfer of the task of supplying goods and services that hitherto were the responsibility of the public sector to the private sector. The uncomfortable fact remains that the propagation of decentralization and privatization as the way to make governments more efficient has accompanied the gathering momentum of globalization. Thus, devolution of powers to sub-national governments has serious implications: first, the goal of devolution not only is to lessen the weight of responsibility carried by higher levels of government but also to foster an *opinion* that lower-level government means less and more efficient government. Secondly, the ability of governments to have a *rational design* of their public sector, in consonance with the wishes of their people, is being constrained by the dictate of fiscal harmonization in many matters particularly in taxation and also by a gradual erosion of tax bases. Finally, since sub-national debt and deficits have been a contributory factor in macro imbalance in developing countries, attention has to be given to reforms at the regional level with prescriptions that further chisel the policy space of sub-national governments.

Globalization episodes improved fiscal discipline at all levels of government for macroeconomic stability; measures initiated by the IMF and World Bank, the Washington Consensus, privatization and liberalization constitute the key elements of the economic framework that attracts both foreign and domestic investment. Does this trend imply an increased indebtedness and a resultant vulnerability for sub-national governments in the developing world? If it does, globalization can impinge on the ability of regional governments to design their public sector in an irreversible and serious fashion. To understand the impact of globalization on the indebtedness of sub-national governments, we cast a look at the Indian experience.

We conduct simple empirical exercises for Indian sub-national governments to shed light on this important issue of indebtedness. To do this we posit equation (A): the task of the equation is to explain state indebtedness of sub-national governments in India. SDEF measures the fiscal deficit of a state as a percentage of gross state's domestic product (GSDP). Two types of explanatory variables are used: annual inflation rate (INF) as a proxy for federal budgetary indiscipline and annual import growth (M) as a proxy for globalization. It is important to note that globalization in India in the 1990s meant a gradual dismantling of the impediments and barriers to imports. The sample period begins in 1989 and ends in 2002. The basic postulated equation is

$$SDEF = c + a_1 M + a_2 INF + u \tag{A}$$

Where c is a constant and u is the typical error term. Inflation figures (INF) are collected from RBI (2004) and import growth (M) is collected from import figures given by RBI, DGCl&S (2004). Fiscal deficits of 19 important states of India (out of 26) are collected from the 11th Finance Commission, Government of India (2000, Annex II.4, pp. 180–5). Table 4.1 presents a summary of the findings. The Indian Government offers a three-tier classification of Indian states: high-income states (H), middle-income states (M) and low-income states (L). We have taken the same classification and excluded states where urban sectors are less important.

Table 4.1 Responsiveness of fiscal deficits of Indian states to globalization (1989–2000)

States	Coefficient a_1 (globalization)	Coefficient a_2 (inflation)	R^2
5 high-income states	0.02	0.05	0.48
5 middle-income states	0.025	0.08	0.40
9 low-income states	0.05	0.23	0.34
19 overall	0.037	0.24	0.38

Source: Computed from RBI, DGCI&S (2004); the 11th Finance Commission, Government of India (2000), Annex II.4, pp. 180–5.

Before we discuss these findings we must keep in mind that these estimates are based on a small number of observations. Both the inflation rate and growth rate of imports have the expected sign on the indebtedness of sub-national governments (H, M and L alike). An increase in unanticipated inflation rate increases the indebtedness of sub-national governments – given the pre-committed budgetary transfers and tax allocations by the Central Government. An increase in import growth, as a proxy for increasing pace of globalization, increases the indebtedness of sub-national governments. Both these effects are statistically significant for 15 out of 19 states and also in groups, as the results show. It is also interesting to note that the magnitude of the effect of mismanagement of budgetary affairs, measured by inflation on sub-national debt (a_2) is larger than the magnitude of the effect of globalization (a_1) for all states. It is to be noted that we could not establish causality due to insufficient data. However, we are able to establish that all the states included in our analysis are major states and represent the status of significant indebtedness along with an increased pace of globalization as reflected in an increase in import growth.

How are individual states coping with debt repayments? Are the poor states more indebted than the rich? The picture is complex, as depicted in Table 4.2. We classify states as H, M and L and use a five-tier classification of degree of indebtedness of sub-national governments. These are high (interest payment as a percentage of revenue receipts in excess of 25%), high–medium (20%–25%), medium (15%–20%), low (10%–15%) and very low (less than 10%).

Table 4.2 shows that there is little correlation between the economic status of a state and its level/degree of indebtedness. Out of the four most indebted states one is high-income (H), one is middle-income (M) and two are low-income (L) states. Out of the three least indebted states,

Table 4.2 Degree of indebtedness and economic status of 19 Indian states, 1996–98

	High	High-medium	Medium	Low	Very Low
H	1	0	0	3	1
M	1	0	2	2	0
L	2	2	1	2	2

Source: The 11th Finance Commission, Government of India (2000), p. 102.

one belongs to the group of high-income states (H) and two are from the group of low-income states (L). The message is, at best, mixed. Although there is no trend, it would be instructive to analyse the link between sub-national debts and provision of local public goods.

Local public goods and urban crises: evidence from India

Globalization in India has been accompanied by a rapid era of urbanization since the early 1990s – 60% of Indian GDP is currently generated in the urban sector of India with about 350m urban population (30% of Indian population). The rapid urbanization and under-investment in urban infrastructure have resulted in serious gaps in demand for and supply of local goods in Indian cities. Urban households have limited access to potable water and adequate sewerage, drainage, sanitation, and waste disposal facilities. To improve the supply of local goods and to prevent further environmental degradation, the Indian Government is according increasing priority to urban infrastructure development and to strengthening of local governments. The 1992 74th Constitutional Amendment embodies a commitment to devolve greater authority and responsibility for urban management from the states to municipalities/local governments. Despite recent trends in decentralized governance, the gaps between demand and supply of local goods with limited infrastructural services has widened in urban areas. It is contended urban crises are partly a spin-off of the indebtedness of state and federal and local governments.

We have shown that economic growth with increased pace of globalization has made most of the Indian states heavily indebted. The Indian Government in its pursuit of macroeconomic stabilization packages has reduced its commitment to local funding. The obvious corollary is that urban bodies have little resources and enormous responsibilities. Here we now establish that local governments have been forced to reduce expenditure on (per capita) the core local goods and social infrastructures in real terms. This serious problem has not gone unnoticed: the Indian Government has introduced a series of measures since 1992 to devolve more power to local governments to redress this problem (the Eight and Ninth Five-Year Plans). The World Bank and the Asian Development Bank recommended a string of policy measures and introduced a number of projects to improve the quality of local goods and social infrastructure in the urban areas under several schemes. How serious is this problem of under-provision of urban local goods? We offer a very grim picture in Table 4.3 that clearly shows a serious under-provision of local goods and some kind of a local government failure in the 1990s in India. To convey this message, we explain the following detail:

Definition 1: Following the recommendation (norms) of the Zakaria Committee (1963) we define D as the minimum per capita expenditure on core (urban) local goods in India. This is an absolutist approach to define the basic minimum local goods (urban water supply, roads, basic public health facilities, primary schooling), which are *acceptable* to Indian society (see Gangopadhyay and Nath 2001a). The Government of India upgraded this norm of minimum per capita expenditure in 1997–98. We have used the inflation data and figures of urban population growth to calculate D as given in Table 4.3.

Definition 2: We define S as the actual per capita expenditure on core local goods. The data on local expenditure was collected in the Report of the 11th Finance Commission, Government of India (2000) and the population figures were collected from the Population Census (2001) published by the Registrar General of India.

Definition 3: We define a shortfall as the difference between the minimum (D) and the actual per capita expenditure (S). If $(D - S) > 0$, then there is a shortfall and a surplus if $(D - S) < 0$.

Definition 4: We define an index of local government failure G as $(D - S)/D$, which represents the inadequacy of a local government to supply the (updated) minimum per capita expenditure on core local goods as recommended by the Zakaria Committee (1963). Note that if $D - S > 0$ then $G < 1$ and the higher (lower) the value of G the larger (smaller) is the local government failure. For $D \leq S$ there is no local government failure. As the value of G increases it indicates a rise in the level of government failure.

Table 4.3 Index of local government failure

D (INR)	220	239.8	269.38	293.6	320	348.8	380.25	414.47	% change
High-income states (5)									
S (INR)	116.39	148.31	181.5	198.6	188.96	200.25	239.88	277.83	
(D−S)	103.61	91.49	87.88	95.00	131.04	148.8	140.37	136.64	
G=(D−S)/D	0.479	0.381	0.326	0.324	0.409	0.425	0.369	0.329	31.30%
S*	46.18	55.08	65.66	70.46	71.25	87.00	98.84	109.77	
(D−S*)	173.82	184.72	203.72	223.14	248.72	261.8	281.41	304.7	
G=(D−S*)/D	0.79	0.77	0.756	0.76	0.777	0.75	0.74	0.735	6.90%
Middle-income states (5)									
S	40	48.15	52.5	61.81	65.53	84.53	97.63	129.07	
(S−D)	180	191.65	216.88	231.78	254.47	264.27	282.62	285.4	
G=(D−S)/D	0.81	0.8	0.805	0.789	0.795	0.7576	0.74	0.6885	15%
Low-income states (9)									
S	37.8	43.24	53.8	54.79	62.47	68.13	78.14	82	
(S−D)	182	196.56	215.58	238.81	237.53	280.67	302.11	332	
G=(D−S)/D	0.82	0.819	0.8	0.813	0.8047	0.8046	0.7945	0.801	2.30%
Overall picture (all states)									
S (All States)	64.47	63.6	70	72	62.91	69.68	76.17	70	
(S−D)	155.53	176.2	199.38	221.6	257.1	179.12	304.08	344.47	
G=(D−S)/D	0.734	0.74	0.754	0.803	0.8002	0.7996	0.83	0.84	−14.50%
Maharashtra									
S	327	428	529	583	542	540	663	782	
(D−S) < 0	−107	−189	−259.6	−289.4	−222	−191.2	−282.75	−367.53	
S/D	1.48	1.78	1.96	1.98	1.69	1.57	1.74	1.88	27%
Years	1990	1991	1992	1993	1994	1995	1996	1997	Improvement in G

Notes: S*: Per capita local expenditure in high-income states excluding Maharashtra; INR: Indian rupee.
Source: 11th Finance Commission (2000), Government of India and Population census (2001), Registrar General, Government of India.

As Table 4.3 demonstrates, during the 1990s all Indian states (except Maharashtra that homes the mega city Mumbai) experienced some kind of serious local government failure in providing the basic minimal (urban) local goods to urban residents. One can safely state that all local governments (except that of Maharashtra) could only provide less than one-third of the per capita expenditure on local goods deemed as the basic minimum. During this phase, the Indian economy experienced considerable globalization, increased pace of urbanization and an era of unprecedented economic growth. Nevertheless the picture of urban life is pretty dismal – the basic minimum of local goods was not offered to more than 300m people. The shortfall, or gap, in the provision of local goods against the backdrop of the Zakaria norm is also amazingly high (more than 75%). This serious under-provision of local goods below the (recommended) absolute minimum is called *urban crises* in this work. This study does not argue that there is a statistical causality that runs from globalization to urban crises. However, the study highlights the possibility of serious urban crises because of privatization, decentralization, tax competition and devolution that typically accompany various doses of globalization.

Table 4.3 also points out an important dimension of interstate comparison of local government failure. During 1990–97 the local government failure improved by 31.3% in five high-income states. If we exclude the exceptional performance of Maharashtra, this increase in local government failure is 6.9% for four high-income states. Five middle-income show improvement in local government failure by 15% during the same period. It is important to note that nine low-income states posted 2.3% improvement in local government failure. While there is improvement in local government failure, in low- to high-income states, the picture is very bleak for the very poor states (not reported in the table). This conclusion is based on the overall picture of all Indian states showing 14.5% deterioration in local government failure. In the following section, we try to understand the theoretical foundation of urban crises.

Theoretical underpinning: local public goods and decentralization

The decentralization theorem of Oates (1972) suggests that local governments in advanced nations are effective in balancing the *preferences* and *cost* thereby achieving a mix of local goods that efficiently satisfies the local demand. However, such an effective allocation may be blocked by interest group influence (see Borge and Rattsø 1993; Borge et al. 1995) that may lead to inefficiency in allocation even in advanced nations. It is quite likely that conflicting interests of urban settlers in developing nations can also block an efficient allocation. The median voter model posits that local goods are supplied through a majority rule voting process. As a result, the supply response of a local government coincides with the preferences of the median voter (see Gangopadhyay and Nath 2001b; Rubinfeld 1987; Bowen 1943; Downs 1957). Such a notion is inconsistent with a local government that provides many local goods and is influenced by powerful political parties (see Borge et al. 1995; p. 137). In such a scenario different groups of voters struggle to enforce their influences on local government (see Craig and Inman, 1985; Renaud and van Winden 1991). As a result the paradigm of direct democracy has severe limitations in explaining the supply responses by local governments even in advanced industrial nations. The median-voter model may have very limited applicability in developing nations. In the context of advanced industrial nations the Tiebout (1956) hypothesis provides the theoretical underpinning of efficient local expenditure.

In this chapter we develop a model by applying the probabilistic voting theorem (see Wittman 1989) to explain an electoral equilibrium that, in turn, determines the supply of local goods in a developing nation.[1] The heart of the matter is that local taxes and goods typically entail political costs and benefits that a self-seeking government, driven by electoral motive, will want to exploit (see Gangopadhyay 2002). An incumbent local government will naturally choose a tax-service package to maximize the probability of its re-election. We start off with the political characteristics of voters and then apply the probabilistic voting theorem to determine the electoral equilibrium to determine the equilibrium urban tax-service package. The following section offers a simple model to explain the equilibrium nature of local government failure and urban crises.

A simple model: why do the local governments fail?

We postulate that there are N residents in an urban jurisdiction and these residents belong to two distinct groups of voters, namely, the rich and the poor. Out of these N voters, N^R are rich and N^P are poor. To keep the analysis tractable we also assume that the budget is to be allocated between two local goods – water supply (W) and roads and maintenance (Z). We develop a two-stage game to determine the equilibrium provision. At Stage I, the incumbent government announces local tax rates. Given the grants and aids, these tax rates will determine the size of the budget of the local government. At Stage II the incumbent allocates the budget between local goods W and Z. An election takes place at the local level at the end of Stage II. The goal of the incumbent is to get re-elected in the election.

We assume that voters have *ideal points* in terms of the allocation of budget. Voters from the same group have the same ideal point. As the actual allocation diverges from the ideal point of a group, more and more voters from this group will withdraw electoral support for the incumbent government. On the other hand, we assume, both groups dislike taxes; hence the higher (lower) the tax rate on a group the lower (higher) is the political support of this group to the incumbent. An electoral outcome is formed at the end of Stage II – given these tax rates at Stage I and the allocation of budget at Stage II. The incumbent maximizes votes in the election by choosing these taxes at Stage I and the budgetary allocation at Stage II, given the expected electoral outcome at the end of Stage II. If information is complete, in the relevant rational expectations equilibrium all players of the game correctly predict the electoral outcome and the incumbent adopts optimal taxes at Stage I and optimal budgetary allocation at Stage II wherefrom the overall equilibrium of the game evolves. In order to solve this game we apply the logic of backward induction: we start off with Stage II and characterize the electoral outcome. Rationality and complete information ensure that all players will form expectations by looking ahead and foreseeing the electoral outcome. At the overall Nash equilibrium of the game the incumbent chooses local taxes and a budgetary allocation to achieve an electoral outcome that maximizes the votes and, thereby, the probability of its re-election.

The precise sequence of moves

The game has two stages when specific decisions and events take place. We highlight these stages as Stage I and Stage II of the game. Before the game unfolds, important determinants of the game are exogenously given and we call them the history. We describe the sequence as:

History:

- Local government receives grant, aids and project-tied funds that we label as F. F is given exogenously.
- There are two distinct groups of residents/voters, namely the rich (R) and the poor (P) who have *ideal points* in the allocation of the local government budget.
- Voters' characteristics are a part of history.

Stage I:

- Local government announces individual tax rates T_R and T_P on the rich and the poor, respectively.
- These tax rates yield the revenue, T, of the local government.
- Thus the budget of the local government B is determined as:

$$B = T + F \qquad (1a)$$

Stage II:

- Local government allocates B between W and Z. That is,

$$B = W + Z = T + F \qquad (1b)$$

- The election takes place after the allocation of budget B at the end of Stage II.

Figure 4.1 summarizes the time-structure of these decisions.

Budgetary allocations of Stage II and payoff functions

In our simple model there are two groups of residents, R and P, and two local goods, W and Z. Preferences of these two groups over these two local goods are assumed to be quasi-linear. The ideal points are presented in the Figure 4.2.

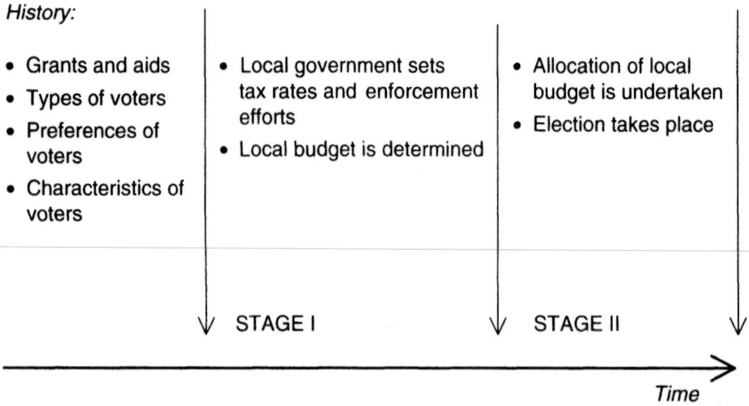

History:

• Grants and aids	• Local government sets tax rates and enforcement efforts	• Allocation of local budget is undertaken
• Types of voters		
• Preferences of voters	• Local budget is determined	• Election takes place
• Characteristics of voters		

STAGE I   STAGE II

Time

Figure 4.1   Time-structure of decisions

	W	Z
R	ϕ_R	$1 - \phi_R$
P	ϕ_P	$1 - \phi_P$

Notes: R: rich, P: poor, W: water supply, Z: roads and maintenance.

Figure 4.2 Ideal points of residents/voters

ϕ_R and $(1 - \phi_R)$ are respectively the split of the budget into W and Z as desired by the rich. As the actual allocation deviates from ϕ_R, a typical rich resident suffers a welfare loss. We similarly define ϕ_P. Let ϕ be the actual allocation of the budget by the local government. The utility function of a rich resident, U^R, is specified as

$$U^R = -(\phi_R - \phi)^2 \tag{1c}$$

The utility function of a typical poor resident is U^P:

$$U^P = -(\phi_P - \phi)^2 \tag{1d}$$

Let us call V total votes that the incumbent receives in the municipal election at the end of Stage II and V^R and V^P be the votes cast in favour of the incumbent by the rich and the poor, respectively. The goal of the incumbent is to maximize the probability of its re-election by maximizing votes. The payoff function of the incumbent, U^G, is simply the total votes that it receives in the election:

$$U^G = V^R + V^P \tag{2a}$$

Electoral framework of Stage II

In order to determine the provision of local goods we now look at the electoral equilibrium of Stage II. We apply the probabilistic voting theorem to explain the electoral equilibrium. It is assumed that the government seeks political support from both of these groups. It is possible that the local government succumbs to sectarian interests and rent-seekers and, hence, adopts a tax-service package for the benefit of one group of voters only (see Craig and Inman 1985; Renaud and van Winden 1991). However, under certain conditions, it can be shown that the local government has an incentive to represents a coalition of both these groups (see Gangopadhyay 2000).

Within a group voters have identical preference. Their preferences are represented by utility functions (1c) and (1d). Following the basic tenet of the probabilistic voting theorem, we write S^R and S^P as the sensitivity variables of these groups of voters. S^R represents the extent to which rich voters decrease their support/vote for the political party in response to a unit divergence between actual allocation and these voters' preferred allocation. S^P is defined in a similar fashion for poor voters. We specify the votes-to-offer function of the rich as the following:

$$V^R = N^R(1 + S^R U^R)\lambda^R \qquad (2b)$$

where V^R labels the votes that the incumbent receives from the rich, N^R denotes total number of rich residents, and λ^R is the proportion of rich residents who vote for the incumbent if the allocation equals the ideal point of the rich. We write the votes-to-offer function of the poor as:

$$V^P = N^P(1 + S^P U^P)\lambda^P \qquad (2c)$$

where V^P labels the votes that the incumbent receives from the poor, N^P and λ^P respectively denote the number of poor residents and the proportion of poor residents who vote for the incumbent if the allocation equals the ideal point of the poor resident. Given the tax rate T_R on the rich, we express the sensitivity variable of the rich, S^R, as the following:

$$S^R = 1 - [(\phi_R - \phi)^2 / T_R] < 1 \qquad (3a)$$

Similarly, we write S^P as:

$$S^P = 1 - [(\phi_P - \phi)^2 / T_P] < 1 \qquad (3b)$$

It is important to note that the sensitivity variable is positively related to the tax burden of voters and also to the divergence between the ideal point and the actual allocation. It is assumed that $(\phi_R - \phi) > 0$ and $(\phi_P - \phi) > 0$. Otherwise, we express the sensitivity function in terms of $(1 - \phi_R)$ and $(1 - \phi_P)$. Based on the above we offer the main result of this chapter in the following proposition.

Proposition 1: An *under-provision-equilibrium* characterizes the proposed game in which the incumbent maximizes its probability of re-election by simply choosing low taxes and inadequate provision of local goods.

Proof: The goal of the incumbent is to maximize (2a) by optimally choosing ϕ at Stage II and setting T_R and T_P at Stage I. Substituting (2b) and (2c) into (2a) yields the following optimization scheme for the incumbent at Stage II:

$$\text{Maximize } \{N^R(1+S^R U^R)\lambda^R + N^P(1+S^P U^P)\lambda^P\}$$

$$\{\phi\} \tag{3c}$$

Subject to (3a) and (3b)

The first order condition for the above optimization at Stage II is reduced to the following:

$$(\phi_R - \phi)N^R\lambda^R(1-(\phi_R-\phi)^2/T_R)+(\phi_P-\phi)N^P$$
$$\lambda^P(1-(\phi_P-\phi)^2/T_P) = 0 \tag{3d}$$

In the overall equilibrium, the incumbent chooses T_R and T_P at Stage I to maximize its probability of re-election in Stage II. One set of values of T_R and T_P at Stage I that will maximize votes cast in favour of the incumbent in the election is the following:

$$(1-(\phi_R - \phi)^2/T_R)) = 0 \tag{4a}$$

That is,

$$T_{R^*} = (\phi_R - \phi)^2 \tag{4b}$$

$$T_{P^*} = (\phi_P - \phi)^2 \tag{4c}$$

What is interesting is that the incumbent has the leeway to choose ϕ. One possibility to get re-elected is to set $\phi = \phi_P$, $T_P = 0$ and $T_{R^*} = (\phi_R - \phi_P)^2$. At this equilibrium the poor pay no taxes for local goods while the rich pay a little. The result is an under-provision equilibrium in which the local government raises very little resources locally and supplies inadequate local goods. QED.

This equilibrium leads to the vicious cycle of urban crises:

- *Why are local goods inadequate in supply?*
  It is because local governments have little resources.
- *Why do local governments have little resources?*
  It is because local taxes are low.

- *Why are local taxes low?*
  It is because local governments supply very little local goods.

Conclusion

Globalization has unleashed serious changes in various areas of the economic and social milieu of developing nations. It has been accompanied by a cascading gale of urbanization and sweeping changes in the ability of governments to have a rational design of their public sector that is in consonance with the wishes of their people. For example, despite a very impressive era of economic growth that accompanied globalization and urbanization in India during the 1990s, the picture of urban life is shown to be pretty dismal. The shortfall, or gap, in the provision of local goods against the norm is alarmingly high (more than 75%). We call this serious under-provision *urban crises*. These trends, however, have varying regional consequences as some regions will attract more business than those economically less-developed.

We argue that the urban crises reflect a local government failure that has an equilibrium nature: we find that the main problem of local governance in developing nations is the inability, or lack of willingness, of local governments to balance the *preference* and the *cost* of providing local goods. The heart of the problem is the low level of local taxes that is driven by the electoral motive of local governments. At these low taxes local governments are simply unable to provide adequate local goods. This tax-service package, however, creates an electoral equilibrium that ensures the political survival of a local government over time. Hence there is no incentive for these governments to improve local goods by increasing local taxes. Increases in grants and aids will have little effect on local goods supply, as they will end up in the coffer of corrupt bureaucrats and politicians. This is akin to the problem of incorrect pricing of a product in a market that is insulated from the forces of competition. *How to improve the quality of local goods?* There are two ways in which one expects an improvement. First of all, it is necessary to revamp the local tax system so that residents pay a decent price for a decent service and also ensure minimum resources are spent on these local goods (Zakaria Committee 1963). Secondly, in consonance with the era of decentralization and deregulation, we suggest that it may be necessary to introduce Tiebout-type competitive forces in providing local goods in order to redress urban crises in developing nations. Local tax reforms and forces of competition are necessary to break the electoral equilibrium that taxes little and provides minimal local goods.

Note

1. The probabilistic voting model is a recent development in political theory to counter the time-honoured predictions of traditional political theory: for centuries social thinkers argued that democratic governments are plagued by the absence of a stable electoral equilibrium and the risk of expropriation of minorities by majorities. This model establishes the existence of a stable voting equilibrium.

Bibliography

Bewley, T. (1981), 'A critique of Tiebout's theory of local public expenditure', *Econometrica*, **49**(3), 713–34.

Borge, L., J. Rattsø and R. Sørensen (1995), 'Local government service production: the politics of allocative sluggishness', *Public Choice*, 82, 135–57.

Borge, L. et al. (1993), 'The restructuring process in small and large municipalities: a dynamic model of local government priorities in norway', *Applied Economics*, 25(5), 589–98.

Bowen, H.R. (1943), 'The interpretation of voting in the allocation of resources'. *Quarterly Journal of Economics*, 58, 27–48.

Craig, S. and R.P. Inman (1985), 'Education, welfare and the "new" federalism: state budgeting in a federalist public economy', in H. Rosen (ed.), *Studies in the State and Local Public Finance*, pp. 187–227, Chicago: Chicago University Press.

Downs, A. (1957), *An Economic Theory of Democracy*, Harper and Row, New York.

Gangopadhyay, P. (2000), 'Coase theorem and coalitional stability: the principle of equal relative concession', *Theory and Decision*, 49, March, 179–91.

Gangopadhyay, P. (2002). 'Politics and nature of competition in oligopolistic markets', in A. Woodland (ed.), *Economic Theory and International Trade: Essays in Honour of Murray Kemp*, Cheltenham: Edward Elgar, pp. 78–85.

Gangopadhyay, P. and Shyam Nath (1989), 'Optimal mix of urban local goods: a game theoretic approach', *National Institute of Public Finance and Policy*, 5/89; July.

Gangopadhyay, P. and Shyam Nath (2001a), 'Bargaining, coalitions and local expenditure', *Urban Studies*, **38**(13), 2379–91.

Gangopadhyay, P. and Shyam Nath (2001b), 'Deprivation and incidence of urban public services', *Review of Urban and Regional Development Studies*, 13(3), 207–20.

Government of India (1980–88). Central Statistical Organisation, Annual Statistical Abstract. New Delhi.

Government of West Bengal (1986). West Bengal Municipal Finance Commission Report. Calcutta.

Henderson, J.V. (1985), 'The Tiebout Model: Bring Back the Entrepreneurs', *Journal of Political Economy*. 93(20), April, 248–64.

Kaul, I. (2003), *Providing Global Public Goods: Managing Globalization*, UNDP.

Krugman, P. and R.L. Elizondo (1996), 'Trade policy and the Third World metropolis', *Journal of Development Economics*, **49**, 137–50.

Oates, W. (1972), *Fiscal Federalism*, New York: Harcourt Brace & Javanovich.

Population Census (2001), Registrar General, Government of India, New Delhi.

RBI (2004), <http://www.indiaonestop.com/inflation.htm>.

RBI, DGCI&S (2004), http://www.indiaonestop.com/exim%20compo.htm.

Renaud, P. and F. van Winden (1991), 'Behavior and budgetary autonomy of local governments: a multi-level model applied to the netherlands', *European Journal of Political Economy*, **7**, 547–77.

Report (2000), The 11th Finance Commission, Ministry of Finance, Government of India, pp. 1–330, New Delhi.

Richardson, H.W. (2004), *The Impact of Globalisation on Urban Development*, Heidelberg, Springer.

Rubinfeld, D. (1987), 'The economics of local public sector', in A. Auerbach and M. Feldstein (eds), *Handbook of Public Economics*, pp. 571–645. Amsterdam: North-Holland.

Samuelson, P.A. (1954), 'The pure theory of public expenditure', *Review of Economics and Statistics*, **36**, 387–9.

Tiebout, C. (1956). 'A pure theory of local expenditure', *Journal of Political Economy*, **64**, 416–24.

UNDP (1993). Human Development Report, New York: Oxford University Press.

World Bank (1985), 'Urban Public Finance in Developing Countries, A Case Study of Metropolitan Bombay', Urban Development Report, No. 76–113, Bombay.

Wittman, P. (1989), 'Why Democracies Produce Efficient Results', *Journal of Political Economy*, 1395–424.

Zakaria, P. (1963). The Zakaria Committee Report, Government of India, New Delhi.

Part II

Labour Market Distortions and Inequalities

5
Globalization, Labor Markets and Gender: Human Security Challenges from Cross-Border Sourcing in Services

*Nahid Aslanbeigui and Gale Summerfield**

Globalization has transformed labor markets with mixed results. In the more developed countries (MDCs), a 'risk regime' has replaced the economic security afforded by mass production, collective bargaining and full-employment macroeconomic policy. As some workers celebrate opportunities created by the dynamic new world, others bemoan the insecurity resulting from flexible labor markets: unemployment, temporary jobs, and an expanding informal economy (Beck 2000). Bhagwati's optimism about the positive impact of trade on real wages of the unskilled may perhaps resonate with some workers in the United States (US) (2004, p. 126). But American service workers displaced in 2001–03 may only remember that a large percentage of them had not found employment by January 2004 or were re-employed at much lower pay, even with full-time positions (Jensen and Kletzer 2005).

Foreign direct investment has created more than 42 million jobs in export-processing zones (EPZs) globally (ILO 2004). Many workers in less developed countries (LDCs),[1] especially women, have migrated for jobs that may pay a premium over the national wage rates. The same jobs, however, have been criticized for long hours, involuntary overtime, underpayment of wages, and unsafe work environments (Pyle 2001). EPZs usually hire workers who migrate internally. International migration has also increased dramatically.

The estimated number of migrant workers – 120 million inclusive of their families (International Organization for Migration 2003, p.307) – combines those who migrate voluntarily in search of better opportunities and millions of women and children who are trafficked annually as domestic or sex workers. Even eternal optimists are disturbed by the rising number of trafficked humans and their plight (Bhagwati 2004, pp. 72, 89).

Prior to the 1990s changes in global employment patterns were determined by the production and trade of goods – more than half the displaced workers in the US were located in the manufacturing sector. In the past decade, however, labor markets have experienced a significant departure from old patterns. Increasingly, more service jobs move across the borders, nearshore or offshore, to captive centers or foreign-owned companies. Multinational companies (MNCs) have searched the globe for cheap qualified workers. Seventy percent of American workers displaced in 2001–03 were in non-manufacturing (Jensen and Kletzer 2005, p. 1). To date an estimated 300 000–995 000 US workers have lost their jobs because of cross-border sourcing in services (CBSS). The number of jobs at risk (14 million) is much higher, however (Center for American Progress 2004).

The service sector is the largest employer in MDCs.[2] Workers in tradable services do not live at the margins of society; they earn more and are better educated relative to workers in manufacturing or non-tradable services (Jensen and Kletzer 2005, p. 20). Thus, it is not surprising that CBSS has unleashed such a heated debate. Led by CNN's Lou Dobbs, the court of public opinion accuses MNCs of 'exporting' their countries, robbing the middle classes of jobs and comfortable living standards. There is mounting pressure on governments to reduce, if not eliminate, CBSS.

On the other side of the debate stand prominent mainstream economists who are sanguine about the consequences. Bhagwati et al. (2004) remind Americans that 70 percent of jobs require the service provider and consumer to be in each other's vicinity and argue that CBSS replaces lower-value jobs – bound to be eliminated by technology anyway – with better ones (2004, p. 31). Jeffrey Sachs and his co-authors predict that CBSS will help the American economy grow by an average annual rate of 0.2 percent until 2010 (Bajpai et al. 2004, p. 64). A comprehensive study by the McKinsey Global Institute (MGI 2005) agrees with these economists: the minuscule employment effects pale in comparison to the resulting lower prices for consumers, higher profit margins for firms, and future alleviation of labor shortages as the population ages.

Much of the debate on CBSS is focused on macroeconomic variables: aggregate labor productivity, growth, unemployment, and prices. Missing from the discussion are domestic and global redistributions in labor markets along gender lines. This chapter is a step toward filling the vacuum. After explaining our choice of terminology, we concentrate on the gender impact of CBSS on MDCs, LDCs and the globe. Since space is limited, we concentrate on the US and India, with references to China.[3] Given the dynamic, and therefore uncertain, nature of future labor market outcomes, the conclusion highlights the need for gender-conscious measures that provide economic security for workers world-wide.

Terminology

Pioneers in CBSS began with back-office business operations in finance, banking and insurance and software development and maintenance in the late 1980s and early 1990s (Bajpai et al. 2004). By the beginning of the new millennium, hundreds of MNCs had joined the burgeoning search for cheap, qualified labor world-wide. In the process, an impressive number of occupations were affected, ranging from radiology, software development, and animation to call-center operations, medical transcription, and hedge-fund administration. The Resource Group, a call-center company founded by Pakistani Americans, has stretched the limits by hiring a virtual secretary who can greet visitors to its headquarters in Washington, D.C., direct telephone calls, arrange meetings, order sandwiches and open the door for mail delivery, all from Karachi (Kalita 2005).

The literature on CBSS does not yet have standardized terminology; outsourcing, offshoring, and global sourcing in services refer to the same phenomenon. It is not hard to understand why we prefer cross-border sourcing in services instead. Outsourcing, the most frequently used term, is the least satisfactory because it is not limited to services. A characteristic feature of post-Fordist manufacturing firms is the 'extensive use of independently owned suppliers linked with the buying firm by close communication and joint planning' (Milgrom and Roberts 1990, p. 526). Outside contractors may be located within the country. World-wide, a large number of corporations in insurance, banking and air transportation have contracted out at least some of their information technology (IT) operations to domestic firms because their IT departments are saddled with forty-year-old mainframe technology (*The Economist* 2004). In addition, firms that cross borders may operate out of captive centers instead of contracting the work out to foreign firms.

Offshore outsourcing, a second and better characterization, faces problems of its own. American workers may be replaced by workers who live across the border, but not offshore, in Canada or Mexico; some countries may not have any shores, because they are landlocked. In addition, the term sometimes does not include 'nearshore' operations. It does not make any difference to American workers whether they are displaced by workers in Mexico or India.[4]

We propose changes in other terms as well. CBSS seems to affect two areas. There is a consensus on the scope of IT operations: 'software development and maintenance activities' (Nicholson 2001, p. 9). Back-office activities and customer service are either categorized as ITES (IT enabled services) or BPO (business process outsourcing). A growing number of publications categorize such activities as ITES–BPO services. We eliminate the overlap by using the acronym ICTES: services that are enabled by either information or communication technology.

Gender dimensions of CBSS

The gender impact of CBSS is rarely evaluated (Kelkar et al. 2002 is an exception). Systematic data on the number of jobs crossing borders are not yet available. Sporadic estimates are not disaggregated by gender. Although illuminating, ethnographic studies on gender dimensions of call-center operations are limited in scope (Mirchandani 2004, 2005; Freeman 2001). A detailed report on gender and technology (Hafkin and Taggart 2001) does not contain much on CBSS. This chapter is a step toward filling the vacuum. Since MDCs and LDCs have conflicting interests at least in the short run, we treat each separately, using examples from the US, India and China.

Gender impacts on MDCs: the US

At current trends, the aggregate employment effects of CBSS are not alarming. The majority of service jobs require direct interaction between providers and consumers (Bhagwati et al. 2004). IT professionals will continue to provide custom-made technology services; landscapers will be hired to beautify American gardens; and healthcare workers will care for patients, an increasingly significant phenomenon as the population ages.

CBSS can reduce the price of services, increasing domestic demand. Cheaper IT services, for example, may result in the integration of IT into sectors that have not yet been transformed by it: retail trade, healthcare, and construction (Mann 2003, p. 4). New jobs will be created as a result, some of which will likely remain in the country.

The US may lose 3.3 to 6 million service jobs by 2015 (Center for American Progress 2004), a small fraction of the total number of jobs in the country (currently above 120 million). But the Schumpeterian process of creative destruction will also generate jobs. Currently, employment at the low end of the skill spectrum in tradable services is falling. However, there is 'little evidence that tradable service industries or occupations have lower employment growth than non-tradable industries or occupations' (Jensen and Kletzer 2005, p. 20). Although shrinking, the American balance of payments data record a consistent annual surplus in traded services for the past decade (the 1995 surplus was 1.6 times higher than that in 2004) (US Department of Commerce, 2005).

Scholars forecast that MDCs will show healthy employment growth rates in the foreseeable future because of their superior legal and institutional structures. Strong legal frameworks, cutting-edge university education, private and government support for R&D, effective governance (transparency and accountability), rule of law, and protection of (intellectual) property rights will ensure that they remain at the forefront of innovation and product development (Trefler 2005; Dossani 2005; Vernon 1966). Employment will grow where new technology and products are introduced. Firms will seek cheap labor in other countries only when processes are codified and products standardized. At the high-end of the animation industry, for example, three-dimensional (3D) production remains in-house for several reasons: technology is so complex and costs so high that very few firms in the world have such production capability. There is a great deal of tacit knowledge, and significant interaction is necessary among animators, software engineers and technical assistants in lighting, shading and modeling. In 2D animation, however, some tasks have become mechanistic and partitioned, making it possible for the labor-intensive production phase to be outsourced to companies in the Philippines and India (Tschang and Goldstein 2004).

Leading economists seem to agree that the qualitative consequences of CBSS are not different from trade in manufacturing at least in terms of wage and employment. When data are disaggregated by gender, however, results are surprising. Workers displaced in the manufacturing sector are more likely to be male: in 2003, male workers held over 70 percent of the jobs in production occupations (US Department of Labor 2004).[5] In contrast, job displacement in tradable services seems to have affected women more heavily. Except for engineering and computer and mathematical categories, women dominate almost every occupation that is threatened by CBSS, their

Table 5.1 US employment share and salaries of female full-time workers by occupation, 2003

Occupation	Women's share of employment (%)	Women's median annual earnings ($)	Women's earnings as % of men's
Architecture and engineering occupations	17.87	*43 004*	*75.6*
Architects, except naval	25.42	NA	NA
Chemical engineers	1.31	NA	NA
Civil engineers	10.22	NA	NA
Computer hardware engineers	11.34	NA	NA
Electrical and electronics engineers	7.41	NA	NA
Drafters	19.28	NA	NA
Engineering technicians, except drafters	21.20	29 588	69.3
Computer and mathematical occupations	*27.84*	*47 112*	*80.2*
Computer scientists and systems analysts	30.29	45 188	81.0
Computer programmers	26.62	50 596	87.3
Computer software engineers	22.25	52 260	75.2
Computer support specialists	35.50	37 804	94.6
Database administrators	42.25	NA	NA
Network and computer systems administrators	24.69	NA	NA
Network systems and data communication analysts	21.30	42 484	73.4
Operations research analysts	48.07	49 660	83.3
Business and financial operations occupations	*56.50*	*38 688*	*73.3*
Human resources, training and labor relations specialists	69.9	40 248	80.6
Management analysts	44.70	50 804	77.1
Accountants and auditors	58.33	39 312	72.6
Legal occupations	*52.05*	*27 716*	*53.8*
Paralegal and legal assistants	86.55	35 620	NA
Miscellaneous legal support workers	76.31	33 956	NA
Healthcare practitioner and technical occupations	*74.46*	*40 040*	*76.8*
Medical records and health information technicians	97.64	26 104	NA

Office and administrative	*74.32*	*26 676*	*87.9*
support occupations			
First-line	67.86	31 668	79.4
supervisors/managers of			
office and admin support			
Bill and account collectors	70.25	25 532	94.7
Book-keeping, accounting,	91.41	26 624	86.0
and auditing clerks			
Payroll and timekeeping	90.20	28 080	NA
clerks			
Customer service	69.06	26 156	89.9
representatives			
Receptionists and	93.16	23 192	89.2
information clerks			
Human resources assistants,	89.47	30 420	NA
except payroll and			
timekeeping			
Reservation and	68.30	26 104	NA
transportation ticket			
agents and travel clerks			
Secretaries and	96.34	27 612	92.7
administrative assistants			
Computer operators	49.40	26 780	75.3
Data entry keyers	81.25	25 376	92.2
Word processors and typists	91.11	26 780	NA
Insurance claims and policy	85.29	28 392	NA
processing clerks			
Office clerks, general	83.63	26 104	99.9

Source: US Department of Labor, 2004, pp. 12–16.

share exceeding 90 percent in some cases (Table 5.1). The total number of women in all the listed occupations (11 012 000) is nearly twice as many as that of men (5 919 000) (based on the US Department of Labor 2004, pp. 12–16). In 2003, almost 43 percent of the total number of jobs in the US were in office and administrative support, with a 74 percent female share. In addition, jobs in female-dominated occupations seem more susceptible to CBSS. Only 6 percent of the total jobs placed in other countries are projected to be in architecture and engineering occupations. The share of office and administrative support occupations is a significant 50 percent (Table 5.2).

Bajpai et al. (2004) predict no long-term downward pressure on American wages. The number of eliminated jobs is small. Moreover, displaced workers earn wages that are below the national average. The elimination of their jobs should, therefore, raise the national average wage (2004, pp. 59–60). Bhagwati et al. (2004) provide vivid examples of the

Table 5.2 Share of American jobs moving offshore by occupational category (%), 2000–15

Occupational category	2000	2005	2010	2015
Management occupations	0	6	7	9
Business and financial operations	11	10	10	10
Architecture and engineering	3	5	5	6
Legal occupations	2	2	2	2
Office and administrative support occupations	53	50	50	50

Source: Forrester Research Report 2002, in Bajpai et al. 2004.

dynamism of the American economy: for every radiologist who loses a job to India, many other health professionals find employment in treating obesity or performing 'face-lifts' and 'chin tucks' on the aging female baby boomers: 'outsourcing is unlikely to lower the wage level of the displaced US workers *except in the short-term*' (2004, p. 30; emphasis added). But even the short-term costs do not seem to move these authors. They celebrate, for example, Kletzer's 2001 study on job displacement in the manufacturing sector over the 1979–99 period: the rates of re-employment and wage change were no different for workers who were displaced by trade relative to others. Two-thirds of the displaced found jobs within two years, 50 percent at equal or higher pay. Framed differently, however, these data are disappointing: one-third of the displaced workers remained unemployed for more than two years; only 33 percent of the total number displaced found jobs at the same or higher pay. Another 33 percent experienced wage reductions of 15 percent or more.

A new study by Jensen and Kletzer shows that workers displaced by trade – defined as those who leave their jobs or lose them because of plant/company closing/relocation – have a higher rate of loss in jobs and wages compared to those in non-tradable sectors despite being more educated (2005, p. 20). Table 5.3 records the characteristics of displaced workers over a three-year period (2001–03), based on the displaced workers survey of the Bureau of Labor Statistics in January 2004.[6] The re-employment rates (full and part-time combined) range from 69 to 80 percent. The average wage in all the listed industries/occupations has declined, affecting more than 50 percent of those who returned to full-time positions.

Despite steady advances in the past decades, occupations remain highly segregated (Table 5.1). Since women dominate the office and administrative support occupations, which are most threatened by CBSS,

Table 5.3 Characteristics of American displaced workers in tradable services, 2001–03

Characteristic	Manufacturing (industry)	Information (industry)	Professional and business services (industry)	Office and admin. support (occupations)
% full-time before Displacement	96	93	91	89.6
% re-employed	64	72	71	69.1
Of re-employed, % full-time (FT)	80	76	80	75.8
All re-employed, % change in earnings	−32	−57	−34	−22.7
FT to FT, change in earnings (mean)	−21	−40	−18.5	−11.3
FT to FT, % with no loss in earnings	42	36	49	47.1

Source: Jensen and Kletzer 2005, Tables 19–21.

it is more likely that they will bear a disproportionate cost of the transformation caused by comparative advantage in services. Bhagwati et al. (2004) believe that workers will not be burdened except in the short run. The short-run may not be as short as they think, however. The average duration of unemployment has become much longer in recent years (Mukoyama and Şahin 2004). This is partly due to rapid technological change, which increases retraining costs (Baumold and Wolff 1998). In addition to many other obstacles, a quarter of a million dollars stands between Maria, a displaced customer representative, and an operating room, where she can perform plastic surgery on female executives who can afford 'face-lifts' and 'chin tucks.'

When manufacturing was giving way to services, displaced blue-collar workers turned to a service (tertiary) sector that was primarily nontradable. There is no fourth sector for displaced white-collar workers; they must compete with other service workers in a sector that is increasingly more tradable. This exacerbates the potential for increasing 'the number of sectors and workers whose prices and wages will be determined in global markets' (Shelburne 2004). This is not good news for the Marias of the US, who are already at the low-end of the income scale. The median wage for women in office and administrative support is $26 676; and in every occupational category listed in Table 5.1 women earn less than men.

Displaced service workers are not likely to receive generous assistance from the social safety net. The most common protector of unemployed workers is unemployment insurance, which runs out after 26 weeks. The built-in restrictions of this program exclude nearly 60 percent of all unemployed workers. The Trade Adjustment Assistance (TAA), signed into law in 1962 to protect workers displaced by trade, was extended in 2002 to cover agricultural, but not service, workers (Brainard et al. 2005). Currently, a significant number of low-wage, predominantly female, white-collar workers are displaced without much help from the social safety net. Regardless of whether they are replaced by technology or trade, they lack the means to survive long spells of unemployment or to retrain for the high-end jobs that economists so enthusiastically promise will be created.

Gender impacts on LDCs: India and China

As suppliers of cheap labor, developing nations benefit significantly from CBSS, at least in the short run. The benefits, however, vary dramatically across countries. Revenues from IT–ICTES in India have been growing at an average annual rate of 30 percent for the past decade, reaching an estimated $28 billion and comprising 4.1 percent of its GDP in 2005 (NASSCOM 2005). MGI (2005) lists many other countries as potential hubs for CBSS, spanning Asia, Eastern Europe, and Latin America.[7] By 2015 China is predicted to emerge as a major player, having the best risk profile for CBSS (Minevich and Richter 2005). To date, it has concentrated on manufacturing; 30 million of the approximately 42 million EPZ workers around the world are in China (ILO 2004). In the service sector, exports stress high-end services, a trend that may continue in the future (Aggarwal 2004). China's IT sector is fragmented, and although it educates more engineers than India, the proportion qualified for MNC work is much smaller (MGI 2005). Currently, China's IT–ICTES workers lack the necessary language skills despite costing more.

With the exception of South Africa, sub-Sahara is excluded from trade in services. The same considerations that drive MNCs toward India and China prevent them from locating in Africa. The HIV-AIDS epidemic, civil strife, inadequate education, and the wide digital divide – worse for women than men (Hafkin and Taggart 2001) – may exclude this large segment of the world population from the benefits of globalization (Castells 2000, p. 432). In the Middle East Israel is the only country that receives sizeable contracts in services from other countries (MGI 2005). Iran and Arab countries together employ about 700 000 workers in EPZs

(ILO 2004). The experience with these zones may help prepare them for service sourcing. But cultural, economic and political obstacles may prevent the benefits of transnational service work from reaching female workers in the region.

CBSS is a significant source of employment growth for countries that attract MNCs. In India, total employment in IT–ICTES grew about 268 % over 2000–05. Currently, the sector employs more than 1 million workers directly and another 2.5 million indirectly (based on NASSCOM 2005). Even if women did not occupy these positions, they would benefit from growth in household incomes that increases opportunities for consumption, education and investment. But women do profit from employment opportunities directly. An estimated 383 000 women are employed in India's IT–ICTES (Table 5.4). Although comparable data are not available for women in China, women's share of employment in services is significant, ranging from 31 percent to 46 percent (Table 5.5).

The female share of employment in the Indian IT sector is forecast at 35 percent. However, the sector is large enough to include more than half of all women who export their services (Table 5.4). The average

Table 5.4 Women's employment share in Indian IT–ICTES sectors, 2005 forecasts

Sector	Total employed (000)	% female	No. of women employed (000)
IT	697	35	244
ICTES	348	40	139
Total	1045	37	383

Source: Calculated from NASSCOM 2003, 2005.

Table 5.5 Female employment share in China, selected sectors, 2002 (year end)

Sector	% female
Post and telecommunication services	37.3
Finance and insurance	45.9
Banking	41.2
Information and consultative services	38.9
Computer application services	30.8
Technology application + dissemination, science and technology exchange services	35.3
Engineering design	32.1

Source: China Statistical Yearbook 2003, Tables 5-3 and 19-1.

IT salary of an Indian employee ranges between $5000 and $12 000 (Bajpai et al. 2004, Table 5.3), far below that of the average American IT worker ($60 000–$80 000) (Bardhan and Kroll 2003, p. 4). But it is much higher than India's per capita income ($620 in 2004; see World Bank 2005). Earnings in the ICTES sector are lower but vary considerably according to worker characteristics and firm ownership structure. In Mirchandani's survey of call centers in India (2004), workers with at least an undergraduate degree received salaries in the $1440–$2640 range. In Poster's survey (2004), the average operator earned more. MNCs paid higher salaries ($7008) compared to joint-ventures ($5076) and Indian firms ($4536). The age and level of education varied positively with the degree of foreign ownership. Thus, a US-owned call center hired workers in the 22–30 age range who had post-college degrees. In contrast, Indian firms worked with younger high-school graduates (18–20).

Although CBSS creates job opportunities for women, it may not create salaries comparable to men's earnings. Data on wage differentials are either not available or are not disaggregated by occupation. In China, women earn substantially less than men in the private sector, where export firms are likely to be located, as well as in services (Table 5.6). Some scholars have captured the earning differentials in Indian IT–ICTES occupations but only qualitatively (Kelkar et al. 2002). The division of labor adopts the traditional form. Men are concentrated in high-pay, senior management positions, or jobs that carry decision-making power. The story is a familiar one: women occupy less important positions and receive lower pay, because family ties prevent them from putting in 18–hour days, or improving their chances through frequent job searches. Cultural and legal barriers prevent women from traveling and living

Table 5.6   Real annual earnings of female Chinese workers as a percentage of male workers' earnings, 2003

Overall	*71*
By institution	
State-owned enterprises	83
Private firms and self-employment	70
By occupation	
Managerial personnel	89
Technicians and engineers	83
Administrative personnel	80
Workers in manufacturing sector	74
Workers in service sector	78

Source: Dong et al. 2005, Table 10.

alone or working at night (Kelkar et al. 2002; Poster 2004). Although back-office services can be performed in daytime hours, call centers usually operate at night to meet customer demand in North America and Europe. The government has had to relax its regulations in some cases to allow night shifts for women.

Ethnographic studies of Indian IT–ICTES highlight other negative aspects of such jobs (Mirchandani 2004, 2005; Poster 2004). They are found to be repetitive and tedious but stressful. Jobs in call centers are particularly so because of Tayloristic monitoring. Some workers resent assuming false identities, having to change their accent, voice and even names to put their customers at ease. Others feel cut off from their social networks because of working night shifts. The work-force is segregated along gender lines. Women seem to be concentrated in jobs that require 'feminine' skills such as performing emotional labor. Employers consider them better equipped at deferring to 'the authority of the customer,' or 'listening carefully to customer needs and providing information in ways which boost customer self-confidence' (Mirchandani 2005, p. 11).

The gender significance of jobs created by CBSS should not be discounted, however. Monotonous and stressful as they may be, they are by no means undesirable. Feminists have long expressed concern about the disproportionate representation of women in the informal economy (Chen et al. 2005). The new jobs are created in the formal economy. Young single women, who were traditionally prevented from living alone, have acquired the independence to live 'away from their families and male relatives' (Kelkar et al. 2002, p. 75). Some call centers house their workers in 'clean, well-organized structures, which often have entrances decorated with glass and marble' (Mirchandani 2004, p. 367); others offer canteens and recreation rooms (Blobspot.com 2004). In a country where women's educational achievements are systematically below men's at all levels (see Table 5.7), women receive extensive language training, a skill which is transferable to other jobs. They are also immersed in information about other cultures, raising their awareness about their relative position in global labor markets.[8] This consciousness guides some workers to search for better opportunities (Mirchandani 2004, p. 369). Many workers use jobs created by CBSS as a step on the career ladder. Some leave other service industries to enter IT–ICTES because it is 'an emerging phenomenon' (Kelkar et al. 2002, p. 76). Others use their newly found skills to access education or jobs in countries such as the US (Poster 2004, p. 14).[9]

In LDCs, workers suited to IT–ICTES work are a small fraction of the labor force available for such services. As a result increased demand

Table 5.7   Education indicators in India

Indicator	India (2000–01)	
	Female	*Male*
Adult literacy Rate (%)	44	70
Female Share (%)		
Primary schools	43.82	
Middle schools	40.82	
Secondary	38.65	
Colleges/Universities	37.5	

Sources: Government of India 2002.

due to CBSS has put upward pressure on wages in some countries. In 2004, *The Economist* reported that wage inflation in some Indian high-tech companies was 15–17 percent and growing. Such trends can push MNCs toward other countries that have cheaper but qualified labor. Indian workers may therefore lose while workers in Sri Lanka and Bangladesh gain. The gender impact of such changes will depend on cultural, economic and legal barriers in the respective countries. Under a worse scenario, the increased cost of labor may lead to the development of labor-saving technology in MDCs – ironically with Indian or Chinese workers' help – in which case labor, male or female, loses world-wide.

Human security outcomes will be worse for LDC women relative to men regardless of mechanism that displaces labor. Usually, women have a higher relative unemployment rate. In 2003 the urban unemployment rate was 4.5 percent higher for Chinese women compared to men (Dong et al. 2005). In 1999–2000, the female–male unemployment differential in urban areas of India was 2.3 percent (Government of India 2002, Table 36). In LDCs unemployed workers, men or women, cannot rely on a generous social safety net even in the short run because it is either inadequate or non-existent. Special assistance introduced by governments usually has a male bias. In 2000–01, for example, the female share of employment created by poverty alleviation programs in rural India was a mere 27.2 percent (ibid., Table 46).

Global gender impacts of CBSS

The conflicts of globalization are readily apparent in CBSS. On the one hand, workers in MDCs lose their jobs. A significant share of the displaced workers remains unemployed for long durations without much government assistance. Those who are re-employed have a good chance of not having a full-time job, or having one at significantly lower pay. On the other hand, workers in LDCs gain jobs that would not have existed if not for CBSS. Although they earn much less than their northern counterparts, they may earn substantially above their own average national income. The future of these jobs, however, is not certain. Wage pressures in LDCs, or technological advancement or economic downturns in MDCs may transfer jobs from one country to another or eliminate them entirely. Displaced LDC workers are relatively worse off compared to their MDC counterparts because of the lack of government-funded safety nets.

The gender dimensions of labor market conflicts are fascinating. In the US a significant share of the jobs in ICTES is held by women. Although increasing, that share is much lower in countries like India and China (Tables 5.4, 5.5). Thus, the gender composition of the global workforce in ICTES is changing in favor of men. The IT sector seems to move in the opposite direction, however. Although women hold a minority share of jobs in IT world-wide, their share seems to be smaller in the US (Table 5.1) than in India or China (Tables 5.4, 5.5). The global share of women in the IT sector, therefore, seems to be increasing albeit marginally. Consider the case of Microsoft, which has invested considerable resources in global high-tech research and education. The ratio of women to men is highest in the Beijing lab and lowest in Cambridge, UK (Table 5.8).

Many observers neglect class or regional dimensions of the global redistribution of jobs. Although it is true that jobs travel from rich MDCs to poorer LDCs, they are transferred to relatively better-off members of the population who can afford to continue their education.

Table 5.8 Number and share of female employees in Microsoft labs world-wide

	Redmond, USA	Bay Area, USA	S. Valley, USA	Cambridge, UK	China	Bangalore, India
No. of female employees	39	4	3	3	25	NA
Female share	11%	11%	10%	5%	15%	
No. of male employees	331	34	26	61	140	NA
Male share	89%	89%	90%	95%	85%	
Total no.	370	38	29	64	165	24(est)

Source: based on Microsoft 2005.

IT–ICTES jobs also favor urban dwellers, who are young, educated, and can speak fluent English. In India, half of all the students graduate around one of the four hubs for such services: Mumbai, Delhi, Bangalore and Hyderabad (MGI 2005). The rest of the country is relatively untouched by the phenomenon.

Conclusion: 'Into the unknown'

CBSS joins the growing informal economy, transnational migration and export processing as a key cause of shifting employment patterns globally. The distribution of future benefits and costs of such shifts is highly unpredictable. MDCs will draw long-term benefits if they invest in enhancing the skills of the labor force and developing sophisticated technology (Trefler 2005, p. 29). Experience proves that women's employment share drops as the technology content of jobs increases. It is unlikely that LDCs will rob MDCs of their comparative advantage in high-end products. Instead they may try to relieve wage pressures by increasing the education and training of their work-forces. Whether women will benefit from such expenditures depends on the government's awareness of gender bias in investment, education and training in addition to the vigilance of women's groups.

The distribution of costs and benefits will also depend on the frequency and depth of systemic shocks. If East Asia is any indication, global financial crises hurt LDCs more, increasing unemployment rates and poverty many fold. However, financial pressures may force MNCs to restructure possibly increasing the flow of CBSS in the long term. Women suffer heavier losses during economic downturns and gain less when opportunities increase.

The cost and benefits of CBSS may be unpredictable for different regions of the world but its labor displacement consequences are a certainty. Duration of unemployment may be long, affecting the human security of the displaced and their families across the globe. These considerations have prompted economists to call for programs that assist workers in MDCs. In the US, they suggest, TAA should be extended to cover displaced workers in tradable services. Since this move may not cover a significant share of such workers, Brainard et al. (2005) propose government-funded wage insurance. Duration of unemployment may be reduced and firms' motivation to train workers increased if the government pays 50 percent of the difference between the pre- and post-deployment earnings for two years. Such a scheme boosts economic security but leaves training to firms. Since women are crowded in unskilled positions, they will need more training. Higher retraining costs may prevent firms from hiring women. The scheme seems to have a built-in bias against women

There is no reason why social safety nets, adjustment assistance, or wage insurance should be restricted to workers in MDCs. Revenues from the Tobin tax on traded foreign exchange – currently under consideration by Canada, France, Belgium, Germany and the UK – can be used not only to alleviate poverty, but to insure workers who are displaced by trade in services. Along similar lines Pearson (2003) has proposed a Maria tax on exported goods and services worth evaluating.

CBSS transforms global labor markets and threatens human security in the process. Measures that create job opportunities, (re)train workers or protect their incomes need to be gender conscious. Otherwise the consequences of CBSS will be no different from other types of economic transformation where women gain relatively less and lose relatively more.

Notes

* We thank Chun Shing Wong for valuable assistance in the research phase of this project.
1. There is no satisfactory classification for countries that are more or less advanced. Since development is a continuum, and our focus is on the economics of human security, we use MDCs and LDCs fully cognizant of their shortcomings.
2. In May 2003 nearly 90% of the American workforce was concentrated in two categories: sales and related occupations and office and administrative support (US Department of Labor, Bureau of Labor Statistics, Occupational Employment Statistics).
3. The US is at the forefront of CBSS, with the United Kingdom (UK) trailing as a distant second. India is the main provider of services to the US and the UK – the American share of India's IT exports was 69.05% in 2002–03 compared to Europe's 22.25% (Bajpai et al. 2004, p. 44).
4. Bajpai et al. 2004 have devised another phrase: global sourcing in services. Although less problematic, it can refer to domestic activities as well.
5. Most, but not all, production jobs are in manufacturing. Women seem to dominate three production occupation categories: electrical, electronics and electromechanical assemblers (60.24%); pressers, textile, garment and related materials (75%); and sewing machine operators (75.81%). Jobs in these occupations are, however, a small portion (6.71%) of the total number of jobs in production occupations (based on US Department of Labor 2004, Table 2).
6. These numbers should be viewed with a degree of caution owing to the recession in the technology sector at the beginning of the millennium.
7. Latin America and Eastern Europe are not as attractive as Asia because of higher labor costs, although they have the requisite risk, infrastructure, and

education characteristics. They may be able to attract more demand for their workers if CBSS continues to bid wages up in Asia.

8. Some call centers in India accept accounts not just from the US but also Australia, Canada and the UK (Poster 2004, p. 19).

9. Freeman has recorded how women who work in ICTES in Barbados and other Caribbean countries have established side-line higglering businesses. These involve trips to other countries for purchasing products that will be resold to co-workers. They also provide opportunities for 'seeing new sites, enjoying themselves, feeling fashionable and adept at finding "good deals," and in constructing forms of femininity that defy traditional boundaries that are both gendered and formulated along the lines of class' (2001, p. 1026).

References

Aggarwal, Alok (2003), *The Future of IT Industry in India and China*, Evalueserve presentation, <sccie.ucsc.edu/documents/workshops/global_it/2003/Aggarwal.pdf>.

Bajpai, Nirupam, Jeffrey D. Sachs, Rohit Arora, and Hapreet Khurana (2004), 'Global services sourcing: issues of cost and quality', CGSD Working Paper No. 16, Center on Globalization and Sustainable Development, Columbia University.

Bardhan, Ashok D. and Cyntha Kroll (2003), 'The new wave of outsourcing', Fisher Center Research Report 1103, University of California, Berkeley.

Baumol, William J. and Edward N. Wolff (1998), 'Speed of technical progress and length of the average interjob period', Jerome Levy Economics Institute Working Paper No. 234, May.

Beck, Ulrich (2000), *World Risk Society*, Cambridge: Polity Press.

Bhagwati, Jagdish (2004), *In Defense of Globalization*, New York: Oxford University Press.

Bhagwati, J., A. Panagariya and T.N. Srinivasan (2004), 'The muddles over outsourcing', *Journal of Economic Perspectives*, 93–114.

Blobspot.com (2004), Call Center Services India, January 11–16; online at <http://www/callcenterservicesindia.blogspot.com/2004>

Brainard, Lael, Robert E. Litan, and Nicholas Warren (2005), 'A fairer deal for America's workers in a new era of offshoring', prepared for the Brooking Trade Forum, Washington, D.C.

Castells, Manuel (2003), 'The rise of the Fourth World', in David Held and Anthony McGrew (eds) *The Global Tranformations Reader and Introduction to the Globalization Debate*, 2nd edition, Cambridge: Polity Press, pp. 430–9.

Center for American Progress (2004), 'Outsourcing statistics in perspective', March 16, available online at <http://www/americanprogress.org/site/pp.aspz?c=biJR>.

Chen, Martha, Joann Vanek, Francie Lund, James Heintz, with Renana Jhabvala and Christine Bonner (2005), *Progress of the World's Women 2005: Women, Work, and Poverty*, UNDP: New York.

China Statistical Yearbook 2003, compiled by the National Bureau of Statistics of China, China Statistics Press.

Dong, Xiao-Yuan, Jiangchum Yang, Fenglian Due and Sai Ding (2005), 'Women's employment and public-sector restructuring: The case of urban China', in Grace Lee and Malcolm Warner (eds) *Unemployment in China: Economy, Human Resources & Labor Markets*, RoutledgeCurzon: forthcoming.

Dossani, Rafiq (2005), 'Globalization and the outsourcing of services: The impact of Indian offshoring', prepared for the Brookings Trade Forum, Washington, D.C.

The Economist (2004), 'A world of work. A survey of outsourcing', November 13.

Freeman, C. (2001), 'Is local: global as feminine: masculine? Rethinking the gender of globalization', *Signs*, 26(4), 1007–37.

Government of India (2002), *Women and Men in India*, Ministry of Statistics and Programme Implementation, Central Statistical Organization.

Hafkin, N. and Nancy Taggart (2001), 'Gender, information technology, and developing countries: An analytic study', Academy for Educational Development, for the Office of Women in Development Bureau for Global Programs.

International Labour Organization (ILO) (2004) EPZ Employment Statistics, <http://www.ilo.org/public/english/dialogue/sector/themes/epz/stats.htm>.

International Organization for Migration (2003), *World Migration 2003: Managing Migration – Challenges and Responses for People on the Move*, available online at <http://www.iom.int/DOCUMENTS/PUBLICATION/EN>.

Jensen, J. Bradford and Lori G. Kletzer (2005), 'Tradable services: Understanding the scope and impact of services offshoring', Institute for International Economics and University of California, Santa Cruz.

Kalita, S. Mitra (2005), 'Virtual Secretary Puts New Face on Pakistan', *Washington Post*, May 10, p. A01.

Kelkar, Govind, Girija Shrestha and N. Veena (2002), 'IT industry and women's agency: Explorations in Bangalore and Delhi, India', *Gender, Technology and Development*, 6(1), 63–84.

Mann, C.L. (2003), 'Globalization of IT services and white collar jobs: The next wave of productivity growth', Policy Brief PBO3-11, Washington, D.C.: Institute for International Economics.

McKinsey Global Institute (2005), *The Emerging Global Labor Market*, McKinsey and Company.

Microsoft (2005), World-wide Labs, <http://research.microsoft.com/aboutmsr/labs/default.aspx>.

Milgrom, Paul and John Roberts (1990), 'The economics of modern manufacturing: technology, strategy, and organization, *American Economic Review*, 80(2), 511–28.

Minevich, Mike and Frank-Jurgen Richter (2005), *Global Outsourcing Report 2005*, New York: Going Global Ventures, Inc.

Mirchandani, K. (2005), 'Gender eclipsed? Racial hierarchies in transnational call center work', unpublished manuscript, University of Toronto.

Mirchandani, K. (2004), 'Practices of global capital: gaps, cracks and ironies in transnational call centers in India', *Global Networks*, 4(4), 355–73.

Mukoyama, Toshihiko and Ayşegül Şahin (2004), 'Why did the average duration of unemployment become so much longer?', Federal Reserve Bank of New York, Staff Report no. 194, September.

NASSCOM (2005), 'Indian IT Industry Fact Sheet', available online at <http://www.nasscom.org>, accessed on 02/03/05.

NASSCOM (2003), 'NASSCOM survey indicates growth of 24.4% in employment in Indian software and services industry in 2002–03', <http://www.nasscom.org>.

Nicholson, Brian (2001), 'Global software outsourcing: The solution to the IT skill gap', School of Accounting and Finance Workshop Report, University of Manchester, UK.

Pearson, Ruth (2003), 'Feminist responses to economic globalisation: Some examples of past and future practice', *Gender and Development*, 25–34.

Poster, W.R. (2004), 'Who's on the line? Indian call center agents pose as Americans for US-outsourced firms', unpublished paper, University of Illinois at Urbana-Champaign.

Pyle, Jean L. (2001), 'Sex, maids, and export processing: Risks and reasons for gendered global production networks', *International Journal of Politics, Culture and Society*, 15(1), pp. 55–76.

Shelburne, Robert C. (2004), 'Trade and inequality: The role of vertical specialization and outsourcing', in *Global Economy Journal*, 4(2), 1–32, available online at <http://www.bepress.com/gej>.

Trefler, Daniel (2005), 'Offshoring: Threats and opportunities', paper prepared for the Brookings Trade Forum 2005, Washington, D.C.

Tschang, T. and A. Goldstein (2004), 'Production and political economy in the animation industry: Why insourcing and outsourcing occur', paper presented at the DRUID summer conference, June, Elsinore, Denmark.

US Department of Commerce (2005), 'International Economic Accounts', Bureau of Economic Analysis, <http://www.bea.gov/bea/dil.htm>, accessed on September 30.

US Department of Labor (2004), 'Highlights of women's earnings in 2003', Bureau of Labor Statistics, September.

Vernon, R. (1966), 'International Trade and Investment in the Product Cycle', *Quarterly Journal of Economics*, 80(2), 190–207.

World Bank (2005), <http://devdata.worldbank.org/data.query>.

6
How Does Globalization Affect Regional Inequality within a Developing Country? Evidence from China

*Xiaobo Zhang and Kevin Honglin Zhang**

Globalization has integrated the product and financial markets of economies around the world through the driving forces of trade and capital flows across borders. One of the main debates on globalization is the effect of growing economic integration on income distribution. The antiglobalization movement argues that globalization is widening the gap between the haves and the have-nots (Mazur 2000). The pro-globalization position claims that the current wave of globalization since the 1980s has actually promoted economic equality and reduced poverty (Dollar and Kraay 2002).

In view of the importance of the subject, and the wide divergence in positions, many studies have been conducted to assess the role of globalization in income inequality (Cline 1997). However, much of the literature on the relationship between globalization and inequality has focused on developed countries, especially the case of the United States (Freenstra and Hanson 1996; Richardson 1995; Rodrik 1997). The number of studies on this issue for developing countries has been relatively small, and existing studies have been limited to the effects of trade liberalization on wage inequality (Wood 1997; Robbins 1996; Hanson and Harrison 1999) and world income inequality (Kaplinsky 2000). Few studies have shed light on the effect of globalization on regional inequality within a developing country.

Increased trade and capital movements have led to greater specialization in production and the dispersion of specialized production processes to geographically distant locations. Theoretically globalization thus would make a developing country more egalitarian through raising wages of its abundant low-income unskilled labor, because the country has comparative advantage in producing unskilled labor-intensive goods and services (Deardorff and Stern 1994).

However, evidence tells us an opposite story. The average Gini coefficients in the transitional and developing countries rose from about 0.25 to 0.30 in the period from the late 1980s to the mid-1990s, an era of rapid globalization (IMF 1998). This appears to be a significant increase in such a short period of time, since the Gini coefficients tend to be stable in the short term. Has globalization merely coincided with widening income inequality, or has it contributed to the phenomena?

In this study we attempt to tackle this issue by providing evidence from China. Being the largest trading nation and the largest recipient of FDI in the developing world, China has obviously been a major participant in the process of globalization for the past two decades. It is virtually certain for China to become even more important in the world economy in the future because of its huge size, dynamic economic growth, continuing policy reforms, and especially its recent entry into the World Trade Organization. Perhaps, like other developing countries, China's economic integration with the world has been accompanied by growing regional inequality; the income gap between coastal and inland areas especially has risen dramatically since the mid-1980s (Kanbur and Zhang 1999; Zhang and Kanbur 2001). Commentators in China have expressed concern about regional inequality and some even warned that further increases in regional disparities might lead to China's dissolution, like the former Yugoslavia (Hu 1996).

Regional inequality might be a result of many factors such as geographic and institutional barriers in product and factor markets, and possibly globalization. Many studies have examined the factors behind China's widening regional gap, such as factor productivity, institutional bias and development strategies (Tsui 1991; Jian et al. 1996; Fleisher and Chen 1997; and Kanbur and Zhang, 1999). Yet there have been few studies investigating the effect of globalization on regional inequality. This study thus aims to close the gap by assessing to what extent globalization may affect regional inequality in China and to suggest appropriate policies to help lagging inland provinces catch up with the more prosperous coastal areas. In particular, special attention will be paid to the role of foreign trade and inward FDI in China's widening regional inequality. We extend Shorrocks's decomposition method (Shorrocks 1982) to evaluate the effects of globalization and other factors on the rising regional inequality. The empirical results suggest that foreign trade and inward FDI indeed have contributed significantly to China's regional inequality.

Foreign trade, FDI, and regional inequality in China

In recent years, few developments in economic globalization have been more important than the sudden emergence of China as a trading nation and a leading FDI recipient (Lardy 2002). For the two decades since China began to integrate with the world economy in 1978, the role of globalization in the Chinese economy has burgeoned in ways that no one expected.

China's economic reforms and open-door policy have resulted in a phenomenal growth of trade and FDI inflows. Between 1984 and 1998 the value of exports grew 19 percent annually while manufactured exports grew 24 percent per year. By 1994 China exported manufactured goods worth over $100 billion and was the eighth largest exporter in the world. While China accounted for only 0.75 percent of world exports in 1978, its share rose to nearly 4 percent in 1998 (IMF 1999). Changes in FDI flows into China are even more astonishing. From an economy virtually without any foreign investment in the late 1970s, China has become the largest recipient of FDI among the developing countries and globally the second (next only to the US) since 1993. FDI flows into China in 1993–2000 constitute over 30 percent of total FDI in the developing world. By 2000 the total FDI received in China reached as much as $347 billion (UNCTAD 2001).

Table 6.1 indicates the pattern of globalization, economic growth, and regional inequality in China over the period of 1978–98. The degree of China's integration with the world economy may be captured by the rapid increase in foreign trade and FDI flows. The ratio of trade (the sum of exports and imports) to GDP (usually defined as openness) has increased five-fold, from 0.05 to 0.30, during the period of 20 years. This ratio of 0.30 is quite large for a large country like China, contrasting the same ratio of 0.12 for the United States. The importance of FDI in Chinese economy may be seen from the rising share of FDI flows in GDP, which was almost zero in 1978 and reached 6.56 percent in 1994, and then fell slightly to 4.43 percent 1998. China's boom in trade and inward FDI has been accompanied by rapid economic growth. The Chinese economy grew at a rate of about 10 percent in the two decades, resulting in more than a six-fold increase in real GDP. The role of foreign trade and FDI in the Chinese economy has become increasingly important. Many studies have shown that trade and inward FDI have contributed significantly to the outstanding performance of

Table 6.1   Trade, FDI, GDP, and regional inequality

Year	Trade/GDP (exchange rate)	Trade/GDP (PPP)	FDI/GDP (%)	Real GDP (1978=100)	Gini (regional)
1978	9.80	5.19	0.00	100.0	0.22
1980	12.62	7.08	0.04	116.0	0.20
1982	14.55	8.64	0.07	133.3	0.19
1984	16.67	6.36	0.22	170.9	0.19
1986	25.29	7.23	0.41	209.9	0.19
1988	25.61	5.98	0.70	260.5	0.20
1990	29.90	7.33	0.85	283.0	0.20
1992	34.22	6.67	2.55	352.2	0.22
1994	43.67	7.21	6.56	448.7	0.24
1996	36.10	8.36	5.08	536.8	0.24
1998	34.42	8.59	4.43	628.4	0.26
Growth (%)					
1978–84	3.57	1.47		9.34	−1.04
1985–98	3.86	−0.09	11.80	9.48	0.63
1978–98	3.77	1.09		9.63	0.34

Note: FDI/GDP is in percentages. Real GDP is an index with 1978 as a benchmark. Because total trade volume is usually only reported in US dollars, we use both the official exchange rate and the PPP index to derive the trade ratio. The Gini coefficient is calculated by the authors using labor productivity (GDP/Labor) with total labor force as weights at the provincial level.

Source: Author's computation based on SSB (1999) and various issues of *China Statistical Yearbook*.

the Chinese economy (Lardy 1995; Zhang 1999 and 2001). The trade boom not only directly raises Chinese output through production for exports, but also increases productivity through efficient allocation of resources and technological upgrading. The contributions of inward FDI to the Chinese economy include increasing capital formation, transferring technology and management know-how, generating employment, and promoting exports. Both trade and FDI have brought extra gains to the Chinese economy in facilitating China's transition toward a market-oriented system, which in turn has enhanced the income growth. Higher levels of trade and inward FDI in China have stimulated domestic market expansion, contributed to reforms of state-owned enterprises and privatization, and promoted competition (Zhang 1999).

However, the gains of economic growth have not been evenly distributed across regions. As shown in Table 6.1, the regional Gini coefficient rose significantly from 0.19 in 1985 to 0.26 in 1998. While the rise in the regional inequality may be caused by many factors, foreign trade and inward FDI seem to play a certain role, as suggested by the strong correlation between the three indices in the table. To see more details about the link between globalization and regional inequality, we present the patterns of trade, FDI, and per capita income by province for 1986–98 in Table 6.2. A striking feature from the table is that coastal provinces have generated more trade volume (over 86 percent of total) and attracted far more FDI (over 87 percent) than inland provinces.[1] In 1998, the three coastal provinces, Guangdong, Jiangsu, and Shanghai, rank top three, while the three inland provinces, Guizhou, Inner Mongolia, and Jilin, are bottom three in terms of attracting FDI. The above three coastal provinces alone contribute to more than 60 percent of the total foreign trade in 1998. The last two columns of Table 6.2 show GDP per capita by province and region, indicating a widening gap between the two regions (the ratio rises from 1.70 in the 1980s to 2.05 in the 1990s). In fact the coastal provinces enjoyed a higher growth rate than inland regions by three percentage points per year in 1978–98.

To further investigate this issue, we calculate the mean ratios of GDP, domestic capital, education levels, FDI, and foreign trade along the coastal and inland areas in Table 6.3. Two features are discernable from these

Table 6.2 Trade, FDI, and GDP per capita in China by regions, 1986–98

Provinces	Share of value of trade in nation (%)		Share of FDI inflows in nation (%)		GDP per capita (in Chinese Yuan)	
	1986–91	*1992–98*	*1986–91*	*1992–98*	*1986–91*	*1992–98*
Coastal areas	85.96	88.08	91.93	87.42	1449	3055
Inland areas	14.04	11.92	8.04	12.58	853	1489

Note: GDP per capita is expressed in 1986 constant prices.
Sources: Calculated from SSB (1999) and *China Statistical Yearbooks* (*SSB, various years from 1990 to 2000*).

Table 6.3 Coast–inland ratios

Year	GDP	Capital	Education	FDI	Trade
1985	1.12	1.20	1.27	13.23	4.68
1990	1.16	1.27	1.28	16.04	5.93
1995	1.39	1.67	1.24	7.03	4.86
1998	1.45	1.52	1.35	6.82	5.90
Increase (%)	29	26	6	−48	26

Note: Authors' calculation.

mean ratios. First, there indeed exist significant disparities between the coastal and inland areas. GDP in the coastal region is more than 40 percent higher than that in the inland region in 1998. Both the levels of domestic capital and FDI per unit of labor in the coastal region are much higher than those in the inland region. The average year of schooling inland has been over 25 percent less than that in coastal provinces. The share of trade in total GDP in the coastal region has been at least two times higher than in the inland region. It seems that the higher labor productivity in coastal areas is associated closely with more capital input, better education, and higher degree of integration with the world economy.

Second, the coastal–inland gap has increased significantly throughout the period. The GDP gap between the two regions rose by 29 percent between 1985 and 1998. Domestic capital investment has become increasingly concentrated in the coastal region with a rise of 26 percent during the period. The difference in economic openness also has increased by 26 percent. The average year of schooling between the two regions has widened by 6 percent. Most FDI has been concentrated in the coastal areas although the ratio does not indicate a clear trend due to the severe year-to-year fluctuation. It appears that the increased disparity in output levels among regions might have been caused in large part by differences in input levels. The question is: which factors have contributed more to the overall increase in inequality?

It is reasonable to speculate that regional comparative advantages in the context of globalization might be an important factor behind the changes in regional inequality. Figure 6.1 plots the relationship between regional inequality and trade while Figure 6.2 graphs the correlation between FDI and regional inequality. The two figures suggest a positive

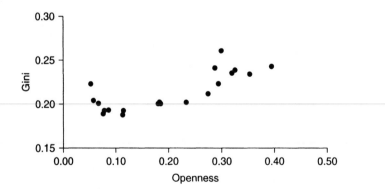

Figure 6.1 Openness and regional inequality

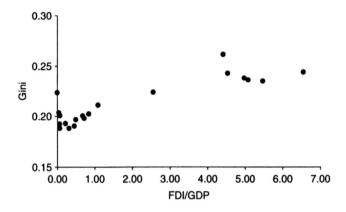

Figure 6.2   FDI and regional inequality

relationship between openness and FDI and inequality. However, we cannot simply infer causation from these two figures. There are possibly many other factors affecting regional inequality as well during this period. A more systematic framework is needed to quantify the contributions of various components to the overall regional disparity.

Model specifications

While there is considerable literature on the causes of China's regional inequality (Lyons 1991; Tsui 1991; Jian et al. 1996; Fleisher and Chen 1997; Kanbur and Zhang 1999; Yang 1999), few studies have systematically examined the role of globalization in China's growing regional inequality. One constraint to assessing the distributional impact of FDI and other production factors is the lack of a suitable analytical framework to decompose the contributions of production factors, such as FDI, toward regional inequality. In the literature, inequality is decomposed based on either exogenous population groups or income sources (Shorrocks 1982 and 1984). The distributional effect of production factors cannot be directly analysed within these existing frameworks. Moreover, because the returns to FDI have not been documented in the official GDP statistics, it is hard to directly evaluate the impact of FDI on inequality. In this chapter, we develop an indirect approach based on Shorrocks's method to quantify the impact of FDI and economic openness on both growth and regional inequality using a panel dataset at the provincial level.

We assume that each region has the same production function at a given time but the regions lie at different points on the production surface. That is to assume that the coefficients are the same across provinces. Following standard procedures in the literature, we assume that the aggregate production functions are of Cobb–Douglas form as follows:

$$Y = AL^{\beta_1} K_D^{\beta_2} K_F^{\beta_3} E^{\beta_4} V^{\beta_5} \qquad (1)$$

where
  Y = total GDP
  A = intercept
  L = labor input
  K_D = domestic capital stocks
  K_F = foreign capital stocks
  E = education
  V = trade-to-GDP ratio
  β_1 = parameters to be estimated.

In equation (1), labor (L) and capital (both K_D and K_F) are traditional inputs in production, and education (E) as an input is suggested by the new growth theory to capture the growth impact of human capital (Barro and Sala-i-Martin 1995). Domestic and foreign capital is treated separately not only to capture their individual effects but also because of the view that growth effects of foreign capital (K_F) may not be identical to those of domestic capital. Inward FDI may foster economic growth in a host country through transferring technology and expanding exports, in addition to contribution to capital formation and employment (Borenstein et al. 1998; Caves 1996; Ram and Zhang 2002). There are several ways in which one can rationalize the notion that the openness, defined as the trade-to-GDP ratio (V), may be treated as a production input in the sense that the level of openness affects aggregate output for given levels of other inputs. It has been widely recognized that a high level of openness leads to a better allocation of resources in terms of concepts of comparative advantages and specialization (Krueger 1980; Ram 1987 and 1990; World Bank 1993). Trade liberalization in a developing country may also facilitate exploitation of scale economies due to an enlargement of effective market size, afford greater capacity utilization, and induce more rapid technological changes (Bliss 1988; Edwards 1993; Feder 1983).

Since each region varies by size, it does not make sense to calculate regional inequality using total GDP. Therefore, we use labor productivity to compare the regional difference. Both output and conventional inputs (excluding education and trade) in (1) are divided by the number of laborers L, to yield:

$$\frac{Y}{L} = AL^{\delta-1} \left(\frac{L}{L}\right)^{\beta_1} \left(\frac{K_D}{L}\right)^{\beta_2} \left(\frac{K_F}{L}\right)^{\beta_3} E^{\beta_4} V^{\beta_5}, \tag{2}$$

where $\delta = \sum_{i=1}^{3} \beta_i$. Notably, labor still appears on the right-hand side of equation (2) unless constant returns to scale are imposed on the production function so that $\delta = 1$. As the standard practice in the literature, we assume constant returns to scale.[2] The logarithmic form of equation (2) thus is given by:

$$y = a + \beta_2 k_D + \beta_3 k_F + \beta_4 e + \beta_5 v + \varepsilon, \tag{3}$$

where lower case indicates logarithms. An error term ε is added to represent the stochastic shocks to output and is assumed to be unrelated to the other variables.

Following Shorrocks (1982) the variance of y in equation (3) can be decomposed as:

$$\begin{aligned}
\sigma^2(y) &= \text{cov}(y, \beta_2 k_D) + \text{cov}(y, \beta_3 k_F) + \text{cov}(y, \beta_4 e) + \text{cov}(y, \beta_5 v) + \text{cov}(y, \varepsilon) \\
&= \beta_2 \text{cov}(y, k_D) + \beta_3 \text{cov}(y, k_F) + \beta_4 \text{cov}(y, e) + \beta_5 \text{cov}(y, v) + \sigma^2(\varepsilon),
\end{aligned} \tag{4}$$

where $\sigma^2(y)$ is the variance of y and *cov* $(y, \bullet)$ represents the covariance of y with other variables. Since the right-hand side variables in equation (3) are not correlated with the error term, the covariance of y and ε is equal to the variance of ε. Considering that y is already in the logarithmic form, $\sigma^2(y)$ is a standard inequality measure known as the logarithmic variance (Cowell 1995). It has the property of invariance to scale. According to Shorrocks (1982), the covariance terms on the right-hand side of (4) can be regarded as the contributions of the factor components to total inequality.

Equations (3) and (4) constitute the basis for our panel analysis of the impact of globalization on regional inequality. In particular, we first estimate the labor productivity function specified in (3), and then decompose the inequality into the components of production factors following (4).

Data and empirical results

A panel data set including 28 provinces over the period 1986–98 was constructed from various issues of *China Statistical Yearbook*. Tibet is excluded from the analysis because of the lack of consistent GDP data. Hainan Province is included in Guangdong Province because data for Hainan are not available before 1988 when it became a separate province. Both nominal GDP and annual growth rates of GDP for each province are published in the *China Statistical Yearbook*. We assume that prices were the same for all provinces in the initial year of 1978 and that the nominal GDP was equal to the real GDP. Under this assumption, real GDP estimates for the whole period can be derived from nominal GDP data for 1978 and the published annual growth rates in real GDP.

Although capital investment data is readily available, information on China's capital stocks is rather scarce. There are several studies reporting domestic capital stocks. Fan et al. (2003) constructed capital stocks series from 1978 to 1995 at the provincial level using gross capital formation data with depreciation adjustment. But so far, we have not seen any figures on foreign capital stocks in China. In this chapter, we make efforts to calculate both domestic and foreign capital stocks based on available information.

For domestic capital stocks, we use published information of gross capital formation and fixed asset depreciation. For the period of 1978–95, the data by province are taken from the *Gross Domestic Product of China: 1952–1995*, while for other years, the data are from the *China Statistical Yearbooks*. The gross capital formation is defined as the value of fixed assets and inventory acquired minus the value of fixed assets and inventory disposed. To construct a domestic capital stock series, we use the following procedure. Define the capital stock in time t as the stock in time $t-1$ plus investment minus depreciation with price adjusted.

$$K_t = \frac{I_t - D_t}{P_t} + K_{t-1} \tag{5}$$

where K_t is the capital stock in year t, I_t is the gross capital formation in year t, and D_t is depreciation in year t. P_t is an accumulative price index with year 1978 as 1, which is derived based on the annual price index for fixed assets as published in *China Statistical Yearbooks*. The price index is available by province from 1988 to 1998 but only available at the national level from 1978 to 1987.

To obtain initial values for the capital stock, we used a procedure similar to that of Kohli (1982). That is, we assume that prior to 1978 real investment in each province has grown at a steady rate (r) which is supposed to be the same as the rate of growth of real GDP from 1952 to 1977 in the corresponding province. Thus,

$$K_{1978} = \frac{I_{1978}}{\delta + r}. \tag{6}$$

where δ is the depreciation rate. This approach ensures that the 1978 value of the capital stock is independent of the 1986–98 data used in our analysis. Moreover, given the relatively small capital stock in 1978 and high levels of investment in the following years, the estimates for capital stocks are not sensitive to the 1978 benchmark value of the capital stock. For foreign capital stocks in China we do not need to worry about the initial stocks because virtually no foreign capital flows went to China until 1979. The foreign capital stocks are constructed as follows:

$$K_t = I_t/P_t + (1 - \delta_t)K_{t-1} \tag{7}$$

China Statistical Yearbooks (SSB, 1995) reports the depreciation rate of fixed assets for years from 1952 to 1992. Since 1992, SSB has ceased to publish official depreciation rates. For the years after 1992, we used the 1992 depreciate rate.

FDI data are adjusted using a three-year moving average to overcome the year-to-year fluctuations at the province level. Similar to the domestic capital, FDI is converted to constant values at 1978 using a constant deflator for US dollars. The total trade volume data are from *Comprehensive Statistical Data and Materials on 50 Years of New China*. We use literacy rate among population above 15 years old as proxy for education level. The data are from various issues of *China Population Statistics*.

The labor productivity function outlined in equation (3) is estimated under different specifications. Table 6.4 reports the estimation results. To check the sensitivity of including foreign capital as a separate variable, we also present estimates with an aggregate capital stock. As noted earlier, the values of trade-to-GDP ratio may be subject to the changes in official exchange rate. Considering that exchange rate is year-specific and common to all provinces, including year dummies in estimations can eliminate this particular and other year-specific effects. As all the variables are in logarithmic form, the difference in conversion factor for total trade only affects the year-specific intercepts. In another specification a regime dummy instead of year dummies is included to capture the policy shift toward a more open system beginning from 1992 when the

Table 6.4 Estimation results for labor productivity

Variables	R1	R2	R3	R4	R5	R6
Intercept	-3.160**	-3.103**	-3.102**	-3.445**	-3.592**	-3.690**
	(0.347)	(0.358)	(0.357)	(0.339)	(0.348)	(0.348)
Domestic capital	0.627**	0.635**	0.634**			
	(0.010)	(0.019)	(0.019)			
Foreign capital	0.027*	0.041**	0.043**			
	(0.011)	(0.010)	(0.009)			
Total capital				0.645**	0.666**	0.670**
				(0.018)	(0.018)	(0.018)
Education	0.908**	0.863**	0.863**	0.960**	0.957**	0.986**
	(0.079)	(0.081)	(0.081)	(0.077)	(0.079)	(0.079)
Trade ratio	0.093*	0.056**	0.057**	0.109**	0.088**	0.105**
	(0.019)	(0.017)	(0.017)	(0.015)	(0.015)	(0.013)
Regime dummy (1992–98)		0.009			0.053**	
		(0.024)			(0.022)	
Year dummies	Yes**			Yes**		
Coastal region	0.052**	0.063**	0.058**	0.076**	0.093**	0.067**
	(0.025)	(0.024)	(0.020)	(0.023)	(0.023)	(0.021)
Hausman Test (p-value)	0.958	0.366	0.229	0.780	0.010	0.001
Adjusted R^2	0.939	0.933	0.933	0.939	0.931	0.930

Notes: All variables are in logarithms. GDP, domestic capital, and foreign capital are at the constant price of 1978. The dependent variable is GDP per unit of labor. The Hausman Test is used to test the endogeneity of domestic and foreign capital. Standard errors are in parentheses. * and ** denote statistical significance at the five percent and ten percent level, respectively.

late supreme leader Deng Xiaoping traveled to the south and promoted opening up. Finally, we drop both year dummies and the regime dummy to check the robustness of the estimations.

There might be issues of endogeneity in the regressions. For example, both domestic and foreign capital might be affected by the output level. To check the possible endogeneity issue for capital stocks and openness, we conduct a Hausman Test and present the p-values in the second to last row in the table. Following Greene (2000) we use the lagged dependent variable, lagged capital stocks and trade ratio, current values of other regressors, and exogenous population variable as instruments in the test. For most specifications except for the last two columns, p-values are larger than five percent, implying that the null hypothesis of no endogeneity cannot be rejected.

The adjusted R^2s for the labor productivity functions range from 0.930 to 0.939, implying good fit. The two regressions with year dummies have the highest adjusted R^2s and p-values for the endogneity test. Coefficients for all the variables except for regime dummy in regression R^2 are statistically significant and have expected signs. In general, the results are rather robust to different specifications. However, there are still some slight differences. When the total capital stock is included, the coefficients for the total capital are higher than for the domestic capital stock in regressions with separate capital stocks. The coefficients for the trade ratio also become higher when the aggregate capital stock is used.

Because we assume constant returns to scale, the labor elasticities can be calculated by subtracting the elasticities for domestic capital and foreign capital or total capital from one. The labor elasticities range from 0.323 to 0.355 across the six specifications. Among the production factors and shift variables considered in the estimation, the elasticity of education has the largest value, implying the importance of human capital. The elasticities with respect to domestic capital or total capital also show high values between 0.6 and 0.7. Both regions have greater capital elasticities than labor elasticities. The coefficients for two variables of globalization, foreign capital and trade ratio, are statistically significant and positive despite the smaller values compared to those for domestic capital and education. The significant coefficients for the regional dummy suggest the existence of systematic difference in labor productivity between inland and coastal regions.

Given the estimated coefficients for labor productivity functions, we can now apply the inequality decomposition method outlined in equation (4) to quantify the contributions of the production factors, human capital, and openness to total regional inequality in labor productivity.

Table 6.5 Inequality decomposition by factors

Year	Inequality	Domestic capital	Foreign capital	Education	Foreign trade	Inland/ Coast	Other factors
1986	0.198	0.102	0.011	0.036	0.023	0.006	0.020
		(51.6)	(5.6)	(18.1)	(11.6)	(2.8)	(10.3)
1988	0.213	0.119	0.015	0.036	0.024	0.006	0.012
		(55.9)	(7.1)	(17.2)	(11.2)	(2.9)	(5.8)
1990	0.220	0.136	0.016	0.030	0.025	0.006	0.007
		(61.6)	(7.4)	(13.5)	(11.6)	(2.7)	(3.2)
1992	0.238	0.143	0.017	0.030	0.025	0.007	0.016
		(60.0)	(7.0)	(12.4)	(10.7)	(3.0)	(6.8)
1994	0.259	0.152	0.016	0.030	0.027	0.008	0.025
		(59.0)	(6.2)	(10.9)	(10.5)	(3.3)	(10.1)
1996	0.284	0.169	0.018	0.027	0.032	0.009	0.029
		(59.5)	(6.4)	(9.4)	(11.2)	(3.2)	(10.3)
1998	0.301	0.180	0.019	0.027	0.034	0.010	0.030
		(59.7)	(6.5)	(9.1)	(11.4)	(3.2)	(10.1)
Growth (%)	52.5	39.4	4.3	−4.2	5.8	2.0	5.2
Contribution	100.0	75.1	8.1	−8.0	11.1	3.8	9.9

Notes:
(1) The decomposition method is based on formula outlined in equation (4).
(2) The second column refers to the measure of inequality (log variance). Columns (3)–(8) are contributions to the overall inequality by individual factors.
(3) The total increase in inequality can be expressed as follows: $\frac{\Delta y_t}{y_{t-1}} = \sum_i \frac{x_{it-1}}{y_{t-1}} \frac{\Delta x_{it}}{x_{it-1}} \equiv \sum_i s_{it-1} \frac{\Delta x_{it}}{x_{it-1}}$, where s_{it-1} is the share of the ith factor's contribution to overall inequality in year $t-1$ and $\frac{\Delta x_{it}}{x_{it-1}}$ is the growth rate of the ith factor's contribution from $t-1$ to t.

Table 6.5 presents the overall inequality and the contributions from these factors to total inequality.

The inequality index, measured as the log variance, in the second column in Table 6.5 has increased from 0.198 in 1986 to 0.301 in 1998, indicating a widening gap in labor productivity over the period. The contributions of domestic capital, foreign capital, education, and the trade-to-GDP ratio are 75.1 percent, 8.1 percent, −8.0 percent, and 11.1 percent, respectively, of the total increase in regional inequality.

The uneven distribution of domestic capital has been a dominant factor behind the increase in regional inequality. China has adopted a preferential policy for the coastal regions since the 1980s. Almost all the inland provinces have set up offices or investing companies in the special zones in the coastal areas. Because of the favorable investment policy, even domestic capital has flown to the south and east

(China Development Report 1995). With the trend of fiscal decentraliz-ation, provinces are allowed to keep a larger share of revenues locally, which further reduces the central government's redistribution power and enlarges the existing regional disparity.

Education has been the only equalizing factor. The education disparity between inland and coastal regions has been much smaller and increased rather slower than most other factors as shown in Table 6.3. Despite a slight increase in inequality in education, the covariance between education and labor productivity has declined from 0.036 to 0.027 as shown in the fifth column in Table 6.5. China has been well known for expansion of basic education to its vast population over the past five decades. The widespread access to basic education has been argued to be an asset for the widely shared and participatory economic growth after the economic reforms in China (Sen 1995). Improvement in education not only enhances one's productivity but also increases one's ability to move, therefore reducing regional inequality.

The variation in the degree of globalization across provinces, indicated by foreign trade and foreign capital, explained 19.2 percent of increase in total regional inequality. In short, after controlling for other factors, globalization through foreign trade and foreign capital is still a rather important force behind the widening regional disparity.

In this chapter we argue that the implicit assumption of integrated factor markets underlying the standard analysis does not hold in China. Segregated factor markets can aggravate the distributional impact of changes in regional comparative advantages associated with globaliza-tion. In a closed economy with agriculture as the predominant mode of production, the comparative advantage is mainly determined by the difference in land/labor ratios across regions within a country. When the economy opens its door to the rest of the world a region's compar-ative advantage is evaluated in a broader global context. In that context regions adjacent to more developed economies may enjoy a far better location advantage for trade and development than landlocked regions and therefore may have a faster growth.

For instance, Guangdong province did not enjoy any obvious compar-ative advantage for trade or location advantage for FDI than inland provinces before the open-door policy was adopted in 1978. Labor productivity in Guangdong ranked fourteenth in that year among 30 provinces, which was almost the same as the inland Sichuan province. Since 1978 Guangdong has become the most favored place for foreign investors as well as the largest trading province largely because of its proximity to Hong Kong. Meanwhile, the rank of labor productivity for

Sichuan has declined from fifteenth in 1978 to twenty-third in 1998. Clearly, the relative comparative advantages between the two provinces have changed significantly with global economic integration. In the ideal case with fully integrated factor markets, changes in comparative advantages will not affect regional disparity. With the free movement of labor and capital regional differences in returns to labor and capital can in large part be mitigated. However, because of geographical and institutional barriers, there exist strong segmentations and distortions in China's factor markets, as shown in Kanbur and Zhang (1999) and Yang (1999). Restrictions on rural–urban and regional migrations have been argued to be a major factor contributing to labor market inefficiency.

In addition to segmentations in the labor market, there exist large distortions in China's capital market as well. Over the past two decades, China has implemented a coast-biased development policy in utilizing the locational advantages of coastal regions since the early 1980s. For instance, up to the early 1990s, almost all special economic zones had been established in the coastal provinces, which enjoyed far more favorable polices regarding attracting FDI and foreign trade than the inland regions. As a result, the capital/labor ratio between the coastal and inland regions has increased significantly. Fan et al. (2002) show an increasing variation in marginal returns to capital since 1985, implying the existence of distortions in the capital market.

In summary, globalization has led to changes in regional comparative advantages, which, in turn, have aggravated regional inequality due to segmentations in labor and capital markets.

Conclusion

The world economy has become increasingly integrated through cross-border trade and capital movements. The correlation between globalization and widening income inequality has led to a growing concern about the distributional impact of globalization, in particular its detrimental effect on the more vulnerable populations and regions. While there has been a large body of literature on the issue, studies about effects of globalization on regional inequality within a developing country have been limited. The purpose of this study is to close this gap through providing a method for investigating the impact of globalization on regional inequality in developing countries and applying the method to China. Using a provincial level data set for the period of 1986–98, we estimate a model that quantitatively decomposes the effects of foreign trade and inward FDI on Chinese regional inequality. The estimates suggest that globalization through foreign trade and FDI indeed played an important role in worsening Chinese regional inequality. The increasing trend of regional disparity can be largely explained by the uneven distribution of production factors and variations in openness among regions. Both domestic and foreign capital investments have been concentrated in the more developed coastal region, leading to a faster growth in these areas. Even after controlling for many other factors, we find FDI and trade have played important roles in contributing to changes in overall regional inequality. This finding is in contrast to theoretical predictions of the standard trade model that implicitly assumes integrated factor markets. Our empirical finding can be explained by the fact that China's factor markets have been rather segmented. Because of the segmentation, most gains from globalization have gone to just part of the country, leading to widening regional disparity.

With its entry into the WTO, China is expected to become more integrated with the rest of the world, probably resulting in large changes in regional comparative advantages. If the government continues to favor the coastal region in its investment strategy, then regional disparity will widen. Further liberalizing the economy in the inland region is an important development strategy for the government both to promote economic growth and reduce regional inequality. In general, removing distortions in factor markets will help mitigate the negative distributional effect of the globalization process. To further promote the nine-year compulsory basic education as widely as possible is also likely to be an effective strategy to ensure that people from all regions participate in and share the benefits of globalization.

Notes

* This is a modified version of the paper published in the *Journal of Development Studies* 39(4), 47–67, April 2003. We acknowledge with thanks the permission given to us to use the copyright material.
1. In order to better analyse these issues, we divide China into two zones: the coastal zone including Beijing, Liaoning, Tianjin, Hebei, Shandong, Jiangsu, Shanghai, Zhejiang, Fujian, Guangdong and Guangxi; the inland zone comprising all the remaining provinces. Haninan is included in Guangdong province.
2. The assumption of constant returns to scale might be restrictive. But without imposing this assumption, labor would appear in the right-hand side of equation (3), making it harder to explain the results.

References

Barro, Robert and Xavier Sala-i-Martin (1995), *Economic Growth*, London: McGraw-Hill.

Bliss, Christopher (1988), 'Trade and development', in Henry Chenery and T.N. Srinivasan (eds) *Handbook of Development Economic*, II, Amsterdam; New York: North-Holland.

Borenstein, E., J. De Gregorio, and J.-W. Lee (1998), 'How does Foreign Direct Investment affect economic growth?', *Journal of International Economics*, 45, 115–35.

Caves, Richard (1996), *Multinational Enterprise and Economic Analysis*, 2nd edition, Cambridge and New York: Cambridge University Press.

China State Statistics Bureau (SSB) (1995), *China Development Report*, Beijing: China Statistical Press.

China State Statistics Bureau (SSB) (1997), *The Gross Domestic Product of China*, Dalian: Dongbei University of Finance and Economics Press.

China State Statistics Bureau (SSB), *China Statistical Yearbook*, various issues, Beijing: China Statistical Press.

China State Statistics Bureau (SSB), *China Population Statistics*, various issues, Beijing: China Statistical Press.

China State Statistics Bureau (SSB) (1999), *Comprehensive Statistical Data and Materials on 50 Years of New China*, Beijing: China Statistical Press.

Cline, William (1997), *Trade and Income Distribution*, Washington, D.C.: Institute for International Economics.

Cowell, Frank (1995), *Measuring Inequality*, 2nd edn, London and New York: Prentice Hall/Harvester Wheatsheaf.

Deardorff, A. and R. Stern (1994), *The Stolper-Samuelson Theorem: A Golden Jubilee*, Ann Arbor: University of Michigan Press.

Dollar, David and Aart Kraay (2002), 'Spreading the wealth', *Foreign Affairs*, 81(1), 120–33.

Edwards, W. (1993), 'Openness, trade liberalization, and growth in developing countries', *Journal of Economic Literature*, 31(3), 1358–93.

Fan, Shenggen, Xiaobo Zhang and Sherman Robinson (2003), 'Structural change and economic growth in China', *Review of Development Economics*, 7(3), 360–77.

Feder, Gershon (1983), 'On exports and economic growth', *Journal of Development Economics*, 12, 59–73.

Feenstra, R. and G. Hanson (1996), 'Foreign investment, outsourcing and relative wages', in R. Feenstra and D. Irwin (eds) *The Political Economy of Trade: Papers in Honor of Jagdish Bhagwati*, Cambridge: MIT Press.

Fleisher, Belton M. and Chen Jian (1997), 'The coast–noncoast income gap: productivity, and regional economic policy in China', *Journal of Comparative Economics*, 25 (2), 220–36.

Greene, H. William (2000), *Econometric Analysis*, New Jersey: Prentice Hall.

Hanson, G. and A. Harrison (1999), 'Trade liberalization and wage inequality in Mexico', *Industrial and Labor Relations Review*, 52, 271–88.

Hu, Angang (1996), 'Excessively large regional gaps are too risky', *Chinese Economic Studies*, 29(6), 72–5.

International Monetary Fund (1999), *International Financial Statistics Yearbook*, Washington, D.C.: IMF.

IMF Fiscal Affais Department (1998), 'Should equity be a goal of economy policy?', *The Economic Issues Series*, No.16.

Jian, Tianlun, Jefferey, Sachs and Andrew, Warner (1996), 'Trends in regional inequality in China', *China Economic Review*, **7**(1), 1–21.

Kanbur, Ravi and Xiaobo, Zhang (1999), 'Which regional inequality? The evolution of rural–urban and inland–coastal inequality in China, 1983–1995', *Journal of Comparative Economics*, **27**, 686–701.

Kaplinsky, Raphael (2000), 'Globalisation and unequalization: What can be learned from value chain analysis?', *Journal of Development Studies*, **37**(2), 117–46.

Kohli, U. (1982), 'A gross national product function and the derived demand for imports and exports', *Canadian Journal of Economics*, **18**, 369–86.

Krueger, Ann (1980), 'Trade policy as an input to development', *American Economic Review*, **70**, May, 288–92.

Lardy, Nicholas R. (1995), *China in the World Economy*, Washington, D.C.: Institute for International Economics.

Lardy, Nicholas R. (2002), *Integrating China into the Global Economy*, Washington, D.C.: Brookings Institution.

Lyons, Thomas P. (1991), 'Interprovincial disparities in China: Output and consumption, 1952–1987', *Economic Development and Cultural Change*, **39**(3), 471–506.

Mazur, Jay (2000), 'Labor's new internationalism', *Foreign Affairs*, **81**(1), 79–93.

Ram, Rati (1987), 'Exports and economic growth in developing countries: Evidence from time-series and cross-section data', *Economic Development and Cultural Change*, **36**(1), 51–72.

Ram, Rati (1990), 'Imports and economic growth: A cross-country study', *Economia Internazionale/International Economics*, **43**(1), 45–66.

Ram, Rati and Kevin H. Zhang (2002), 'Foreign direct investment and economic growth: Evidence from cross-country data for the 1990s', *Economic Development and Cultural Change*, **51**(1), 205–15.

Richardson, J. (1995), 'Income inequality and trade: How to think, what to conclude', *Journal of Economic Perspectives*, (9), 33–55.

Robbins, D. (1996), 'HOS hits facts: Facts win; Evidence on trade and wages in the developing world', developing discussion paper no. 557, Harvard Institute for International Development.

Rodrik, Dani (1997), *Has Globalization Gone Too Far?* Washington D.C.: Institute for International Economics.

Sen, Amartya Kumar (1995), 'Economic development and social change: India and China in comparative perspectives', Development Economics Research Programme Discusion Paper No. 67. Suntory and Toyota International Centres, London School of Economics and Political Science, London.

Shorrocks, Anthony F. (1982), 'Inequality decomposition by factor components', *Econometrica*, **50**(1), 193–211.

Shorrocks, Anthony F. (1984), 'Inequality decomposition by population subgroups', *Econometrics*, **52**(6), 1369–85.

Tsui, Kai-yuen (1991), 'China's regional inequality, 1952–1985', *Journal of Comparative Economics*, **15**(1), 1–21.

United Nations Conference on Trade and Development (UNCTAD) (2001), *World Investment Report 1998 and 2001*, New York: United Nations.

Wood, A. (1997), 'Openness and wage inequality in developing countries: The Latin American challenge to East Asian conventional wisdom', *World Bank Economic Review*, **11**, 33–57.

World Bank (1993), *The East Asian Miracle: Economic Growth and Public Policy*, London: Oxford University Press.

Yang, Danis (1999), 'Urban-biased policies and rising income inequality in China', *American Economic Review* (Paper and Proceedings), **89**(2), 306–10.

Zhang, Kevin H. (1999), 'How does FDI interact with economic growth in a large developing country? The case of China', *Economic Systems*, **23**(4), 291–303.

Zhang, Kevin H. (2001), 'Roads to prosperity: Assessing the impact of FDI on economic growth in China', *Economia Internazionale/International Economics*, **54**(1), 113–25.

Zhang, Xiaobo and Ravi Kanbur (2001), 'What Difference Do Polarisation Measures Make?', *Journal of Development Studies*, **37**(3), February, 85–98.

7
Flexicurity, Casualization and Informalization of Global Labour Markets

Johannes D. Schmidt

This chapter attempts to examine how global restructuring has impacted labour markets in the North and the South. The point of departure is that although the discourse on globalization has enshrined workfare as a new socio-economic objective for capitalist societies, the results of this strategy have left much to be desired. In fact, globalization has had a huge impact on the increase of unemployment and the de-regulation of labour markets, which is interpreted as a move towards varieties of flexibility with a concomitant removal of worker protection, lowering of social protection and weakening of labour unions. Sociologically speaking this implies a loss of social cohesion and individualization of human security and a collapse of stable social structures and traditional institutions in both North and South.

What we are witnessing is a change of work arrangements in the North with an accompanying loss of the social relevance of the workplace and of labour-based social organizations. Another measure is the extent of so-called 'a-typical' work such as part-time employment and fixed-term contracts. A third has been the introduction of flexicurity as a possible response. The new phase in capitalism encapsulated in the term globalization is associated with the rise of new concepts such as 'postindustrialization', 'risk-, information-, or network-society', all of which draw upon the changing nature of work and labour markets.

In the South casual work is the price paid for the introduction of flexibility by the international financial institutions (IFIs), transnational corporations (TNCs) and local governments. A related impact is that trade unions have lost bargaining power and a continuation of the neo-liberal thrust towards reduced protective regulation is seemingly the result. De-regulation and the withdrawal of the state have contributed to the creation of a new reserve army of unemployed workers and a new trend towards informalization of labour markets. The chapter is divided into five parts. The first part briefly explores the impact of globalization on redistribution strategies; part two takes a closer look at the relationship between the so-called labour market flexibility and the 'race-to-the-bottom'; part three is devoted to the impact of globalization in the North; part four on the impact in the South. The conclusion discusses various types of resistance against neo-liberal globalization.

Situating the shift to workfare theoretically

Globalization is currently the catch-phrase of our times. In its neoliberal conceptualization as both project, process and outcome it denotes the economic layer of juridical and political deregulation, social flexibilization and economic liberalization. It is based on the thinking of neo-classical economic orthodoxy and inextricably linked to the liberalization of commodity, labour and capital markets.[1] In the neoclassical variant globalization in the labour market is seen as qualitatively different from globalization in goods/asset markets. Ideally speaking, according to this school of economics, the factor of production (labour services) crosses national boundaries embodied in individuals – denoted as international migration (Chiswick and Hatton 2003: 65; Bordo et al. 2003).

In reality, the neo-classical variant of globalization creates a benign picture of the impact of economic liberalization and deregulation where conflicts and contradictions disappear and the concomitant policy prescriptions follow natural laws. It represents globalization as actively decoupling the firm from its relationship with state and society, rendering it 'footloose' and infinitely mobile. However, neo-liberal forms of discipline are indeed bureaucratized and institutionalized, and operate with different degrees of intensity across a range of 'public' and 'private' spheres, in various state and civil society complexes (Gill 2003: 131). The state itself has become an active proponent of privatization and deregulative measures of labour markets in the promotion of what in essence is capital accumulation. Furthermore, neo-classical theory 'purports to describe international economic relations on the basis of comparative advantage among nations endowed with equal bargaining power. It is a model in which the reality of profits, power and exploitation is expunged' (Clairmont 1996: 35). This line of thinking is based on an intellectual and ideological hegemony of the North and its linked intellectual dependency of the South (Gosovic 2000)[2] with grave consequences for the developing countries.

Globalization has been an integral part of capitalist development since its very beginning. 'The accumulation of capital has always been a profoundly geographical and spatial affair. Without the possibilities inherent in geographical expansion, spatial reorganization, and uneven geographical development, capitalism would long ago have ceased to function as a political-economic system' (Harvey 2000: 20, 24–5).[3] This means that it can be interpreted as the empowerment of capital relative to labour and the intensification of social relations so that local happenings are shaped by events occuring many miles away, and vice versa. Harvey reminds us that capitalism is under the impulsion to accelerate turnover-time, to speed up the circulation of capital, and consequently to revolutionize the time horizon of development. Secondly, capitalism is under the impulsion to eliminate all spatial barriers, to 'annihilate space through time' as Marx put it, but it can only do so through the production of fixed space. Coupled with the deregulation of finance, and the twin information revolution cum monopolization of media power, and finally the reduction of cost and time of moving commodities and people or 'overcoming space', as Harvey notes, have altogether created immense contradictions. According to these tendencies wider spaces for private profit maximization strategies are created and thus exploited by economic actors on a world-wide scale. It is now possible to avoid the expensive time-consuming regulations belonging to the shield of social protection which traditionally guarantees human and/or socio-economic security.

This perspective is grounded in a materialist international political economy approach but adds an ideational and relational perspective to the understanding of globalization as 'a set of complex, contradictory processes in which gender, race, ethnicity, and class play an important role' (Marchand and Runyan 2000: 11). Coupled to this notion, globalization itself tends to reinforce and exacerbate existing inequalities, including gender, but is also embedded in a highly gendered and uneven discourse.

Globalization then is a process where market mechanisms increasingly transform various types of politically and collectively decided regulations with new ones catering to specific economic interests. This implies increasing levels of privatization, monetary liberalization, reductions in tariffs, labour market flexibilization and fiscal discipline. The impact of these neo-liberal approaches and policies opens up for competition between workers and the prospects of 'downward levelling' in wages and work conditions (Southall and Bezuidenhout 2004: 128). International labour competition is not a new phenomenon but has changed its form and become more intensive in tandem with the internationalization of capital and production. 'First, international competition is now more direct because it occurs through actual job substitution; second, it is now also more extreme in that the workers involved have greater disparities in their wages, employment standards and political rights.' (Winthers 1996, cf. Hutchison and Brown: 2001: 15). The point is that while earlier competition between workers in the North saw labour gains through productivity-based bargaining, the latest version of globalization produces a 'race to the bottom' for wages, working conditions and organizing capacities.

With the new discourse of neo-liberalism, capitalism has been transformed from one of praise for the most productive period of human history to one of blaming the dirigism of both Keynesian (welfare statist) and Listian (economic nationalist) macro-economics (Schmidt and Hersh forthcoming). The result has been the dismantling of the so-called European social model and a transformation of the developmental state in East Asia. Although a convergence in social policy terms is emerging, there are also important differences between various institutions and actors in the global economy as well as new types of social resistances to these changes.

Labour market flexibility and the race to the bottom

In the mainstream neo-classical economic theory labour markets are universal, ahistorical and asocial. This is demonstrated by Fine who notes that to be 'unemployed, it is necessary to acknowledge that capitalist employment is the predominant form taken by work or labour, that a wage system is involved. In other words, we need to know what is different about the labour market in historical and social terms as well as by comparison with other commodities that do not experience chronic unemployment (a term that is used with extreme reluctance when describing markets other than labour)' (2003: 83–4). Their theories promise affluence, liberation of the individual, time for leisure and joy but the reality proves different. One of the main proponents of neo-classical globalization admits that 'wages of low-skill workers will fall in markets that face cheap imports. Second, that economic insecurity will increase for almost everyone: As economic change speeds up, nobody has a job for life. Third, the patterns of existing income support and other forms of subsidy will become more explicit and therefore harder to sustain . . . Fears one through three . . . have some basis in reality' (Crook 2003: 550). In this mode labour becomes a commodity and less a production factor and in a Marxian sense both production and consumption is marked by alienation. Thus labour power employed by capital is the source of value (and surplus value) (Fine 2003: 87). Implicitly the theory operates with 'externalities' such as flexible labour markets and increase of labour productivity.

Flexibility encompasses almost all spheres of social organization in both North and South. 'It is presented as synonymous with deregulatory government, lean production and the flexible firm, the decollectivization of industrial relations and the overall dissolution of work and employment into a fluid and transient form' (Amoore 2002: 23–9). Following this thinking there are two problems. It omits the social relations and masks the political power and social contests that surrounds the restructuring of work. It means that there is no acknowledgement of the constitution of market forces and technological development by the social forces engendered by the production process in specific places and at specific historical moments. It also provides a disciplinary ethos and concrete strategies for adjusting to and coping with globalization.

The term itself serves to constrain political and social debate about the restructuring of work and labour markets as it imposes the view that there is no alternative. The resulting impact of globalization and flexibility is obviously that all social change will conform and converge. A 'race to the bottom' seems to be implied by its call for a decrease in regulation levels of labour relations, but also seeks to exert a downward pressure on welfare and social benefits that are presumed to 'inhibit' the incentive to work.[4]

These contradictory processes and the downward levelling of regulations are closely linked to the liberalization of international trade and integration of world markets. Lowering economic barriers has opened enormous opportunities for TNCs with a dramatic increase in mergers and acquisitions across borders rising ten-fold between 1988 and 2000. Since 1998, 103 countries have offered concessions to foreign TNCs such as tax holidays, direct subsidies and special exemptions on import duties.[5] This competition war to attract highly mobile foreign capital able to switch production easily between countries leads to a 'race to the bottom' with respect to fiscality, environment and labour standards.

Another feature of this evolution is the 'feminization of labour' through the unprecedented increase in the numbers of women workers in the formal and especially informal labour force. Women are hardest hit by flexibilization and casualization in order to keep wages and labour costs down and productivity up. In addition the increase in part-time employment has gone hand in hand with increases in multiple job holding and casual/temporary jobs particularly for women.

There are clear signs of a global trend towards informalization of labour, lowering of wages and increasing unemployment as the most prominent outcomes of uneven neo-liberal globalization and increasing inequalities between North and South.

The empirical evidence for these claims is documented in Table 7.1 which shows that, 'the world work force continues its upward climb. The ILO's findings indicate that the differentials between the world's labour force by income and regional groups are widening. Percentage share of the high income group is expected to dive from 21% to 11%; that of the low income group to spurt from 52% to 61%' (Clairmont 1996: 345).

As shown in Table 7.2 global unemployment stood at 185.2 million in 2004 adding more than 40 million without job in a decade which

Table 7.1 Growth of world labour force (1965–2025) (millions of workers)

Income groups	1965	1995	2025	Annual compound growth rates (1965–2025)
World	1329	2476	3656	1.7
	(100)[a]	(100)[a]	(100)[a]	
High	272	382	395	0.7
	(21)	(15)	(11)	
Middle	363	658	1.020	1.7
	(27)	(27)	(28)	
Low	694	1436	2241	2.0
	(52)	(58)	(61)	

Note: [a] Figures in brackets are percentages.
Source: International Labour Force (cf. Clairmont 1996: 345).

Table 7.2 Unemployment in the world, 1994, 1999, 2001–2004 (millions)

Year	1994	1999	2001	2002	2003	2004
Total	140.3	170.3	174.3	180.9	185.2	184.7
Male	82.8	99.5	102.8	107.0	110.0	109.7
Female	57.5	70.9	71.5	73.8	75.2	75.1

Source: ILO 2005. Differences from earlier estimates are due to revisions of the IMF estimates of GDP growth used in the model.

was supposed to have been the Golden Years of neo-liberal globalization (ILO 2005: 1).

Table 7.3 indicates that there are huge differences between North and South in terms of change in unemployment rate although Asia seems to differ from the general trend of formal high unemployment. ILO figures show that of the 2.8 billion workers in the world, half have wages below the US$2 a day poverty line. Among these working poor, 535 million live with their families in extreme poverty on less than US$1 a day (ILO 2005: 2, also see Table 7.4). One consequence has been a tremendous growth of informal and causual work. According to ILO, the urban informal economy was the primary job generator during the 1990s in Latin America. In Africa, the informal economy generated more than 90 per cent of all new jobs in the region in the 1990s.

Since the 1970s labour markets in the North have been characterized by high unemployment rates. New technologies encourage decentralized production. Increasingly jobs are out-sourced and sub-contracted as companies seek greater flexibility and lower costs. Decentralized processes also enable firms to marginalize trade unions and neutralize labour conflicts. Globalization contributes to increased flexibility world-wide through market-based networks that promote a diversity of contractual arrangements between capital and labour. The numbers of full-time, career-seeking and long-term employees have fallen (Morris 2003: 7).

These non-traditional labour arrangements are also evident throughout the economies of most developing nations, but 'half the planet's labour force (1995) live in poor countries where per capita income is below $700. These are official numbers that deliberately circumvent the quasi-slave labour of tens of millions of children that are deliberately unrecorded as in Bangladesh and Pakistan – votaries of the Free World' (Clairmont 1996: 345). Another impact has been growing inequalities between the North and the South: 'The income gap between the fifth of the world's people living in the richest countries and the fifth in the poorest was 74 to 1 in 1997, up from 60 to 1 in 1990 and 30 to 1 in 1960' (UNDP 1999: 3).

Nevertheless, it is not possible to conceive of globalization as a one-way, inexorable path towards economic integration and a global labour market. Economic forces do not autonomously impact 'institutions and markets in an unmediated fashion, abstracted from the social and political setting in which they are embedded. Indeed, uneven development of globalisation is to be expected and whether there is levelling up or down in specific regional integration exercises, for example, will depend

Table 7.3 Labour market indicators

Region	Change in unemployment rate (percentage point)	Unemployment rate (%)			GDP growth rate (%)			Employment-to-population ratio (%)		Annual labour force growth rate (%)	Annual GDP growth rate (%)
	1999–2004	1994	2003	2004	2003	2004	2005	1994	2004	1994–2004	1994–2004
World	0.0	5.5	6.3	6.1	3.9	5.0	4.3	62.4	61.8	1.6	4.1
Developed economies and European Union	0.2	8.2	7.4	7.2	2.1	3.5	2.9	55.9	56.8	0.6	2.7
Central and Eastern Europe (non-EU) and CIS	−1.9	6.5	8.4	8.3	7.0	7.4	6.1	56.5	51.6	−0.1	1.6
East Asia	−0.2	2.5	3.3	3.3	7.9	8.3	6.8	78.2	76.4	1.3	8.1
South East Asia and the Pacific	0.8	4.1	6.5	6.4	4.8	5.7	5.3	66.8	66.7	2.4	4.3
South Asia	0.8	4.0	4.8	4.7	6.9	6.3	6.5	56.2	56.1	2.2	5.8
Latin America and the Caribbean	−0.9	7.0	9.3	8.6	1.8	4.6	3.6	55.6	56.0	2.1	2.7
Middle East and North Africa	−0.2	12.4	11.7	11.7	5.9	4.8	4.6	43.9	47.3	3.4	4.0
Sub-Saharan Africa	0.3	9.8	10.0	10.1	3.5	4.4	5.6	65.5	65.6	2.7	3.3

Source: ILO 2005. Differences from ealier estimates are due to revisions of the IMF estimates of GDP growth used in the model as well as new regional groupings.

Table 7.4 Global working poverty (WP), 1994 to 2004

Year	$1 WP estimate (in millions)	Share of $1 WP in global employment	$2 WP estimate (in millions)	Share of $2 WP in global employment
1994	611	25.3%	1.325	54.9%
1995	621	25.4%	1.300	53.2%
1996	551	22.2%	1.289	51.9%
1997	569	22.5%	1.299	51.3%
1998	581	22.6%	1.338	52.1%
1999	569	21.8%	1.368	52.4%
2000	561	21.1%	1.364	51.3%
2001	563	20.8%	1.372	50.8%
2002	561	20.4%	1.382	50.4%
2003	550	19.7%	1.387	49.7%
2004	535	18.8%	1.382	48.7%

Source: Kapsos 2004.

on the balance of social and political forces involved' (Munck 2004: 4). What this implies is the fact that the size of the economy matters as well as the strength of the state and the balance of social forces to resist external and domestic policies of neo-liberal globalization.

From flexicurity to insecurity in the North

The most dramatic change in labour markets as an effect of globalization has been the growth of insecurity understood as fear of job loss. 'One concept which has become increasingly popular among policy-makers is "employability": the argument is that individuals can no longer anticipate unbroken employment within a single organization but can avoid labour market vulnerability by acquiring valued competences, including adaptibility itself. This is the basis on which the European Commision (1997) envisages a "balance" between flexibility and security' (Hyman 2004: 25; also EU Commision 1997). This is denoted by the term 'flexicurity'.

The idea about flexicurity is derived from the Dutch labour market debate and has become the new overall policy of the European Union in its attempt to distance itself from the US. It can be defined as: 'a policy strategy that attempts, synchronically and in a deliberate way, to enhance the flexibility of labour markets, the work organisation and labour relations on the one hand, and to enhance security – employment security and social security – notably for weaker groups in and outside the labour market on the other hand' (Wilthagen and Rogowski 2002: 250). This cause has been relatively successful in the Scandinavian economies and to some degree in the Netherlands. In the rest of the EU it has not achieved the same success because of a variety of reasons such as emphasis on Fordist or industrial types of flexibility and income security.

By blaming the victims this rhetoric in fact can be seen as a way of individualizing unemployment and deficient job opportunities and scapegoating the unemployed for their own marginalization; or, as Lowe (1998: 248) puts it, 'the concept of "life-long learning" is shifting the onus of human resource development onto the individual'.

A purely supply-side labour market policy aimed at increasing individual 'employability' is likely to result primarily in a more qualified cohort of unemployed; a frustrating mismatch between enhanced skills and the limited skill content of available jobs (particularly in the expanding service sector); and perhaps also in a demographic shift in the structure of employment and unemployment. However, the concept of employability is in principle one that can be made appealing to trade union policy. This would imply the coordination and integration of demands which unions have indeed often embraced: first, for enhanced individual entitlements to education and training, and for flexible opportunities to benefit from these throughout the working life of individuals; second, for more effective (and worker-oriented) provision both by employers and by education and training institutions; third, for demand-side policies to encourage employment growth and, no less importantly, to provide appropriate employment opportunities for 'upskilled' workers. As Lowe argues (1998: 249), 'job quality could be a basis for collective action, especially among well-educated young workers whose expectations are still high'.

The policy strategy of flexicurity thus has limited relevance in small parts of Europe only. In particular because the social wage is being eroded and regular employment is increasingly treated as a luxury that cannot be afforded.

Turning to the US, 'real wages are below their level of 1973' (Bienefeld 2000: 48). Estimates from 2001 showed that one-third of all US workers are identified as contingent workers and this appear to be a conservative estimate (Parker 2002: 109). Conventional fixed-term employment, in manufacturing and services, is being swiftly replaced by part-time, low paid, non-unionized labour. Unionized labour in manufacturing fell from 42 per cent in 1950 to less than 14 per cent in 1994 (Clairmont

1996: 45). The intention of employers has been to eliminate unions, cut labour costs, gain greater control over the labour process and increase their profits, as was done in earlier phases of industrial capitalism.

Since the 1980s labour markets in the US have been characterized by falling wages and growing inequalities while Europe has been cast in a high structural long-term unemployment, for both the lowest deciles of the labour market (Cuyvers and Rayp 2001). These trends have emerged as a result of the transfer of production and manufacturing to low-wage countries. The proportionate decline in the US manufacturing work-force has had dramatic impacts for the de-industrialization of the US war economy and increasing unemployment in the goods-producing and manufacturing sectors. The 'lucky' laid-off workers have been able to obtain employment in the low-paid service sector which increased, relative to the total labour force, from 66.7 per cent in 1970 to 80.5 per cent in 2000 (Berberoglu 2003: 101).

What we are witnessing is jobless growth in the North, that is, economic growth rates with growing unemployment. With the predominance of financial capital and a permanent stage of surplus production the manufacturing sector cannot find new outlets for its production. 'Only a minute fraction of all industrial jobs were generated within the TNC manufacturing sector, a job sector that is being rapidly degutted. Over the past decade, the world's Top 500 corporations shed over 400 000 workers yearly. There are no signs of a turning point as any casual perusal of the financial press would confirm. Job exterminism continues to move in concert with TNC expansion' (Clairmont 1996: 45).

It seems that the European model of social capitalism increasingly is converging with the American model of market fundamentalism. Proponents of the neo-liberal discourse claim that in the long run the benefits of globalization will eventually trickle down but unfortunately in the long run we are all dead, as Keynes said.

Deregulation, casualization and informalization of work in the South

When discussing the situation in the Third World it is unavoidable to include the role of the IFIs. The IMF attached more than 50 structural policy conditions to the typical three-year loan disbursed through its Extended Fund Facility in the 1990s and nine to 15 structural conditions to its typical one-year standby arrangement. Their scale and scope were unlike anything in the institution's prior history. The IMF moved into areas such as corporate, behavior, accounting methods and principles, attacks on corruption, promotion of good governance, and so on (Eichengreen and James 2003: 535). These interventions have had a huge impact on labour market policies in the developing countries and have been a direct cause for the increases in unemployment and informalization of labour. This has led the Bank to claim that: 'Governments and workers are adjusting to a changing world. The legacy of the past can make change difficult or frightening. Yet realization of a new world of work . . . is fundamentally a question of sound choices in the international and the domestic realm' (World Bank 1995: 11).

The aftermath of the East Asian crisis in 1997 offers an illustration of the ideological blindfold by the 'Washington consensus' when it contended that, 'East Asian labor markets are fairly flexible, with fewer institutional or policy-driven rigidities than European or Latin American markets – minimum wage policies are limited, wage-setting practices are flexible, and wages and productivity growth are closely linked. As a result, fewer sharp contrasts existed between formal, privileged workers and rural, informal workers' (World Bank 1998, cf. De Meyer 2001: 161). The reality is that not only were the IMF and the World Bank responsible for the outset of the crisis by pressing for the encouragement of speculative capital through account liberalization from the constraints of previous regulation, but the draconian crisis management programmes and conditionalities resulted in the ultimately negative growth rates and record unemployment rates in 1998, where 'over 1 million people in Thailand and 21 million in Indonesia fell below the poverty line' (Bello 2002: 66–7). When Asian governments were forced to accept financial 'relief', Washington imposed conditions that clearly targeted ordinary workers. 'A standard message was to increase labor market flexibility, and the not-so-subtle subtext was to lower wages and lay off workers,' as Stiglitz asserted. He also stressed that: 'In East Asia, it was reckless lending by international banks and other financial institutions, combined with reckless borrowing by domestic financial institutions . . . which may have precipitated the crisis. But the costs, in terms of soaring unemployment and plummeting wages, were borne by the workers' (Aslam 2000). Flexibility can be seen as a response to globalization which increases competition but at the same time East Asia illustrates that it has been accompanied by weakened trade unions and an authoritarian political system.

The same trends can be seen in China where the government is promoting a high-speed, export-led growth model highly dependent on FDI. China has become the largest recipient of FDI in the world, and the government has actively courted investment with tax benefits, infrastructure, and highly repressive and exploitative labour conditions. TNCs now account for more than 45 per cent share of industrial output, greater than the 30 per cent share of state firms. This investment has been largely diverted from other peripheral countries, especially in East Asia, that had previously depended on it to cater to their own export-led growth. China's success thus poses a serious competitive threat to other peripheral countries. It is tied, for example, to growing economic strains and instabilities in South Korea and Mexico (Hart-Landsberg and Burkett 2005). However, China is losing more manufacturing jobs than the United States. For the entire economy between 1995 and 2002, China lost 15 million manufacturing jobs, compared with 2 million in the US. The entrance of China as a major exporter based on increasingly flexible labour-market policies has been accompanied by a tremendous growth in the informalization of labour accompanied by petty crime, prostitution and menial labour. Urban joblessness, unheard of when the Maoist government provided cradle-to-grave employment, now averages around 8–9 per cent. Reliable numbers are not available, but some estimate there are at least 19 million Chinese who are out of work; tens of millions more are unaccounted for by the Labour Department.

The entrance of China as a major player has also had grave consequences for a country like Mexico where a similar situation as the one in East Asia can be observed. In the aftermath of the Peso crisis and buoyed by the North American Free Trade Agreement (NAFTA), Mexico in the 1990s was the bustling factory floor of the Americas. But since 2000, as China rose to assume that role, more than 270 000 Mexicans have lost assembly jobs, hundreds of factories have closed their doors, and Mexico's trade deficit with China has grown to more than $5 billion. The ubiquitous 'Made in China' stamp, found on everything from toys to textiles to statues of Our Lady of Guadalupe, has become the incarnation of the single greatest perceived threat to Mexico's economic prosperity and a symbol of the pitfalls of globalization (Farrell et al. 2005). In this vein, China's rise to prominence in the global economy coupled with the dominance of neo-liberal globalization are thus affecting internal developments in other parts of the Third World as well.

The Asian, African and Latin American situations indicate a worsening in unemployment and labour market conditions. In addition, unemployment rates in many countries mask widespread under-employment. The working poor are largely invisible in official statistics. Billions of women and men do not have work that taps their individual creativity and utilizes their productive potential. For the most part women's work remains undervalued and unaccounted for. The informal sector for the majority provides precarious employment and insecure living conditions. As noted above, many nations have cut back social and employment-related benefit programmes while corporations cut pension, health and other social insurance benefits. Human security – from public security to health and food security, to education and shelter – is a real experience only for a minority. Informal structures and logics of individual as well as institutional and administrational action of citizens are responsible for an increasing insecurity of peoples. Many of them are losing social security protection when they are excluded from the formal working place. Public security is diminishing owing to the fiscal crises and then being privatized so that only the rich are able to buy security as a market commodity. The private supply on markets is only accessible for those who dispose monetary purchasing power, and for the great majority informal provision of formerly public goods becomes a condition of survival (Altvater 2005).

The growing importance of the informal sector is followed by huge increases in organized crime in providing employment opportunities. In many cases this is seen as the only viable survival strategy. Restructuring of formal sector enterprises in market economies and state-owned enterprises in transition economies has resulted in a proliferation of activities in the informal and criminal economy. The proportion of urban employment in the parallel economy is about one-third in Asia and the Pacific, three-fifths in Africa and two-fifths in Latin America. New jobs are primarily being created in the informal economy where workers generally face greater insecurity and have less protection. This has led to social marginalization of informal workers who are generally unrecognized, unrecorded, unorganized, unrepresented, unregulated, unregistered and unprotected.

Work in the informal economy is generally of low skill and low productivity; working conditions can be unsafe and unhealthy; and workers usually work long hours and receive low pay. Women tend to comprise between 60 and 80 per cent of total informal employment and are generally concentrated in a narrow range of activities with lower-skill, lower-pay tasks (food processing, garment sewing and domestic services) (ILO 2005: 6). The result is that while global per capita income tripled over the period 1960–94, there were over 100 countries in the 1990s with per capita incomes lower than in the 1980s, or in some cases, lower than in the 1970s and 1960s. This implies that the reliance on the growth of the informal sector and its concomitant illegal and criminal activities has an increasing impact on social and human security.

Concluding remarks on the need for alternatives

The prospects of achieving full employment have permanently receded. Unemployment has soared everywhere. It is also evident that it is not possible for all countries to pursue the strategy of flexicurity as it demands an embedded social compact between labour, employees and the state. The developmental state in East Asia is gone, again perhaps with the exception of China where a developmental state with 'Chinese characteristics' has emerged. The nature of work has changed tremendously to a greater level of informalization and the reliance on casual labour. Indeed we can observe a trend towards 'Thirdworldization' of labour markets in the North, especially in the United States.

In a more strategic perspective this implies that capital has gone global while labour organization remains national. One reason is that trade unionism is no longer a struggle with capital but a trench war against the tax-payer probably because the public sector is easier terrain for trade union recruitment and the concomitant difficulties of organizing workers in trade unions exposed to globalization. Also in Eastern Europe, South Africa, India and Brazil organized trade unionism has become weaker, divided and reduced to confrontational politics (MacShane 2004; Munck 2004), but with important exceptions.

As Bienefeld notes 'competitive market forces are amoral, unsentimental and enormously powerful. In arm's-length markets, goods and services compete without reference to the social or human conditions of their production. In the process, they become commodities; socially disengaged use values. And, when their appearance and their performance characteristics (their 'use values') are equivalent, the cheapest ones survive. The question of whether the lowest price was made possible by superior organization, by better technology or by the intense exploitation of labor is of no concern to the market, unless people, acting through a political process, make it so' (2000: 46–7). Work-force growth and TNC labour demolition strategies, 'to remain internationally competitive' (to use their pedestrian refurbished rationalization), will augment joblessness with further soaring inequalities as their concomitant (Clairmont 1996: 346).

The issue is that there is a historical trend towards forms of production organization in which capital no longer needs to pay for the reproduction of labour power. At the same time, participation in the global market-place means that the domestic market is no longer needed to serve the self-expansion of capital. Jobless growth is what the present phase of capitalism is all about. 'It is this process of globalization rather than any claimed imbalance in the national accounts between public and private sector growth (the fiscal deficit), nor any demographic imbalance (the greying population) that is the main reason for the perceived need to shed and restructure the welfare state which has become the dominant political project in all advanced countries since the 1980s' (Hoogvelt 1997, 113). Coupled with the fact that there is a 'race to the bottom' in terms of job flight and a competition of lowering standards, regulations and laws it is interesting to note that so far the responses from labour in the North are re-active and in most cases have relied on a defensive and protectionist strategy.

The question is what types of resistance are reliable and which are unsustainable in both a short-term and longer-term perspective. Ellen Meiksin Wood criticizes those anti-capitalists who focus on TNCs and international agencies. She points out that many of the arguments used against these organizations are not anti-capitalist, but anti-global. The real issue is that globalization is a consequence of capitalism, not a cause of exploitation. Instead Wood forcefully argues that nation-states are still the most reliable guarantors of capital accumulation, and therefore states should remain the focus of opposition movements. She is correct when she argues that: 'While we can imagine capital continuing its daily operations with barely a hiccup if the WTO were destroyed, it is inconceivable that those operations would long survive the destruction of the local state.' And 'capitalism whether national or global, is driven by certain systemic imperatives of competition, profit maximization and accumulation, which inevitably require putting "exchange values" above "use values" and profit above people.' The point is that the capitalist state has always performed a very important function: 'controlling the mobility of labour, while preserving capital's freedom of movement' (Wood 2003: 131, 133, 134).

Globalization can not create prosperity for all, only the illusion of it. Globalization per se is not a new phenomenon but rather a rethoric invoked by governments in the North in order to justify their voluntary surrender to the financial markets. '[F]ar from being – as we are constantly told – the inevitable result of the growth of foreign trade, deindustrialization, growing inequality and the retrenchment of social policies are the result of *domestic political decisions* that reflect the tipping of the balance of class forces in favour of the owners of capital.' (Bourdieu and Wacquant 2001; Hersh 2004). This is why there are increasing signs of popular and worker-organized resistance against the impact of globalization and 'a revolt against the idea that labor, rather than investors or management, should pay the cost of corporate globalization' (Pfaff 1997).

Notes

1. Neo-liberalism emerged out of an 'unholy alliance' between neo-classical economics, which provided most of the analytical tools, and what may be called the Austrian-Libertarian tradition, which provided the underlying political and moral philosophy. It is an 'unholy alliance', because the gap between these two intellectual traditions is not a minor one, as those who are familiar with, for example, Hayek's scathing criticism of neo-classical economics would know (see Chang 2001: 1). It is also interesting to note that it was in a Latin American economy, Chile, that it was implemented for the first time under the dictatorship of Augosto Pinochet.
2. This hegemony is closely related to the launch of other imperatives and co-optations of words such as 'the end of conflict', 'the end of class struggle', 'the end of ideology', 'partnership', 'stakeholders' and so on. See Gosovic (2000).
3. For this and the following, see Harvey (2000).
4. The term 'race to the bottom' reflects the notion that global economic competition encourages deregulation. This causes the state to lose its redistribution role and its capacity to offer services to citizens, since taxation revenues would decline. In short, the governments with the lowest standards and income taxes would emerge as the winners, since they would be the ones attracting companies to set up operations in their territory, see Brawley (2003: 59).
5. For this and the following, see Morris (2003).

References

Altvater, Elmar (2004), 'Globalization and the informalization of the urban space', in Johannes D. Schmidt, *Development Studies and Political Ecology in a North South Perspective*, Occasional Papers No. 5, DIR, Aalborg University, Denmark.

Amoore, Louise (2002), *Globalization Contested: An International Political Economy of Work*, Manchester and New York: Manchester University Press.

Aslam, Abid (2000), 'World Bank dissident invokes Asian workers' woes', *Asia Times*, January 12.

Bello, Walden (2002), *Deglobalization: Ideas for a New World Economy*, London: Zed Books.

Berberoglu, Berch (2003), *Globalization of Capital and the Nation-State*, Lanham and Oxford: Rowan and Littlefield.

Bienefeld, Manfred (2000) 'Globalization and social change. Drowning in the icy waters of commercial calculation', in Johannes D. Schmidt and Jacques Hersh (eds) *Globalization and Social Change*, London: Routledge.

Bordo, Michael D., Alan M. Taylor and Jeffrey G. Williamson (eds) (2003), *Globalization in Historical Perspective*, Chicago: University of Chicago Press.

Bourdieu, Pierre and Loïc Wacquant (2001), 'Neoliberal newspeak: Notes on the new planetary vulgate', *Radical Philosophy*, 105, January.

Brawley, Mark R. (2003), *The Politics of Globalization*, Toronto: Broadview Press.

Chang, Ha-Joon (2001) 'Breaking the mould. An institutionalist political economy alternative to the neoliberal theory of the market and the state', Paper Number 6, May, Geneva: United Nations Research Institute for Social Development.

Chiswick, Barry R. and Timothy J. Hatton (2003), 'International migration and the integration of labor markets', in Bordo et al.

Clairmont, Frederic F. (1996), *The Rise and Fall of Economic Liberalism. The Making of the Economic Gulag*, Penang, Malaysia: Southbound and Third World Network.

Crook, Clive (2003), 'Globalization in Interdisciplinary Perspective'. A panel, in Bordo et al.

Cuyvers, Ludo and Glenn Rayp (2001), 'Globalisation and wages in industrial countries: Theory and empirical evidence', in Ludo Cuyvers (ed.) *Globalisation and Social Development: European and Southeast Asian Evidence*, Cheltenham, UK: Edward Elgar.

De Meyer, Tim (2001), 'ILO fundamental principles and rights to work in Asia Pacific: Emerging standards for emerging markets', in Cuyvers and Rayp.

Eichengreen, Barry and Harold James (2003), 'Monetary and financial reform in two eras of globalization', in Bordo et al.

European Commission (1997), 'Partnership for a new organisation of work', Luxembourg: Office of Official Publications from the European Communities, in Hyman (2004).

Farrell, Diana, Antonio Puron and Jaana K. Remes (2005), 'Beyond cheap labor: Lessons for developing economies', *McKinsey Quarterly*, 1, March.

Fine, Ben (2003), 'Contesting labour markets', in Alfredo Saad-Filho (ed.) *Anti-Capitalism. A Marxist Introduction*, London: Pluto.

Gill, Stephen (2003), *Power and Resistance in the New World Order*, Basingstoke: Palgrave Macmillan.

Gosovic, Branislav (2000), 'Intellectual hegemony in the context of globalisation', in Denis Benn and Kenneth Hall (eds) *Globalisation: A Calculus of Inequality Perspectives from the South*, Kingston, Jamaica: Ian Raddle Publishers.

Hart-Landsberg, Martin and Paul Burkett (2005), 'Thinking about China', <http://mrzine.monthlyreview.org/mhlpb300705.html>.

Harvey, David (2000), 'Globalization in Question', in Johannes D. Schmidt and Jacques Hersh (eds), *Globalization and Social Change*, London: Routledge.

Hersh, Jacques (2004), 'Oldspeak/newspeak of (neo)liberalism on development', *Interdisciplinary Journal of International Studies*, 2(1), 3–19 (also avalilabe at <http://www.ijis.auc.dk>).

Hoogvelt, Ankie (1997), *Globalization and the Postcolonial World*, London: Macmillan.

Hutchison, Jane and Andrew Brown (2001), 'Organising Labour in Globalising Asia: An Introduction', in (eds) *Organising Labour in Globalising Asia*, London: Routledge.

Hyman, Richard (2004), 'An emerging agenda for trade unions?' In Munck.

ILO (2005), 'Global employment trends brief', February, Geneva <http://www.ilo.org/public/english/employment/strat/download/get05en.pdf>.

Kapsos, S. (2004), 'Estimating growth requirements for reducing working poverty: Can the world halve working poverty by 2015?', Employment Strategy Paper no. 2004/14, IMF, Geneva.

Lowe, Graham (1998), 'The future of work: Implications for unions', in *Relations industrielles*, 53.

MacShane, Denis (2004), Foreword in Munck.

Marchand, Marianne H. and Anne Sisson Runyan (2000), 'Feminist sightings of global restructuring: conceptualizations and reconceptualizations', in (eds) *Gender and Global Restructuring. Sightings, Sites and Resistances*, London: Routledge.

Morris, Elizabeth (2003), 'Globalization and research priorities for labour markets in Southeast Asia', ILO, Geneva, <http://www.globalpolicy.org/globaliz/econ/2003/iloglob.pdf>.

Munck, Ronaldo (ed.) (2004) *Labour and Globalization. Results and Prospects*, Liverpool: Liverpool University Press.

Munck, Ronaldo (2004), 'Introduction: Globalisation and Labour Transnationalism', in Munck.

Parker, Robert E. (2002), 'The global economy and changes in the nature of contingent work', in Berch Berberoglu (ed.) *Labor and Capital in the Age of Globalization*, Boston: Rowan and Littlefield.

Pfaff, William (1997), 'Why should workers bear the brunt of globalization pain?', *International Herald Tribune*, New York, January 13.

Polet, Francois and CETRI (ed.) (2004), *The Globalisation of Resistance: The State of Struggle*, London: Pluto Press.

Schmidt, Johannes D. and Jacques Hersh (forthcoming) 'Neoliberal globalization: Workfare without welfare', *Journal of Globalizations*, 3(1).

Southall, Roger and Andries Bezuidenhout (2004), 'International solidarity and labour in South Africa', in Munck.

UNDP (1999), *Human Development Report 1999*, New York: Oxford University Press.

Wilthagen, T. (1998), 'Flexicurity: A new paradigm for labour market policy reform?', Berlin, WZB Discussion Paper FSI.

Wilthagen, T. and R. Rogowski (2002), 'Legal Regulation of Transitional Labour Markets', in G. Schmid and B. Gazier (eds), *The Dynamics of Full Employment: Social Integration through Transitional Labour Markets*, Cheltenham: Edward Elgar.

Winthers, Jeffrey A. (1996), *Power in Motion: Capital Mobility and the Indonesian State*, Ithaca and London: Cornell University Press.

Wood, Ellen Meiksins (2003), 'Globalisation and the state: Where is the power of capital?', in Alfredo Saad-Filho (ed.) *Anti-Capitalism. A Marxist Introduction*, London: Pluto Press.

World Bank (1995), 'Workers in an Integrating World', *World Development Report*, New York: Oxford University Press.

World Bank (1998), *East Asia: The Road to Recovery*, Washington D.C.: Cf. World Bank. De Meyer.

8
Race to the Bottom: the Impact of Globalization on Labor Markets – a Review of Empirical and Theoretical Evidence

Ozay Mehmet

Some years ago Rodrik (1997) argued that globalization has gone too far with the negative outweighing its positive impacts. A major concern of policy-makers and researchers in this context is that foreign direct investment (FDI) may relocate inferior, low-wage jobs from high-income countries to labor-abundant economies forcing a competitive downward decline in wages all around, known as 'race to the bottom' (RTB) (Wilson 1996, Klevorick 1996, Brown et al. 1996, Singh and Zammit 2004). The RTB issue places labor market dynamics to the forefront of the globalization debate. Surprisingly, and in contrast to the political and moral debate on workers' rights and labor standards issues, the economics of the labor market has received very little attention to date, although in the wake of the Asian currency collapse, the subject is becoming more topical (Jomo (ed.) 2003). This chapter seeks to make a small contribution in this field.

The chapter is organized in five parts as follows. Following this introduction part two gives a general review of globalization, direct foreign investment (FDI), and labor market dynamics. The third examines empirical evidence within the framework of a standard neo-classical labor market model featuring FDI. This model was previously applied in a group of four Asian countries and the results reported in an earlier article (Mehmet and Tavakoli 2003). These results are briefly summarized here as well. Part four provides an updated overview of labor market conditions in these four Asian economies, especially in the light of the Asian currency collapse that highlighted the critical need for a 'social safety net'. The final part discusses some policy implications of the results for labor market policy.

Globalization, FDI and the labor market

The link between globalization and labor market dynamics is an important one, especially in the case of labor-abundant developing countries where there is a general shortage of productive jobs. If FDI inflows into a developing economy fail to increase demand for labor its other social benefits will be offset or reduced by increasing labor market imbalance. Specifically, rising excess labor may push wages down, and if this condition is coupled in the home-country labor market with job losses due to outflow of FDI, then an RTB phenomenon will emerge. It is, therefore, essential that economists and policy-makers concern themselves with labor market dynamics in the context of globalization.

For trade economists the issue of the labor market is not a new one. In classic Ricardian trade theory, labor was the single factor of production and comparative advantage was based on differences in labor productivity. Global free trade optimum was a full employment equilibrium. However, in the traditional trade models there is no room for legislation to protect workers and their basic rights to organize. This amounts to an assumption that the labor market is 'a level playing field' manifesting full flexibility and perfect information. The neo-classical models such as the Stolper–Samuelson and Mundell connect trade to labor markets on the basis of these assumptions. According to the Stolper–Samuelson model the relative factor rewards change in the wake of a move from the autarky to free trade, such that factors in trade-oriented industries gain at the expense of other sectors. In the Mundell model factor movements have equivalent consequences for relative factor rewards to arm's-length trade. These models predict that international trade and labor market flexibility increase employment, foster growth, and faster growth leads to higher wages (Greenaway and Nelson 2001).

However, both industrialized and developing countries are now having second thoughts about the negative result of free trade and capital mobility in the age of globalization. 'The industrialized nations, which earlier vigorously preached the virtues of free trade, now worry about its vices. Many DCs feel marginalized in emerging world economy and wonder their fear of trade was not justified after all' (Ghose 2000, 281). In fact, one effect of globalization, which trade and development economists have recognized, is the deteriorating position of low-skilled relative to high-skilled workers in developed countries. It is observed that 'within almost all OECD countries, the least-qualified section of the labor force lost out in the 1980s and 1990s either in terms of a decline in their wages relative to the most skilled, or in terms of the relative likelihood of their being in work, or both' (Greenaway and Nelson 2001, 2). The fact is that a global competition generates pressures to lower wages and labor standards across the world. One pressure arises when profit-seeking firms seek to escape from collective bargaining and relocate operations to lower-cost foreign locations in which there is no collective bargaining and other labor rights which are well-established in rich, industrialized countries. As a result of these omissions, labor in developing-country labor markets may be subject to exploitation, that is, under-payment of wages relative to marginal product of labor.

The presence of labor exploitation in developing countries in contrast to social safety nets and legislated labor rights in developed countries, give to potential RTB in the global economy. National and MNE competition generates cost minimization strategies which have potentially adverse effects on wages and on the levels and conditions of employment. Globally employers and owners of FDI gain bargaining strength vis-à-vis workers and unions in that when firms go international, employers are able to substitute cheaper foreign labor for domestic workers. Capital wins, labor loses in a zero-sum framework.

The threat of plant relocation or investing abroad rather than at home is a powerful leverage that owners of FDI can utilize against workers and governments alike. In the process the regulatory capacity of governments is being weakened; therefore, there are more responses to compete for more FDI and export markets (Lee 1996, 492). The net effect of these pressures is that demand for labor in the global labor market tends to become more elastic when the labor market becomes more exposed to foreign competition (Rodrik 1997, 16). In an empirical test of this hypothesis, reported below, we provide support for this tendency.

The labor market impacts of trade can be explained from two different views (Campbell 1994). One is 'the upward convergence' view. According to this view, a greater openness in North/South trade raises the burden of adjustment on high-cost environment. Lower costs (particularly in labor-intensive production in DCs) are a legitimate source of comparative advantage, and complementary division of labor in which North buys more labor-intensive cheap products and sells more of its more capital-intensive products. The other is 'the downward convergence' view, which is that competition through trade rarely finds countries exchanging different goods only on the basis of their complementary and discrete comparative advantages. During the passage of some complementary equilibrium in the cross-border division of labor, there is less room for North production that combines high costs and low skills. It is the unskilled worker in North who is most vulnerable to the expansion of international trade.

In the 1980s many DCs liberalized their economies to international trade and private capital inflows such as FDI and foreign portfolio investment. Since the mid-1980s FDI has been a main source, and by far the largest, of private capital flows to these countries. On average, FDI accounted for about 50 percent of the private capital inflows during the 1990s (Moran 1998:16). The positive effects of FDI in the 1980s and 1990s forced policy-makers in DCs to rely on FDI, complementary to international trade, as an important source of economic growth.

The neo-classical growth model has been applied broadly to test empirically how FDI could affect economic growth. The modern growth model has also emphasized the endogenous technological change as a result of access to better technologies through FDI in order to enhance the economic growth (Bacao Reis, 2001, 411)

FDI is included in the neo-classical growth model to show how it affects the economic growth positively (Papanek 1973, Most and Van Den Berg 1996, de Mello 1997, Borensztein et al. 1998). It is also shown that the more open the economy to international investors the more there is to gain from FDI. It is further shown that the effect of FDI on economy has expanded faster in DCs with export-promoting industries (EPI) strategy compared to import-substituting industries (ISI) strategy (Balasubramanan et al. 1996). A major limitation of these studies is that they generally do not take into account the feedback response of labor market adjustments on economic growth.

Empirical evidence

The empirical evidence regarding the effect of globalization on labor market adjustments is mixed. At one extreme Krugman (1994) argues that the impact of globalization is relatively minor. According to his finding, 'imports of manufacturing goods are still only 2 percent of the combined GDP of the OECD. The conventional wisdom is that trade flows of this limited magnitude cannot explain the large changes in relative factor prices that have occurred' (quoted in Rodrik 1997, 14). Krugman has also argued more positively about the effect of globalization on developing countries stating that 'bad jobs' created by FDI are better than 'no jobs'. Another study shows that MNEs are primarily 'home-centered' (Hirst and Thompson 1996, 96). In this context a study based on a large sample of data to four industrialized countries

(Germany, Japan, the United Kingdom, and the United States) for 1987 and 1992–93 shows that between 70 and 75 percent of MNEs value added was produced on home territory. Another view is that there has been a qualitative change in global economic environment affecting workers across the world and this has had some impact (Lee 1996, 493). On the other hand, there is an increasing number of studies focused on the impact of globalization on labor markets in developing countries. Weeks (1999) considers 17 countries in Latin America for the period 1970–97 to analyse gains and losses during the major changes in economic policy that occurred over two decades. Through the 1980s and 1990s every government in Latin America (with the exception of Cuba's) reduced both trade regulations and capital controls. The labor market impact of this trade liberalization can be estimated on the basis of an unemployment equation for these countries during the 1990s. The outcomes for labor markets are mixed. In fact, 'labor's gains in the 1990s, when economic growth quickened, have been meager, even negative in some countries' (Weeks 1999, 152). In fact, as a consequence of public and private downsizing, facilitated by labor market reforms, trade liberalization had the effect of increasing unemployment by making it easier to dismiss workers. Therefore, the review of labor market conditions in Latin America shows that gains from trade growth were not passed to workers in most countries (Weeks 1999, 162). It is argued that effective bargaining power is required to distribute gains to labor. Hence, the role of trade unions is reaffirmed. But the neo-classical literature, in its foundation as well as in the current context of globalization, has an anti-trade union bias. The effect of trade unions on wage determination is observed to be negative. The current bias against trade union in Latin America reflects the political changes of the past two decades. Throughout Latin America the strength of trade unions has declined dramatically. The liberalizing trading regimes for these countries have been associated with the reduction of workers' rights and the concentration of wealth (Weeks 1999, 166).

Studies covering trade and labor markets in both developed and developing countries are rare. One exception is Ghose (2000) based on a sample of two industrialized countries (the United States and Japan) and six Asian DCs (China, India, Indonesia, Malaysia, Philippines, and Taiwan). This study shows that there is no convincing and theoretical evidence for believing that growth of trade between developed and developing countries has been responsible for the deterioration in labor standards in either group of countries. As a result of trade expansion labor standards improved in all countries except the United States and

Philippines, and there was deterioration only in the United States where employment stagnated and real wages declined (Ghose 2000, 302). On balance, evidence so far on the labor market effects of trade is still inconclusive. However, trade liberalization is suspected as a major contributing factor in growing international economic inequality and it is feared that it is leading to a deterioration of global labor standards (Ghose 2000, 281). Clearly, more empirical evidence is required to settle this debate.

In Table 8.1 the growth rate and average value of main variables are summarized for four Asian countries (namely, China, Philippines, Singapore and Thailand), during four different periods. Time-series data

Table 8.1 Real GDP growth rate, gross domestic investment/GDP ratio, FDI/GDP ratio, FDI/total investment ratio, labor growth rate, and real capital growth rate (in percentage), 1971–98

Variable	Country	China	Philippines	Singapore	Thailand
GDP growth	1971–80	–	5.8	7.7	7.1
rate	1981–90	10.1	1.0*	6.0	7.6
	1991–98	10.4	3.6	7.6	4.9
	1971–98	9.7[1]	2.8	7.3	7.2
(Gross domestic	1971–80	–	21.5	36.4	24.2
investment)/GDP	1981–90	28.7[2]	21.9	39.4	29.8
	1991–98	33.9	22.4	35.9	37.2
	1971–98	31.0	21.9	37.3	29.9
FDI/GDP	1971–80	–	2.6	5.4	5.6
	1981–90	4.4[3]	7.2	9.0	11.4
	1991–98	38.1	15.7	5.4	18.8
	1971–98	20.2[3]	8.0	6.7	11.4
FDI/(Total	1971–80	–	1.1	12.6	2.3
investment)	1981–90	1.5[3]	3.4	18.8	3.4
	1991–98	9.7	6.5	12.9	5.5
	1971–98	5.4[3]	3.5	14.9	3.6
Labor growth	1971–80	2.0[4]	2.9	4.7	3.9
rate	1981–90	3.6	2.8	2.3	2.8
	1991–98	11.4	3.1	3.0	0.4
	1971–98	3.0[4]	3.0	3.5	2.9
Capital growth	1971–80	–	18.8	18.9	15.5
rate	1981–90	16.3	1.0*	10.4	11.5
	1991–98	12.2[1]	6.5	9.0	9.8
	1971–98	14.4	7.2	11.8	12.4

Notes: (1) Based on 1979; (2) based on 1981; (3) based on 1982; (4) based on 1974. * In 1984 a high inflation rate started.

are used to cover two recent decades of globalization, but these data are limited to wage rate information availability too. Data are collected from different sources: the IMF, ILO, and Asian Development Bank. All values are in real terms, using a proper price index. The main variables selected relate to the economic performance of each country. As it is observed the growth rate of real GDP is high in China. Among four countries the economic performance of China is outstanding; on the other hand, Philippines has a low economic performance. The growth rate of real GDP is at the lowest level in the latter country. During the 1980s Philippines was faced with high inflation and stagnation, both real and nominal output and capital stock declining significantly in the second half of the 1980s. The FDI ratio with respect to total investment (domestic and FDI) is at the lowest level in Thailand and on average it is roughly the same in Philippines.

Findings and results

An earlier econometric study (Mehmet and Takavoli 2003) focused on four Asian countries, namely China, Philippines, Singapore and Thailand, which have been among the leading recipients of FDI, and we reported on the impact of FDI on labor market performance. The choice of these four was significantly determined by data availability. We now summarize and highlight some of our findings.

All four countries, except Singapore, are large, labor-abundant countries and production tends to be relatively labor-intensive compared with labor markets in industrialized countries. But there are differences between them in terms of labor market conditions captured by the output elasticity with respect to labor, that is, the percentage contribution of output to percentage employment creation. This output elasticity with respect to labor is positive (0.864) and higher than the output elasticity with respect to capital (0.146) for the period 1984–98 for Philippines to confirm the labor intensive pattern of growth. For Singapore and Thailand the growth model is estimated for two different periods for comparison.

From Table 8.2 it is observed that the highest output elasticity with respect to labor corresponds to Philippines. China is in second position. The lowest elasticity is for Thailand during 1980–98. The effects of FDI on economic growth, measured by FDI/GDP ratio, are different among countries. In the cases of Philippines and Singapore the effects are positive and significant, regardless of time periods. In China, on the other hand, the FDI effect is positive only in the 1990s, where in fact the FDI growth is increasing tremendously. Its effect is not positive

Table 8.2 The output–labor (L), output–capital (K), elasticities and FDI effect on economic growth (GDP growth rate (y) as a dependent variable)

Variable	China 1984–98	Philippines 1984–98	Singapore 1979–96	Singapore 1970–98	Thailand 1980–98	Thailand 1972–98
Constant term	14.1 (1.4)	2.172 (1.1)	–	–	–	–
L-growth rate (l)	0.610 (3.6)***	1.078 (2.0)**	0.392 (1.8)*	0.513 (2.3)**	0.465 (2.8)**	0.513 (3.8)***
K-growth rate (k)	0.532 (2.0)**	0.348 (3.6)***	0.217 (2.4)**	0.131 (3.3)***	0.317 (4.2)***	0.309 (6.4)***
FDI/GDP ratio (f)	-1.376 (3.7)***	0.467 (5.2)***	0.288 (1.9)*	0.387 (2.8)***	-0.133 (4.8)***	-0.122 (3.5)***
D.f	1.335 (3.8)***	–	–	–	0.255 (3.4)***	0.240 (2.5)**
Trend	-0.794 (3.8)***	-0.453 (3.7)***	–	–	–	–
Dummy (D)	–	–	4.190 (4.5)***	2.838 (2.5)**	2.496 (2.0)**	2.551 (1.9)*
R-squared adjusted	0.805	0.743	0.380	0.264	0.870	0.717
F-Stat.	12.5	7.7	3.1	4.2	31.0	17.4
D.W.	2.8	1.9	1.9	1.8	1.5	2.2
N	15	15	18	28	19	27

Notes:
(1) t-statistics are in brackets. *10%, **5%, and ***1% significant.
(2) China: the L-growth rate (l) is in one period lagged-form, and (domestic gross investment/GDP) ratio is used for K-growth rate (k). The dummy variable is as D: 1992–98 = 1, and 1983–91 = 0.
(3) Singapore: the dummy variable is as 1988–98 = 1, 1983–87 = 0.
(4) Thailand: the dummy variable is as 1985–96 = 1, 1972–84 = 0, and 1997–98 = 0.
Source: Mehmet and Tavakoli 2003.

in the 1980s. It seems the total effect of FDI is washed out during the whole period of 1984–98. But this could be because of lack information over a long period of time. But there is no doubt that the effect of FDI is positive on Chinese economic growth, particularly during the 1990s. In Thailand the story is different from that of China. FDI started to increase significantly in Thailand from the mid-1980s. Since then, however, the FDI effect has been significant but uncertain, our results showing a small negative effect on growth of −0.133 for the shorter and −0.122 for the longer period.

Overall, the effect of FDI is more effective in Philippines and Singapore and less effective in China, less certain in the case of Thailand.

One percent increase in FDI affects by 0.467 percent and 0.288 percent the economic growth in Philippines and Singapore, respectively. We now turn to our major issue: the effect of FDI on demand for labor and wages. The evidence from our estimation is presented in Tables 8.3 and 8.4. The major finding is that, as a result of global competition for FDI, the demand for labor gets more elastic. The last row in both tables show that the lowest effect of FDI on demand elasticity of labor is in China, where its absolute value increases from 2.169 to 2.268; that is, just about 5 percent, slightly less in the case of Thailand. The FDI increases demand elasticity for labor by about 15 percent higher in Singapore. By far the greatest impact is observed in the Philippines, where labor elasticity rises about 35 percent.

Tables 8.3 and 8.4 also give evidence on the negative effect of FDI, measured by FDI/ total investment ratio on demand for labor, lowering the real wage rate in the host developing economy. On average, 1 percent

Table 8.3 Demand for labor and FDI (real wage rate as a dependent variable), China and Philippines

Variable	China: 1982–98		Philippines: 1980–95	
	With FDI	*Without FDI*	*With FDI*	*Without FDI*
FDI/(Total investments) ratio	−0.003 (2.4)**	– –	0.0478 (3.2)***	– –
Labor elasticity	−2.268	−2.169	−1.101	−0.812

Notes: *10%, **5%, and ***1% significant. t-statistics are in brackets.
Source: Mehmet and Tavakoli 2003.

Table 8.4 Demand for labor and FDI (real wage rate as a dependent variable), Singapore and Thailand

Variable	Singapore: 1983–1997		Thailand: 1980–1998	
	With FDI	*Without FDI*	*With FDI*	*Without FDI*
FDI/(Total investments) ratio	−0.039 (2.3)**	–	0.0337 (1.0)***	–
Labor elasticity	−1.098	−1.034	−0.592	−0.569

Notes: *10%, **5%, and ***1% significant. t-statistics are in brackets.
Source: Mehmet and Tavakoli 2003.

increase in FDI ratio affects the real wage in Philippines by −0.0478 percent, −0.0337 percent in Thailand, −0.003 percent in China, and in Singapore by about −0.4 percent. This suggests that labor's purchasing power has declined as a result of globalization in each country. In turn this finding implies that the social benefits of FDI in host countries is limited. When the real wage rate is declining as a result of foreign enterprise competition with domestic firms in DCs, then the labor productivity is affected negatively, and consequently economic growth will have a negative labor market impact.

Policy implications: Is there an escape from RTB?

The empirical results reported in this chapter show, at least for the period studied, a negative effect of FDI in the four countries analysed, namely, China, Philippines, Singapore, and Thailand. As a result of FDI inflows, demand for labor in the global labor market becomes more elastic.

What higher elasticity of demand for labor means is that, given unlimited labor supply demonstrated by the infinitely elastic supply schedule in the host country, FDI inflow expands employment at subsistence wage-rate. That is to say, foreign direct investment creates inferior, low-wage jobs. At the same time, in the labor market of the home country, (i.e. in the high-income country from where FDI originates) the wage rate declines in the wake of relocation of jobs as an integral part of FDI. Together these effects imply an RTB globally.

There are, however, two counter-arguments here. First, evidence of RTB may be a transitional process, likely to disappear as FDI inflows continue and the host-country experiences sustained growth. This can only be determined in time. Secondly, as Kruger has argued, even if FDI does generate second-rate jobs, these may be better than no jobs in labor-abundant, high-poverty host-countries. This argument, however valid during a transition, cannot be used as a justification for labor exploitation, especially in the medium and long terms.

The second argument centers on the possible prospect of inferior jobs generated by a RTB becoming a more permanent fixture of globalization. This question, in turn, leads to the following one: What are the possible motives behind FDI leading to RTB? As in the case of footloose industries, this kind of FDI may be prompted by the search, indeed greed, for global profits by MNCs. In other words, if and where the key motive behind FDI is cost-reduction for greater profit to be remitted back by MNCs to the home country at the expense of the host country, then RTB is indeed a serious worry implying a systemic labor exploitation in a global zero-sum game. In this context, labor exploitation in low-income countries may turn out to be a necessary evil of globalization, at least in the transition to an eventual steady-state development. In the shorter term, however, if this is indeed the case, then globalization may reduce, not enhance, welfare in developing countries and it may even do so globally on the basis of the 'one-man one-vote' principle of giving the same weight to each person's welfare.

What is the way out of this dilemma? There are two alternative action programs: international and national. The former is to introduce minimum labor standards into the regulation of international trade and finance with the overall aim of promoting and maintaining a 'level playing field'. The International Labor Office (ILO) has, based on long years of experience, drafted a set of *core labor standards* for this purpose and relies on *moral suasion* to uphold these standards. Unlike the World Bank and IMF, ILO has no *conditionality*, or 'big stick' to coerce or punish countries violating labor standards. The ILO also may appear 'soft' in comparison with the World Trade Organization (WTO) regulating inter-national trade and taking legal action against countries found guilty of dumping and other unfair trade practices (Mendes and Mehmet 2003). For all these reasons the ILO approach may be less than acceptable for those social critics of unfair labor practices by countries that systemat-ically violate worker rights in total disregard of decent labor standards. The ILO approach, however, is not without merit (Singh and Zammit 2004). The fact is that it is difficult to promote a 'level' global labor market unless all trading countries subscribe to a common set of 'playing rules'. That may be a long time coming.

In the meantime, remedial action may be required at the national level. This is the logic of pro-active labor policy. Pro-active labor market policy is required at the host country level to minimize the worst forms of exploitation in the name of globalization. In the short term social safety nets and protective legislation are required to protect workers, especially vulnerable groups such as women and children, while in the global public policy arena minimum core labor standards are required as part of global governance (Mendes and Mehmet 2003). In the medium and longer term, pro-active labor market policy interventions are needed to screen FDI inflows to ensure that these do not transfer anti-labor technologies into labor-abundant economies. There is evidence that capital intensity of output is rising steadily globally, meaning that per unit of output more capital is employed than labor or, put differently, employment growth is lagging behind both the growth of new entrants into the labor force as well as the growth of ouput.

In labor-abundant developing countries, production must become more labor-friendly. Without harming productive efficiency, economic and industrial policies must promote job opportunities to absorb into productive employment new entrants of young school leavers and higher education graduates. Tax policies and regional development projects in under-developed regions must provide extra incentives to potential investors for job creation. The intent here, it should be noted, is productive job creation that actually contributes to poverty reduction and creation of value-added.

Even then job creation incentives may appear to be in conflict with current World Bank–IMF priorities intended to eliminate subsidies, but this WB–IMF thinking is strictly against unproductive subsidies. By contrast what is being defended here is productive job creation. If and when investment incentives in under-developed, labor-abundant regions actually reduces poverty and raises value-added, then such incentives may be justified.

Additionally pro-active labor market policies in the medium and longer term would entail policy interventions aimed at enhancing labor productivity through skill training and human capital formation via technical and vocational education. In regions with high levels of illiteracy, expansion of primary schooling would, of course, have to precede skill development through human capital formation.

Conclusion

This chapter has demonstrated evidence in support of RTB in the wake of relocation of FDI from high-income (home) countries to low-income (host) countries. The core of our analysis is increasing elasticity of demand for labor in the global labor market. This implies that there is a downward pressure on wages in home countries, while in the host country employment expands at subsistence wage levels with 'bad jobs' becoming the rule. In the process, there is a global impoverization of workers globally as FDI operates as a corporate tool of squeezing labor at both the home and host country ends of the labor market.

Is the RTB evidence temporary? As it reflects a corporate strategy of maximizing global profits, there is no expectation that the RTB will be self-adjusting. In other words, it may not automatically correct itself. FDI, just in the case of footloose industries, will simply move forever internationally across borders always attracted by the magnet of cheap labor at the poverty, subsistence wage.

In the final analysis, and in view of the unlikely event (for the foreseeable future) of collective international action on the adoption of core labor standards as discussed above, host countries need to take stock of the technology they import and to determine what kind of employment policy they ought to follow in the light of the labor abundance and labor force growth they face. They do possess some productive policy options, within the context of a pro-active labor market policy, as outlined above.

References

Asian Development Bank (2000), *Key Indicators of Developing and Pacific Countries*, Vol. XXXI, Oxford: Oxford University Press.

Bacao Reis, A. (2001), 'On the welfare effects of foreign investments', *Journal of International Economics*, 54(2): 4111–427.

Balasubramanan, V.N., M. Salisu and D. Saford (1996), 'FDI and growth in EP and IS countries', *Economic Journal*, 106 (Jan.): 92–105.

Bhagwati, J. and R.E. Hudec (eds) (1996), *Fair Trade and Harmonization, Prerequisites for Free Trade? Vol 1, Economic Analysis*, Cambridge, Mass: MIT Press.

Borensztein, E., J. de Gregorio and L.-W. Lee (1998), 'How does FDI affect economic growth?', *Journal of International Economics*, 45: 115–35.

Brown, D.K., A.V. Deardorff and R.M. Stern (1996), 'International labor standards and trade: A theoretical analysis', in Bhagwati and Hudec (eds).

Campbell, D. (1994), 'Foreign labour immobility and the quality of employment', *International Labour Review*, 132: 185–204.

de Mello, L.R., Jr (1997), 'FDI in DCs and growth: A selected survey', *Journal of Development Studies*, 34(1): 1–34.

Ghose, A.K. (2000), 'Trade liberalization, employment, and global inequality', *International Labour Review*, 139(3): 281–305.

Greenaway, D. and D. Nelson (2001), 'The assessment: Globalization and labour-market adjustment', *Oxford Review of Economic Policy*, 16(3): 1–11.

Hirst, P. and G. Thompson (1996), *Globalization in Question: The International Economy and the Possibilities of Governance*, Cambridge: Polity Press.

IFC (1997), *Foreign Direct Investment, Report No.5*, Washington D.C.: World Bank.

International Labour Office. *Yearbook of Labour Statistics*, various issues, Geneva: ILO.

International Monetary Fund, *International Financial Statistics Yearbook*, various issues, Washington D.C.: IMF.

Jomo, K.S. (ed.) (2003), *Southeast Asian Paper Tigers? From Miracle to Debacle and Beyond*, London and New York: RoutledgeCurzon.

Klevorick, A.K. (1996), 'Reflections on the race to the bottom', in Bhagwati and Hudec (eds).

Krugman, P. (1994), 'Does the Third World growth hurt first world prosperity?', *Harvard Business Review*, 72(4): 113–24.

Lee, E.P. (1996), 'Globalization and employment: Is anxiety justified?', *International Labour Review*, 135(5): 485–97.

Mehmet, O. and A. Tavakoli (2003), 'Does foreign direct investment cause a race to the bottom: Evidence from four Asian countries', *Journal of the Asia Pacific Economy*, 8(2): 133–56.

Mendes, E. and O. Mehmet (2003), *Global Governance, Economy and Law. Waiting for Justice*, London and New York: Routledge.

Moran, T.H. (1998), *Foreign Direct Investment and Development*, Washington D.C.: Institute of International Economics.

Most, S.J. and H. Van Den Berg (1996), 'Growth in Africa: Does source of investment matter?', *Applied Economics*, 28(9): 1427–33.

Papanek, G.F. (1973), 'Aid, foreign private investment, savings growth in less developing countries', *Journal of Political Economy*, 81(1): 120–30.

Rodrik, D. (1997), *Has Globalization Gone Too Far?*, Washington D.C.: Institute for International Economics.

Singh, A. and A. Zammit (2004), 'Labor standards and the "Race to the Bottom": Rethinking globalization and workers' rights from the developmental and solidaristic perspectives', *Oxford Review of Economic Policy*, 80(1): 85–103.

Weeks, J. (1999), 'Wages, employment and workers' rights in Latin America, 1970–1998', *International Labour Review*, 138(2): 152–69.

Wilson, J.D. (1996), 'Capital mobility and environmental standards: Is there a theoretical basis for race to the bottom?', in Bhagwati and Hudec (eds).

Part III
Capital, Technology and Finance

9
Globalization and the Agrarian Question: Peasants' Conflicts in Africa and Asia*

Samir Amin

This chapter focuses on land tenure reforms required for large parts of Africa and Asia in the event of future developments that are designed to benefit the whole of society, its working classes in particular and, of course, the peasants (over half the population of Asia and Africa), and seek the reduction of inequality and the radical eradication of 'poverty'. This option is one that institutions and mechanisms that are actually generating poverty refuse to promote.

This development paradigm involves a combination of a 'mixed' macro economy (combining private enterprise with public planning) based on the democratization of market management and the state and its interventions, and a decision to opt for agricultural development based on peasant family farms.

The implementation of this set of basic principles, for which it would clearly be necessary to define specific methods for each country and phase of development, would lead to the formation of an 'alternative' on a national scale. It would, of course, need to be accompanied by an evolution of practices to support it both regionally and globally through the construction of an alternative globalization that would be negotiated rather than imposed unilaterally by dominant transnational capital, the collective imperialism of the triad (the United States, Europe, Japan) and United States hegemonic tendencies.

We aim to deal here only with a single aspect of this complex problem, namely, the rules governing access to the use of farmland. These rules must be created in a way that 'integrates rather than excludes', that is to say, a way that allows all farmers the right of access to land, which is a fundamental condition of the continued existence of a 'peasant society'. This basic right is certainly not enough by itself. It would have to be supported by policies enabling peasant family farms to produce their goods in a way that would ensure the growth of national production (which in turn would guarantee a secure food supply for the country) and a parallel improvement in the real income of all the peasants concerned. It is a question of implementing a range of macro-economic proposals and adequate forms of politically managing these, and ensuring that negotiations on the organization of international exchange systems are subject to the requirements of the former. These aspects of the problem are not discussed here. Rather, as access to land depends on tenure status, the 'reforms' related to this are the subject for discussion.

The language used in this area is often imprecise because of the lack of sufficient conceptualization. In French the terms *réformes foncières* (land reforms), *réformes agraires* (agrarian reforms) and sometimes *lois concernant le domaine national* (state land laws), *transformations des modes d'exploitation* (transformation of farming methods) and in English the terms 'land tenure' and 'land system' are often used interchangeably.

First of all, two types of 'tenure status' (or systems of land tenure) must be defined: those based on the private ownership of farm land and those that are not.

Land tenure based on private ownership of land

Here the owner has, to use the terms of Roman law, *usus* (the right to use an asset), *fructus* (the right to appropriate the returns from the asset) and *abusus* (the right to transfer). This right is 'absolute' in the sense that the owner can farm his land himself, rent it out or even abstain from farming. The property may be given away or sold and it forms part of assets that can be inherited.

This right is often less absolute than it appears. In all cases use is subject to public order laws (such as those prohibiting its unlawful use for the cultivation of stupefacients) and increasingly to environmental regulations. In some countries, where an agrarian reform has been carried through, a limit has been established for the maximum surface area an individual or family can own (see below). The rights of tenant farmers (duration and guarantee of the lease, amount of land rent) limit those of the owners in varying degrees to the extent of affording the tenant farmer the major benefit of the protection of the state and its agricultural policies (this is the case in France). Freedom to choose his crops is not always the rule. In Egypt, from earliest times, the state agricultural services establish the proportion of land allotted to different crops depending on their irrigation requirements.

This system of land ownership is modern inasmuch as it is the product of the constitution of ('really existing') historic capitalism which originated in western Europe (England) in the first place) and among the Europeans who colonized America. It was established through the destruction of the 'customary' systems for regulating access to land, even in Europe. The statutes of feudal Europe were based on the superposition of rights to the same land: those of the peasant concerned and other members of a village community (serfs or freemen), those of the feudal lord and those of the king. The assault on these rights took the form of 'enclosures' in England, imitated in different ways in all European countries during the course of the nineteenth century. Marx denounced this radical transformation, which excluded the majority of peasants from access to use of land, turning them into proletariat emigrants to the towns (forced by circumstances) or, in the case of those who stayed, into farm labourers or tenant farmers, which he regarded as numbering among the type of measures of primitive accumulation that dispossessed the producers of property or denied them the means of production.

The use of the terms of Roman law (*usus* and *abusus*) to describe the status of modern bourgeois ownership perhaps indicates that the latter had distant 'roots', in this case, those of land ownership in the Roman Empire and more precisely those of pro-slavery latifundist ownership. The fact remains that as these particular forms of ownership have disappeared in feudal Europe, we cannot talk of the 'continuity' of a 'Western' concept of ownership (itself associated with 'individualism' and of the values it represents) which has, in fact, never existed.

The rhetoric of capitalist discourse about itself – 'liberal' ideology – has not only produced this myth of 'Western continuity'. It has, above all, produced another even more dangerous myth, namely that of the 'absolute and superior rationale' of economic management based on the private and exclusive ownership of the means of production, which it considers farmland to be. In fact, according to conventional economics, the 'market', that is to say the transferability of ownership of capital and land, determines the optimal (most efficient) use of these 'factors of production'. So, according to this principle, land becomes 'merchandise like any other', transferable at the 'market' price, in order to guarantee that the best use is made of it both for the owner concerned and society as a whole. This is nothing but mere tautology yet it is the one upon which all ('vulgar', which is to say acritical, to use Marx's terms) bourgeois economic discourse is based. This same rhetoric is used to legitimize the principle of land ownership by dint of the fact that it alone can guarantee that the farmer who invests in improving his yield per hectare and the productivity of his work (and that of any employees) will not suddenly be dispossessed of the fruit of his labour and savings. This is not the case and other forms of regulating the right to use the land can produce similar results. In sum, this dominant discourse uses the conclusions that it sees fit to draw from the construction of Western modernity in order to propose them as the only necessary 'rules' for the advancement of all other peoples. To make land everywhere private property in the current sense of the term, as practised in capitalist centres, is to spread the policy of 'enclosures' the world over; in other words, to hasten the dispossession of the peasants. This course of action is not new: it began and continued during earlier centuries of the global expansion of capitalism in the context of colonial systems in particular. Today the World Trade Organization (WTO) intends only to accelerate the process even though the destruction that would result from this capitalist approach is increasingly foreseeable and predictable. Resistance to this option by the peasants and peoples affected should make it possible to build a real and genuinely human alternative.

Land tenure systems not based on private ownership of land

As we can see, this definition is negative – *not* based on private property – and therefore cannot designate a homogeneous group since access to land is regulated in all human societies; however, it is regulated either by 'customary authorities', 'modern authorities', the state or more specifically, and more often, by a group of institutions and practices involving individuals, communities and the state.

'Customary' administration (expressed in terms of customary law or known as such) has always (or almost always) ruled out private property (in the modern sense) and always guaranteed access to land for all the families (rather than the individuals) concerned; in other words, those that are part of a 'village community' that is distinct and can be identified as such. Yet it has (almost) always never guaranteed 'equal' right to land. In the first place, it most often excluded 'foreigners' (usually the vestiges of conquered peoples), 'slaves' (of differing status) and shared land unequally depending on clan membership, lineage, caste or status ('chiefs', 'free men', etc.). So there is no reason to heap excessive praise upon these traditional rights as a number of anti-imperialist national ideologues unfortunately do. Progress will certainly require them to be challenged.

Customary administration has almost never been the system used in 'independent villages'. These have always been part of stable or changing, sound or precarious state groupings depending on circumstances but very rarely have they been absent. So the rights of use of the communities and families that comprised them have always been limited by those of the state that levied taxes (which is why I describe the vast family of pre-modern production methods as 'tributory').

These complex forms of 'customary' administration, which differ from one time and place to another, only persist, in the best of cases, in extremely deteriorated forms and have been under attack by the dominant rationale of world capitalism for at least two centuries (in Asia and in Africa), sometimes five (in Latin America).

In this respect India is probably one of the clearest examples. Before British colonization, access to land was managed by 'village communities', or more precisely by their upper ruling castes–classes, though excluding lower castes, the Dalits, who were treated as a kind of collective slave class similar to the Hilotes of Sparta. These communities were, in turn, controlled and exploited by the imperial Mughal state and its vassals (Rajahs and other rulers' states) which levied tribute. The British raised the status of the zamindars, formerly land revenue collectors, to that of 'owners' who thus became large allied landowners in spite of tradition although they upheld 'tradition' when it suited them, for example, by 'respecting' the exclusion of Dalits from access to land. Independent India has not challenged this serious colonial inheritance which is the cause of the incredible poverty of the majority of its peasantry and then after of its urban proletariat (cf. Amin 2004). The solution to these problems and the building of a viable economy for the peasant majority is therefore through an agrarian reform in the strictest sense of the term (see below for the meaning of this proposal). The European colonizations of Southeast Asia and that of the United States in the Philippines resulted in similar developments. The 'enlightened despotic' regimes of the east (the Ottoman Empire, the Egypt of Mohamed Ali, the Shahs of Iran) also by and large established private ownership in the modern sense of the term to the benefit of a new class wrongly described as 'feudal' (by most historical Marxist thinking) recruited from among the senior ranks of their power system.

As a result of this, private ownership of land has since affected the majority of farm land, especially the best of it, throughout Asia outside China, Vietnam and the former Soviet republics of central Asia and there are only remnants of deteriorated para-customary systems in the poorest regions that are of the least value to the dominant capitalist farming in particular. This structure differs widely juxtaposing large landowners (country capitalists to use the terminology I proposed), rich peasants, middle peasants, poor peasants and the landless. There is no peasant 'organization' or 'movement' that transcends these acute class conflicts.

In Arab Africa, South Africa, Zimbabwe and Kenya, the colonizers (with the exception of Egypt) granted their colonists (or the Boers in South Africa) 'modern' private properties of a generally latifundist type. This legacy has certainly been brought to an end in Algeria but here the peasantry had almost disappeared, proletarized (and reduced to vagrancy) by the extension of colonial lands, whereas in Morocco and Tunisia the local bourgeoisie took them over (which was also the case to some extent in Kenya). In Zimbabwe, the revolution has challenged the legacy of colonialization to the benefit, in part, of new middle owners of urban rather than rural origin and, in part, of 'poor peasant communities'. South Africa still remains outside this movement. The remnants of deteriorated para-customary systems that survive in the 'poor' regions of Morocco or Berber Algeria and the former Bantustans of South Africa are threatened with private appropriation from inside and outside the societies concerned. In all these situations scrutiny of the peasant struggles (and possibly those of the organizations that support them) is required: are we talking about 'rich peasant' movements and demands in conflict with some orientation of state policy (and the influences of the dominant world system on them), or of poor and landless peasants? Can they form an 'alliance' against the dominant (so-called 'neo-liberal') system? Under what conditions? To what extent? Can the demands – expressed or otherwise – of poor and landless peasants be 'forgotten'?

In intertropical Africa the apparent survival of 'customary' systems is certainly more visible because here the model of colonization took a different and unique direction, known in French (the term has no translation in English) as *economie de traite*. The administration of access to land was left to the so-called 'customary' authorities, however, controlled by the colonial state (through traditional clan leaders, legitimate or otherwise, created by the administration). The purpose of this control was to force peasants to produce a quota of specific products for export (peanuts, cotton, coffee, cocoa) over and above what they required for their own subsistence. Maintaining a system of land tenure that did not rely on private property suited colonization since no land rent entered into composition of the prices of the designated products. This resulted in land being wasted, destroyed by the expansion of crops, sometimes permanently (as illustrated by the desertification of peanut producing areas of Senegal). Yet again capitalism showed that its 'short term rationale', an integral part of its dominant rationale, was in fact the cause of an ecological disaster. The combination of subsistence farming and the production of products for export also meant that the peasants were paid almost nothing for their work. To talk in these circumstances of a 'customary land tenure system' is going far too far. It is a new regime that preserves only the appearance of 'traditions' and often the least valuable of these.

China and Vietnam provide a unique example of a an access to land administration system that is based neither on private ownership or on 'customs' but on a new revolutionary right unknown elsewhere. It is the right of all peasants (defined as inhabitants of a village) to equal access to land and I stress the use of equal. This right is the finest accomplishment of the Chinese and Vietnamese revolutions.

In China, and even more so in Vietnam which was more extensively colonized, 'former' land tenure systems (those that I have described as 'tributary') were already quite eroded by dominant capitalism. The former ruling classes of the imperial power system had turned most of the agricultural land into private or quasi-private property, whereas the development of capitalism encouraged the formation of new rich peasant classes. Mao Zedong was first followed by the Chinese and Vietnamese communists, to have defined a revolutionary agrarian strategy based on the mobilization of the majority of poor, landless and middle peasants. From the outset, the triumph of this revolution made it possible to abolish the private ownership of land, which was replaced by that of the state, and organize new forms of equal access to land for all peasants. This organization has passed through several successive phases including that inspired by the Soviet model based on production cooperatives. The limited achievements made by the latter have led both countries to return to peasant family farming. Is this model viable? Can it lead to a sustained improvement in production without bringing about an excess of rural manpower? Under what conditions? What supporting policies does it require of the state? What types of political management can meet the challenge?

Ideally, the model involves the dual affirmation of the rights of the state (sole owner) and of the usufructuary (the peasant family). It guarantees equal distribution of the village land among all of the families. It prohibits any use of it, such as renting, other than for family farming. It guarantees that the proceeds of investments made by the usufructuary return to him in the short term through his right of ownership of all farm produce (which is freely marketed, although the state guarantees a minimum price), and in the long term by inheritance of usufruct to the exclusive benefit of children remaining on the farm (any person who emigrates from the village loses his right of access to the land which is then redistributed). As this involves rich land but also small (even tiny) farms, the system is only viable as long as the vertical investment (the green revolution with no large scale industrialization) is equally efficient to allow the increase of production per rural worker as does horizontal investment (the expansion of farming supported by increased industrialization).

Has this 'ideal' model ever been implemented? Certainly something close to it has (for example, during the time of Deng Xiaoping in China). However, the fact remains that although this model ensures a high degree of equality within the village, it has never been able to overcome the inequalities between one community and another that are a function of the quality of the land, the density of the population and the proximity of urban markets. Furthermore, no redistribution system has been up to the challenge (even through the structures of cooperatives and state trade monopolies of the 'Soviet' phase).

More serious is the fact that the system is itself subject to internal and external pressures that undermine its direction and social scale. Access to credit and satisfactory subsidization are subject to bargaining and interventions of all kinds, legitimate or otherwise. 'Equal' access to land is not synonymous with 'equal' access to the best production conditions. The popularization of 'market' ideology contributes to this destabilization. The system tolerates (and has even re-legitimized) farm tenancy and the employment of waged employees. Right-wing discourse – encouraged from abroad – stresses the need to give the peasants in question 'ownership' of the land and to open up the 'farmland market'. It is quite clear that rich peasants (and even agribusiness) seeking to increase their property are behind this discourse.

This system of peasant access to land has been administered thus far by the state and the party, which are one. Clearly one might have thought that it could have been administered by genuine elected village councils. This is certainly necessary as there is hardly any other means of winning the support of the majority and reducing the intrigues of the minority would-be beneficiaries of a more markedly capitalist approach. The 'party dictatorship' has shown itself to be largely inclined to careerism, opportunism and even corruption. Social struggles are currently far from non-existent in rural China and Vietnam. They are no less strongly expressed than elsewhere in the world but they are by and large 'defensive' and concerned with defending the legacy of the revolution – equal right to land for all. This legacy must be defended, especially as it is under greater threat than it may appear despite repeated affirmations from both governments that the 'state ownership of the land will *never* be abolished in favour of private property'. Yet today this defence demands recognition of the right to do so through the organization of those who are affected, that is to say, the peasants.

The forms of organization of agricultural production and land tenure are too varied in Asia and Africa for one single formula of 'alternative peasant social construction' to be recommended for all.

By 'agrarian reform' we must understand the redistribution of private property when it is deemed too unequally divided. It is not a matter of 'reforming the land tenure status' since we are dealing with a land tenure system governed by the principle of ownership. This reform, however, seeks to meet the perfectly legitimate demand of poor and landless peasants and to reduce the political and social power of large landowners. Yet, where it has been implemented, in Asia and Africa after the liberation from former forms of imperialist and colonial domination, this has been done by non-revolutionary hegemonic social blocks in the sense that they were not directed by the dominated poor classes in the majority (except in China and Vietnam, where, in fact, for this reason there has been no 'agrarian reform' in the strict sense of the term but, as I have already said, suppression of the private ownership of land, affirmation of state ownership and implementation of the principle of 'equal' access to the use of the land by all peasants). Elsewhere real reforms dispossessed the only large owners to the eventual benefit of middle and even rich peasants (in the longer term), ignoring the interests of the poor and landless. This has been the case in Egypt and other Arab countries. The reform under way in Zimbabwe may face a similar perspective. In other situations such as in India, Southeast Asia, South Africa and Kenya, reform is still on the agenda of what is needed.

Even where agrarian reform is an immediate unavoidable demand, its long-term success is uncertain as it reinforces an attachment to 'small ownership', which becomes an obstacle to challenging the land tenure system based on private ownership.

Russian history illustrates this tragic situation. The evolution begun after the abolition of serfdom (in 1861), accelerated by the revolution of 1905 then the policies of Stolypin, had already produced a 'demand for ownership' that the revolution of 1917 had consecrated by means of a radical agrarian reform; and, as we know, the new small owners were not happy about giving up their rights to the benefit of the cooperatives created in the 1930s. A 'different approach' based on peasant family economy and generalized small ownership might have been possible but it was not tried.

Yet what about the regions (other than China and Vietnam) in which the land tenure system is not (yet) based on private property? We are, of course, talking about intertropical Africa.

We return here to an old debate. In the late nineteenth century, Marx, in his correspondence with the Russian Narodniks (Vera Zassoulitch among others), dares to state that the absence of private property may be a major advantage for the socialist revolution by allowing the transition from a system of the administration of access to land other than that governed by private ownership but he does not say what forms this new system should take and the use of 'collective', however fair, remains insufficient. Twenty years later Lenin claimed that this possibility no longer existed and had been destroyed by the penetration of capitalism and the spirit of the accompanying private ownership. Was this judgement right or wrong? I cannot say on this matter as it goes beyond my knowledge of Russia. However, the fact remains that Lenin did not consider this matter of crucial importance, having accepted Kautsky's point of view regarding the 'Agrarian question'. Kautsky generalized the scope of the modern European capitalist model and felt that the peasantry was destined to 'disappear' owing to the expansion of capitalism itself. In other words capitalism would have been capable of 'resolving the agrarian question'. Although 80 per cent true for the capitalist centres (the Triad: 15 per cent of the world's population), this proposition does not hold true for the 'rest of the world' (85 per cent). History shows not only that capitalism has not resolved this question for 85 per cent of people but that from the perspective of its continued expansion it can resolve it no longer (other than by perhaps genocide! – not recommended). So it fell to Mao Zedong and the Communist parties of China and Vietnam to find a suitable solution to the challenge.

The question resurfaced during the 1960s with African independence. The national liberation movements of the continent, the states and party-states that arose from them enjoyed, in varying degrees, the support of the peasant majority of their peoples. Their natural propensity to populism led them to conceive of a 'specific (African) socialist approach'. The latter could certainly be described as very moderately radical in its relationship both with dominant imperialism and the local classes associated with its expansion. It did not raise the question of rebuilding peasant society in a humanist and universalist spirit to any lesser extent, a spirit that often proved highly critical of the 'traditions' that the foreign masters had in fact tried to use to their profit. All – or almost all – African countries adopted the same principle, formulated as an 'inalienable right of state ownership' of all land. I do not believe this proclamation to have been a 'mistake', nor do I think that it was motivated by extreme 'statism'.

Examination of the way that the current peasant system really operates and its integration into the capitalist world economy reveals the scale of the challenge. This management is provided by a complex system that is based on both 'custom', private ownership (capitalist) and the rights of the state. The 'custom' in question has degenerated and barely serves to disguise the discourse of bloodthirsty dictators who pay lip service to 'authenticity', which is nothing but a fig leaf that they think hides their thirst for pillage and treachery in the face of imperialism. The only major obstacle to the expansionist tendency of private ownership is the possible resistance of its victims. In some regions that are better able to yield rich crops (irrigated areas and market garden farms) land is bought, sold and rented with no formal land title.

Inalienable state property, which I defend in principle, itself becomes a vehicle for private ownership. Thus, the state can 'provide' the land necessary for the development of a tourist area, a local or foreign agribusiness or even a state farm. The land titles necessary for access to improved areas are distributed in a way that is rarely transparent. In all cases the peasant families who inhabited the areas and are asked to leave are victims of these practices which are an abuse of power. Still, the 'abolition' of inalienable state property in order to transfer it to the occupiers is not feasible in reality (all village lands would have to be registered with the land registry) and if this were attempted it would only allow rural and urban notables to help themselves to the best plots.

The right answer to the challenges of the management of a land tenure system not based on private ownership (as the main system at least) is through state reform and its active involvement in the implementation of a modernized and economically viable and democratic system for administering access to land that rules out, or at least minimizes, inequality. The solution certainly does not lie in a 'return to customs', which would, in fact, be impossible, and would only serve to accentuate inequalities and open the way for savage capitalism.

We cannot say that no African state has ever tried the approach recommended here. In Mali, following independence in September 1961, the

Sudanese Union began what has very wrongly been described as 'collectivization'. In fact, the cooperatives that were set up were not productive cooperatives, production remaining the exclusive responsibility of family farms. It was a form of modernized collective authority that replaced the so-called 'custom' on which colonial authority had depended. The party that took over this new modern power was clearly aware of the challenge and set the objective of abolishing customary forms of power that were deemed to be 'reactionary' even 'feudal'. It is true that this new peasant authority which was formally democratic (those in charge were elected) was in fact only as democratic as the state and the party. However, it had 'modern' responsibilities, namely, to ensure that access to land was administered 'correctly', that is to say, without 'discrimination', to manage loans, the distribution of subsidies (supplied by state trade) and product marketing (also partly the responsibility of state trade). In practice, nepotism and extortion have certainly never been eradicated. The only response to these abuses should have been the progressive democratization of the state and not its 'retreat' as liberalism then imposed (by means of an extremely violent military dictatorship) to the benefit of the traders ('dioulas').

Other experiences in the liberated areas of Guinea Bissau (impelled by theories put forward by Amilcar Cabral) in Burkina Faso at the time of Sankara have also tackled these challenges head on and sometimes produced unquestionable progress that today people try to erase. The creation of elected rural collectives in Senegal is a response the principle of which I would not hesitate to defend. Democracy is a never-ending process, no more so in Europe than in Africa.

What current dominant discourse understands by 'reform of the land tenure system' is quite the opposite from what the construction of a real alternative based on a prosperous peasant economy requires. This discourse, promoted by the propaganda instruments of collective imperialism – the World Bank, numerous cooperation agencies and also a number of NGOs with considerable financial backing – understands land reform to mean the acceleration of the privatization of land and nothing more. The aim is clear: create the conditions that would allow 'modern' islands of (foreign or local) agribusiness to take possession of the land they need in order to expand. Yet the additional produce that these islands could provide (for export or creditworthy local market) will never meet the challenge of the requirements of the creation of a prosperous society for all, which implies the advancement of the peasant family economy as a whole.

So, counter to the above, a land tenure reform conceived from the perspective of the creation of a real, efficient and democratic alternative supported by prosperous peasant family production must define the role of the state (principal inalienable owner) and that of the institutions and mechanisms of administering access to land and the means of production.

I do not exclude here complex mixed formulas that are specific to each country. Private ownership of the land may be acceptable – at least where it is established and held to be legitimate. Its redistribution can or should be reviewed, where necessary, as part of an agrarian reform (South Africa, Zimbabwe and Kenya, with respect to sub-Saharan Africa). I would not even necessarily rule out the controlled clearance of land for agribusiness in all cases. The key lies elsewhere, in the modernization of peasant family farming and the democratization of the management of its integration into the national and global economy.

I have no blueprint to propose for these challenges so I will limit myself to pointing out some of the great problems that such reform poses. The democratic question is indisputably central to the response to the challenge. It is a complex and difficult question that cannot be reduced to insipid discourse about good governance and electoral pluralism. There is an indisputably cultural aspect to the question: democracy leads to the abolition of 'customs' that are hostile to it (prejudice concerning social hierarchies and above all the treatment of women). There are legal and institutional aspects to be considered: the creation of systems of administrative, commercial and personal rights that are consistent with the aims of the plans for social construction and the creation of suitable (generally elected) institutions. However, above all, the progress of democracy will depend definitively on the social power of its defenders. The organization of peasant movements is, in this respect, absolutely irreplaceable. It is only to the extent that peasants are able to express themselves that progress in the direction known as 'participative democracy' (as opposed to the reduction of the problem to the dimension of 'representative democracy') will be able to make headway.

The question of relations between men and women is another aspect of the democratic challenge that is no less essential. Peasant 'family farming' obviously concerns the family, which is to this day characterized almost everywhere by structures that require the submission of women and their exploitation in the work-force. Democratic transformation will not be possible in these conditions without the organized action of the women concerned.

Attention must be given to the question of migration. In general, 'customary' rights exclude 'foreigners' (that is to say, all those who do not belong to the clans, lineage and families that make up the village community in question) from the right to land or place conditions upon their access to it. Migration resulting from colonial and postcolonial development have sometimes been of such a scale that they have over-turned the concepts of ethnic 'homogeneity' in the regions affected by this development. Emigrants from outside the state in question (such as the Burkina Be in Ivory Coast) or those who although formally citizens of the same state are of an 'ethnic' origin other than that of the regions they have made their homes (like the Hausa in the Nigerian state of Plateau), see their rights to the land they have cultivated challenged by short-sighted and chauvinistic political movements that also benefit from foreign support. To throw the 'communitarism' in question into ideological and political disarray and uncompromisingly denounce the paracultural discourse that underpins it has become one of the indispensable conditions of real democratic progress.

The analyses and propositions set out above only concern the status of tenure or rules on access to land. These matters are certainly central to debates on the future of agricultural and food production, peasant societies and the people that comprise them yet they do not cover all aspects of the challenge. Access to land remains devoid of the potential to transform society if the peasant who benefits from it cannot have access to the essential means of production in suitable conditions (credit, seed, subsidies, access to markets). Both national policies and international negotiations that aim to define the context in which prices and revenues are determined are other aspects of the peasant question.

Further information on these questions that go beyond the scope of this chapter can be found in the writings of Jacques Berthelot – the best critical analyst of projects on integrating agricultural and food production into 'world' markets. So I shall restrict myself to reiterating the two main conclusions and proposals reached:

(i) We cannot allow agricultural and food production, and land to be treated as ordinary 'merchandise', and then agree to the need to integrate them into plans for global liberalization promoted by the dominant powers (the United States and Europe) and transnationalized capital.

The agenda of the World Trade Organization (WTO), which inherited the General Agreement on Tariffs and Trade (GATT) in 1995, must quite simply be refused. Opinion in Asia and Africa, beginning with peasant organizations but also all the social and political forces that defend the interests of working classes and those of the nation (and demands for food security in particular), all those who have not given up on a development project worthy of the name, must be persuaded that negotiations entered into as part of the WTO agenda can only result in catastrophe for the peoples of Asia and Africa and threaten to devastate the lives of more than two-and-a-half billion peasants from the two continents while offering them no other prospect than migration to slums, being shut away in 'concentration camps' the construction of which is already planned.

Capitalism has reached a stage where its continued expansion requires the implementation of 'enclosure' policies on a world scale similar to those at the beginning of its development in England, except that today the destruction on a world scale of the 'peasant reserves' of cheap labour will be nothing less than synonymous with the genocide of half of humanity. On one hand the destruction of the peasant societies of Asia and Africa; on the other, some billions in extra profit for world capital and its local associates derived from a socially useless production since it is not destined to address the needs of hundreds of the millions of the extra hungry but only to increase the number of obese in the North and those who emulate them in the South.

So Asian and African states must quite simply be called upon to withdraw from these negotiations and therefore reject decisions taken by the imperialist United States and Europe within the famous 'Green Rooms' of the WTO. This voice must be made to be heard and the governments concerned must be forced to ensure that it is heard in the WTO.

(ii) We can no longer accept the behaviour of the major imperialist powers (the United States and Europe) that together assault the people of the South within the WTO. It must be pointed out that the same powers that try to impose their 'liberalist' proposals unilaterally upon the countries of the South do not abide by these proposals themselves and behave in a way that can only be described as systematic cheating.

The Farm Bill in the United States and the agricultural policy of the European Union violate the very principles that the WTO is trying to impose on others. The 'partnership' projects proposed by the European Union following the Cotonou Convention as of 2008 are 'criminal', to borrow a strong but fair expression from Jacques Berthelot. We can and must hold these powers to account through the authorities of the WTO set up for this purpose. A group of countries from the South not only could but must do it.

Asian and African peasants organized themselves in the previous period of their peoples' liberation struggles. They found their place in powerful historical blocks that enabled them to be victorious over the imperialism of the time. These blocks were sometimes revolutionary (China and Vietnam) and found their main support in rural areas among the majority classes of middle, poor and landless peasants. When, elsewhere, they were led by the national bourgeoisie, or those among the rich and middle status peasants who aspired to becoming bourgeois, large landowners and 'customary' local authorities in the pay of colonization were isolated.

In a new approach the challenge from the new collective imperialism of the triad (United States, Europe, Japan) will only be met if historical blocks form in Asia and Africa that cannot be a *remake* of former ones. The definition of the nature of these blocks, their strategies and their immediate and longer-term objectives in these new circumstances is the challenge facing the alter-globalist movement and its constituent parts of social forums. This is a far more serious challenge than a large number of movements engaged in current struggles may imagine.

New peasant organizations exist in Asia and Africa that support the current visible struggles. Often, when political systems make it impossible for formal organizations to form, social struggles for the campaign take the form of 'movements' with no apparent direction. Where they do exist, these actions and programmes must be more closely examined. What peasant social forces do they represent, whose interests they defend? The majority mass of peasants or the minorities that aspire to find their place in the expansion of dominant global capitalism?

We should be wary of over hasty replies to these complex and difficult questions. We should not 'condemn' many organizations and movements on the pretext that they do not have the support of the majority of peasants for their radical programmes. That would be to ignore the demands of the formation of large alliances and strategies in stages. Neither should we subscribe to the discourse of 'naive alter-globalism' that often sets the tone of forums and fuels the illusion that the world would be set on the right track only by the existence of social movements. This discourse, it is true, is more one common to numerous NGOs – well-meaning maybe – than of peasant and worker organizations.

Note

* The analysis and proposals made in this chapter are only relevant for Asia and Africa. The agrarian issue in Latin America and the Caribbean has its own particular and sometimes unique particularities. Thus, in the Southern Cone of the continent (southern Brazil, Argentina, Uruguay and Chile), modernized, mechanized latifundism that benefits from cheap labour is the method of farming that is best adapted to the demands of a liberal global capitalist system that is even more competitive than the agriculture in the United States and Europe.

References

(i) Reference to peasant struggles in Asia and Africa (China, India, the Philippines, Sri Lanka, Egypt, Ethiopia, Western Africa, South Africa and Zimbabwe) can be found in:

S. Amin et al. (2004), *Les luttes paysannes et ouvrières face aux défis du XXIe siècle [Peasant and Worker Struggles and the Challenges of the 21st Century]*, Les Indes Savantes, Paris. Translations into English, Spanish, Arabic and Chinese are currently under way. See also:
S. Amin (2004), *L'Inde, une grande puissance? [India, a Great Power?]*, October. Available at <http://forumtiersmonde.net> and <http://thirdworldforum.net>.

(ii) Cf. work by Jacques Berthelot on negotiations and proposals for agricultural integration into liberal globalization.

J. Berthelot (2005), *L'agriculture, talon d'Achille de l'OMC [Agriculture, the Achilles Heel of the WTO]*.
Also, *Quels avenirs pour les sociétés paysannes en Afrique de l'Ouest ? [What Future for the Peasant Societies of Western Africa?]* available at <http://thirdworldforum.net>.

(iii) M. Mazoyer and J. Roudard (1997), *Histoire des agricultures du monde [History of World Agriculture]*, Paris: Le Seuil.
(iv) Cf our proposals for the integration of peasants' right to access to land in the charter of universal rights at: <http://forumtiersmonde.net>, section 'Current Programmes': the new Agrarian Question.

10
Globalization, Capital Inflows and Financial Crises

B.N. Ghosh

Capital inflow is supposed to be an important indicator of globalization. Based on this indicator this chapter argues that the global financial crises that occurred in the last phase of the 1990s were due to many factors that could be associated with globalization. By examining the problem of East Asian economies in this context the chapter explains that a dependent type of capitalism was mainly responsible for the financial crisis in these countries that received a hunk of hot money and unregulated capital inflow. Capital market liberalization was not necessary for these economies; they could otherwise have sustained a fairly high growth rate with their high savings rate (around 35 per cent). However, for the purpose of attaining a very high (more than 10 per cent) quantitative growth rate, the required investment in excess of domestic saving was obtained by these countries through foreign borrowing, and they became heavily indebted. Borrowing was high because of the loan-pushing type of lending strategy by the international financial institutions. All these economies opened their capital account before reforming the financial sector and without making the banking sector strong. Capital market liberalization is often dangerous for nascent economies. Some of the developed countries (DCs) introduced it only at the late stage of their development (in the 1970s). Excessive and unregulated capital inflow produced many types of macroeconomic vulnerabilities, such as high debt/reserve ratio, higher deficit in the current account and appreciation of the real exchange rate. The appreciation of real exchange rate reduced exports, which aggravated the macroeconomic vulnerabilities and financial crisis was the natural outcome.

Increased capital inflow augmented a capital intensity in production that possibly reduced employment and wages. Moreover, by increasing the production of exportables, higher capital inflow put the terms of trade against these countries, which led to the situation of immiserizing growth. Capital inflow in such countries was mainly accompanied by hot money that contributed to short-term speculative bubbles; the bubbles then burst with the sudden outflow of this money. The Asian financial crisis teaches a couple of lessons that are worth remembering in the days of neo-liberal globalization: first, capital market liberalization is not generally needed to obtain FDI for a country that has achieved macroeconomic stability (as in the case of China); and second, FDI is not necessarily beneficial all the time for all types of countries.

In a non-regulated and less developed financial system, as in the MIT (Malaysia–Indonesia–Thailand) countries with financial liberalization and the resultant capital flow, banking crisis and currency crisis may mutually reinforce each other through a vicious circle and, in terms of causality, the former often precedes the latter (Kaminsky and Reinhart 2001). This observation seems to square with the facts of the MIT economies.

In a sense, financial crisis can be looked upon as a situation of capability failure, which is rather pervasive in the days of globalization. The fiscal crisis partly manifests government failure to postpone debt or raise new loans, and also policy failures in many directions including macroeconomic mismanagement. In the same way, financial crisis also manifests capability failure on the part of the monetary authority to maintain the stability of the exchange rate, stabilize the interest rate or protect the foreign reserve. The commercial banking system as a whole manifests capability failure in maintaining a balance among liquidity, profitability and solvency. The free market system also manifests capability failure in the sense that it is not able to resolve the problem of financial crisis through its automatic adjustment mechanism in the areas of banking, exchange rate and monetary management. The capability failure in each case is mixed up both as a cause and an effect in a vicious spiral. Many of the syndromes of capability failure are indeed generated by the process of globalization as will be clear from the discussion that follows. The present chapter is an attempt to corroborate the aforesaid hypothesis in the case of the Malaysian economy.

Capital inflow, macroeconomic vulnerabilities and crisis

Evidently, capital inflow is associated both with economic growth and financial crisis. The association between capital inflow and growth has been accepted to be real by many researchers in the case of the emerging market economies in Southeast Asia including Malaysia. The very strong argument in favour of capital inflow is that it supplements domestic saving and boosts investment and growth. Capital inflows are extremely volatile and depend on many push and pull factors. The pull factor from the domestic developing economy is generally the higher interest rate differential compared to the country of origin of capital flow. The demand for larger doses of foreign capital is another very important pull factor that woos the capital flow. The push factors are lower global interest rates and declining marginal efficiency of capital in the developed countries that have already accumulated over time huge amounts of surplus capital. The theory of finance capital suggests that, in the face of declining opportunities for profitable investment possibilities at home, lenders are inclined to practise loan-pushing (Basu 1991) and the investors from the developed capitalist countries take recourse to sending their capital to those emerging countries where the return to capital is much higher. Thus, higher profitability and speculative gains are the two basic push factors behind world capital flows. Cyclical factors such as recession or temporary boom may also act as important factors for the inflow and outflow of capital. The study by Calvo et al. (1993) came to the observation that capital flows to Latin America were fundamentally driven by cyclical factors of recession, balance of payments debacle and low interest rates in the United States. In the same way sudden booms and spurts in economic activities through massive projects may accelerate the demand for capital inflows, as in many of the newly emerging market economies. As for Malaysia, successful completion of structural adjustment programmes in the early 1990s was one of the reasons for increased capital inflow.

It should, however, not be forgotten that capital flows are essentially different from the flow of goods and services across the borders. The former flows may and generally do accompany more uncertainty, higher costs, distortions in the valuation of assets and destabilizing market correction behaviour (Devlin et al. 1995). As a matter of fact, financial flows always give rise to many types of externalities created, and at times exacerbated, by asymmetric information between borrowers and lenders, and in the matter of evaluation of the present and the future. The Minsky type of model (1986) of information asymmetry, which presumes that borrowers know more than the lenders, does not seem to be true in the case of Southeast Asian economies. The fact that Western lenders knew better was implied by their refusal to roll over debts and their decision to ask for payments of old debts immediately before the crisis in Thailand, Korea, Malaysia and Indonesia. Presumably, these lenders were posted with the latest information about the debilitating macro fundamentals of these economies of which the borrowers perhaps were unaware. It cannot be denied that behind the original manifestation of herd behaviour there is the hard-headed exercise of rational estimation in the financial world.

By now it has become pretty clear that different types of capital inflows do create different degrees of volatility in the capital-receiving country. Griffith-Jones (1998) has critically analysed earlier studies that did not find any systematic differences in the degrees of volatility for different types of capital inflows. Thus the pernicious effects of globalization went unnoticed for quite some time, and people naively believed that capital inflow is an unmixed blessing. It is now rather well-established that whereas long-term capital and foreign direct investment are more stable, short-term flows are rather hotter and destabilizing (Cailloux and Griffith-Jones 1997; Frankel and Rose 1996, and Chuhan et al. 1993).

Based on the nature and characteristics of capital inflows, the following five stylized propositions appear to be obvious:

Proposition I: Capital inflows do supplement domestic savings and boost investment and economic growth in some cases.

Proposition II: Capital inflows to developing countries depend on various types of push and pull factors and are influenced by higher interest rate differential and higher marginal productivity of capital.

Proposition III: All capital inflows will not have the same degrees of volatility – while short-term flows are more volatile and destabilizing, long-term flows are more stable and salutary.

Proposition IV: Capital inflows in the situation of uncertainty, asymmetric information, high information cost and other possible distortions can cause errors in subjective valuation. This may lead to sudden and destabilizing market adjustments. The allocation of resources through capital inflow in the situation of information asymmetry and uncertainties that cannot be properly evaluated does not appear to be efficient.

Proposition V: Unless properly managed, and if the proportion of short-term inflow is quite high, capital inflow may lead to financial problems.

Following the Mundell–Fleming Model (1962–63), capital inflow can be said to be a positive function of the interest rate differential between the domestic rate and the world average rate. However, domestic interest rate itself is negatively correlated to the inflow of capital. That is, more and more capital inflow to a developing economy will gradually reduce the domestic interest rate until such time as the domestic rate and the world rate become equal. The model envisages that, with perfect capital mobility and flexible exchange rate, a higher relative domestic interest rate will lead to capital inflow, which will induce expansion and higher growth; but continued capital inflow will bring down the domestic interest rate and stop all expansion. However, the theoretical findings of the model do not square with the empirical facts of many emerging market economies including Malaysia. This issue will be taken up later in this chapter.

Does capital inflow lead to growth?

In order to fully appreciate the macroeconomic fundamentals in their proper perspective in depth and range, it is necessary to traverse beyond the empirics of the domestic economy and study the impacts of capital inflow. In fact, capital inflow in the highly leveraged economy of Malaysia, like many other ASEAN economies, is supposed to be positively correlated to economic growth. Very often capital inflow positively influences economic growth and, in the same way, economic growth by ensuring profitability and higher returns on capital also considerably influences the inflow of capital into the domestic economy. In the case of Malaysia political and economic stability has played no less an important role than other factors that attracted foreign capital. In the case of Malaysia the interdependent nature of economic growth and capital inflow make it imperative for analytical reasons to introduce causality analysis to determine the cause–effect relationship between these two variables. In what follows an analysis based on the Granger test is applied to determine the direction of causality between these variables.

$$KI_t = \alpha_{01} + \alpha_{11} KI_{t-1} + \alpha_{21} KI_{t-2} + \beta_{11} EG_{t-1} + \beta_{21} EG_{t-2} + \varepsilon_{t1}$$

$$EG_t = \alpha_{02} + \alpha_{12} EG_{t-1} + \alpha_{22} EG_{t-2} + \beta_{12} KI_{t-1} + \beta_{22} KI_{t-2} + \varepsilon_{t2}$$

where:

KI_t = capital inflow

KI_{t-i} for $I = 1, 2$ = first and second lags of capital inflow

EG_t = economic growth

EG_{t-i} for $I = 1, 2$ = first and second lags of economic growth

Results of the Granger test is given in Table 10.1.
The results of the Granger test given in Tables 10.1 and 10.2 shows that capital inflow does not cause economic growth, but that economic growth does cause capital inflow. Taking the clue from the Granger test of causality, as elaborated earlier, it is now pertinent to explain the determinants of capital inflow, which has been found to be influenced by economic growth. On the basis of general *a priori* and *a posteriori* information obtained from various theoretical and empirical studies, one can identify seven major variables that are supposed to be phenomenologically related to capital inflow. The formal *exante* relation is shown in the model that follows. The relationship will be tested later by means of a multiple regression analysis.

Table 10.1 Results of specified models

KI & EG (T = 17)

(1) $KI_t = -1530.2621 + 0.3867\ KI_{t-1}{}^{**} + 0.2078\ KI_{t-2}{}^{**} + 305.9209\ EG_{t-1} + 330.7922\ EG_{t-2}$

t; (2.308) (2.672) (0.986) (1.435)

$R^2 = 0.7190$ Adj $R^2 = 0.6066$

$F = 6.396^*$

(2) $EG_t = 4.3539 + 0.6398\ EG_{t-1}{}^{**} - 0.2961\ EG_{t-2}{}^* + 0.0003\ KI_{t-1} - 0.0003\ KI_{t-2}$

t; (2.146) (2.919) (0.974) (−0.967)

$R^2 = 0.4092$ Adj $R^2 = 0.1728$

$F = 1.731$

Notes: *Denotes significance at 1% level.
**Denotes significance at 5% level.

Table 10.2 Hypotheses test

---

(1) $H_0 : \beta_{11} \neq \beta_{21} = 0$ (KI does cause EG)

LM = 12.4287 $\chi^2_{(2,\ 0.01)} = 9.21$

LMF = 16.6317 $F = 6.70$ with $\alpha = 0.01$

The results show that KI does not cause EG.

(2) $H_0 : \beta_{12} \neq \beta_{22} = 0$ (EG does cause KI)

LM = 6.138 $\chi^2_{(2,\ 0.01)} = 9.21$

LMF = 4.502 $F = 6.70$ with $\alpha = 0.01$

The results show that EG does cause KI.

The Model:

$$KIN = f(GDP, OEG, EMP, PGI, GRO, WAG, RI)$$
$$= \beta_0 + \beta_1\ GDP + \beta_2\ OEG + \beta_3\ EMP + \beta_4\ PGI + \beta_5\ GRO + \beta_6\ WAG$$
$$+ \beta_7\ RI + \mu_i$$

Where,

KIN = Capital inflow (RM in million)

GDP = Gross domestic product (RM in million)

PGI = Private and government investment (RM in million)

OEG = Operating and development expenditure by government (RM in million)

EMP = Total number of skilled people employed

GRO = Economic growth (percentage)

WAG = Percentage of average change in the wage rate in Malaysia

RI = Rate of interest (percentage)

β_0 = Intercept

β_1........β_7 = Partial regression coefficients

μ_i = Error term

Data for the present analysis have been collected from various sources such as Economic Reports (Government of Malaysia), International Financial Statistics, Malaysian Five Year Plans and Budget Reports. The analysis is based on time-series data for the period 1975–97. The estimation is based on the OLS method. The data analysis shows that while some independent variables like the GDP, economic growth and the domestic interest rate are positively associated with capital inflow, the variables such as employment, rate of change in the wage level and domestic investment have negative associations. However, these relations in the model have not been found to be statistically significant. Therefore, an attempt has been made to introduce a step-wise method of regression.

The multiple regression model is used to determine the influence of various factors on capital inflow. On the basis of the Forward Elimination Method, the influence of GDP has been found to be significant at one per cent level. The GDP as an independent variable used in the model can explain more than 35 per cent of the variation in capital inflow. The F test which is a measure of overall significance of the estimated regression is found to be significant at one per cent level. Thus it is found at the 99 per cent level of confidence that capital inflow is linearly related to GDP. The fact that GDP positively influences capital inflow has already been proved by the Granger test. The Step-wise Forward

Elimination Method simply corroborates the earlier result. Surprisingly the analysis does not lend support to the Mundell–Fleming thesis, which emphasizes the unique signification of the rate of interest as a determinant of capital inflow.

Macro vulnerability and speculative attack

As is well known, the surge of capital inflow that accompanies globalization leads to monetary and fiscal expansion. The increase in domestic prices, as a result, particularly of non-tradable goods, escalates the domestic wage levels. Wages in the MIT countries (Malaysia, Indonesia and Thailand) grew at the rate of 12 per cent per annum with Malaysia recording the fastest growth of 23 per cent before the financial crisis (Hussain and Radelet 1999, 43), but productivity of labour was lagging behind the wage.

Wage escalation, glut in the world market for some of the Asian products, particularly electronics, and the risk of new competitors such as China and Mexico were mainly responsible for the lackadaisical performance of the export sector. The loss of price competitiveness was one of the very crucial factors responsible for the emerging comparative disadvantage in these countries. Malaysia's export growth rate which was 20.3 per cent on average during 1990–95 plummeted to 5.8 per cent in 1996 (Table 10.3). However, for a non-crisis country such as India with a low degree of globalization, export growth increased from 5.8 to 7.4 per cent during the same period. Thus capital inflow, through its higher price effect, weakened the export sector. Behind the price escalation was the growth of domestic credit expansion. In Malaysia, due to capital inflow, credit expansion recorded a growth from 5.01 per cent in 1988 to 27.7 in 1996 (Table 10.3).

A very potent cause of export slow down was the loss of competitiveness due to appreciation of real exchange rate. The increase in the prices of tradable goods as a result of credit expansion generally increases trade deficits. This causes an appreciation of the real exchange rate as the prices of non-tradable goods increase because of relative price changes. The Balassa–Samuelson theorem suggests that an open economy over the years experiences price escalation of non-tradables. The appreciation reallocates resources from the production of tradable goods to the production of non-tradable goods. The capital inflow and the resultant credit boom are all mostly diverted to the speculative sector, real estate and property markets which generate quick and larger profits. All these lead to the expansion of non-tradable sector, contraction of tradable

Table 10.3   Capital inflow and macro vulnerabilities

Year	Short-term debt/ reserve ratio		Index of real exchange rate		Export growth rate		Current a/c balance	
	Malaysia	India	Malaysia	India	Malaysia	India	Malaysia	India
1990	–	–	100	100	17.4	–	−5.9*	−3.2
1991	47.5	141.5	–	–	16.8	–	−8.9	−0.4
1992	48.9	143.1	–	–	18.5	–	−4.0	−1.0
1993	50.8	67.6	–	–	15.7	5.8	−5.0	−1.7
1994	35.0	59.9	–	–	24.7	–	−6.0	−1.2
1995	34.7	71.7	–	–	26.0	–	−10.0	−1.4
1996	41.6	53.3	–	–	5.8	7.4	−5.0	−1.0
1997	69.2	44.7	73.8	100.8	–	–	−5.1	−1.5

	Growth in domestic credit (%)	Net capital inflow (% of GDP)	Short-term capital as % long-term capital	Domestic rate of interest
1988	5.01	–	57.11	2.6
1989	19.9	3.5	86.011	4.4
1990	17.9	4.2	47.81	6.8
1991	18.4	11.9	771.18	7.8
1992	16.5	15.2	415.75	7.6
1993	12.2	16.2	1422.98	6.5
1994	14.8	9.6	176.66	3.7
1995	29.5	8.5	24.26	5.5
1996	27.7	9.5	1553.53	6.4

Note: * Average of 1990–95.
Sources: IMF, International Financial Statistics, Govt. of India, Economic Survey (1999–2000), Ghosh (2000, 9) Hussain and Radelet (1999, 44), Eichengreen (1999, 144).

sector, appreciation of real exchange rate and larger trade deficit (Corbo and Hernandez 1996).

In all the crisis-ridden East Asian economies the real exchange rate did appreciate substantially (Ghosh 2000, 9). Although it significantly appreciated for Malaysia, for India, which was not affected by the crisis, there was depreciation (see Table 10.3). In the East Asian countries that were linked to dollars in more or less fixed terms, the exporters faced comparative disadvantages. It should be noted that the misalignment (appreciation) brought about by weak macro fundamentals cannot sustain the exchange rate pegging for a long time; and in the event of currency attack, it is difficult to successfully defend the domestic currency, as was the case in Malaysia. Table 10.3 clearly shows that, whereas for a more globalized economy like Malaysia macro fundamentals deteriorated over time to lead to financial turmoil, for a less globalized economy like India, the situation was much better. The first generation model of speculative attack which was popularized by Paul Krugman (1979) suggests that domestic policy of monetary and fiscal expansion leads to a series of persistent balance of payments deficits under a regime of fixed exchange rate. In such a situation there is a run on the domestic country's international reserve and a speculative attack on the currency. The attack is engineered at all because, in the face of declining stock of reserve, speculators know for sure that the fixed exchange rate regime will ultimately collapse and a devaluation of the currency will take place. They soon offload the domestic currency, setting it or converting it to relatively stable foreign assets or currency; in the process the central bank loses its foreign exchange reserve, which was already inadequate, and when the danger point comes the currency collapses. A few macroeconomic indicators such as a huge budget deficit, high interest rate, growing inflation, dwindling foreign exchange reserve, over-valuation of real exchange rate and balance of payments deficits and the like signal any speculative attack. A high short-term debt–reserve ratio, which is supposed to be an important indicator of macro vulnerability, was present in all the crisis-ridden countries of East Asia. In Malaysia it increased from 47.5 in 1991 to 69.2 in 1997. But for a non-crisis country like India the ratio value declined from 141.5 to 44.7. It should be noted that the domestic expansion in a globalized economy, which is the main culprit, comes mainly through capital inflows.

In order to fully appreciate the total impact of macroeconomic fundamentals on crisis it is imperative to juxtapose the picture of the current account balance of payments with the scenario of export, short-term debt–reserve ratio, and the appreciation of the real exchange rate. The current account balance in Malaysia as a percentage of GDP stood at −5.1 which, according to the conventional wisdom, is higher than the danger mark of −4. It was only on an average −1.0 for a non-crisis country like India during 1996 (Table 10.3). There was also a considerable amount of decapitalization over time because the degree of outflow of capital from the MIT economies in the form of profit and dividend repatriation and investment abroad, and this almost offset the capital inflow during the period immediately preceding the crisis. The current account deficits in the MIT countries were pretty high but their export performance was disappointing. As an offshoot the equity prices declined and the real estate bubble burst. This created the problems of insolvency for the players in the stock and property markets and of government's commitment to sustain the currency peg.

In the case of the Asian crisis banking problems and currency problems were inextricably mixed up in a vicious spiral and both became the integral parts of the financial crisis that erupted in 1997. The reasons for the involvement and the impact of the banking system need further elaboration. In the process of globalized development of the Southeast Asian economies, including Malaysia, commercial banks were assigned a crucial role. These banks perform the responsibilities of industrial development in much the same way as the banking system in Schumpeter's model of economic development.[1] These are also the institutions that sustain and promote the system of crony capitalism and state capitalism, which are said to be predominating in Southeast Asia.[2] The implicit government guarantees create moral hazard both for short-term borrowing by banks from abroad, and the international financial institutions lending money to these banks.[3] All these lead to the problems of non-performing loans (NPL), mounting short-term debts and the vulnerability of the banking system. The NPL was extremely high for the crisis-affected economies of Indonesia, Thailand and South Korea. It was \$35 billion (33.01 per cent) for Malaysia in 1997.

There are precisely three channels through which a banking crisis may come about in a globalized economy. First, credit boom following capital inflows may lead to adverse selection,[4] proliferation of non-performing loans, and the weakening of the banking system to the point of crisis, which may be called realization crisis. Second, foreign liabilities of the domestic banking system may be mostly short-dated and pretty high. For instance, offshore liabilities of domestic banks in Malaysia were 9.2 per cent, Indonesia 5.6 per cent and Thailand 26.8 per cent of GNP in 1997 (Radelet and Sachs 1998). In such a situation, the simultaneous calling back of all loans by foreign lenders petrified by panics may actually lead to a bank run. In the same way panic-stricken depositors' attempts to withdraw deposits all at a time may also precipitate banking crisis in a system organized on fractional reserves. Third, a substantial rise in the domestic interest rate to defend the domestic currency in the context of weak macroeconomic fundamentals is likely to engineer a domestic credit squeeze, economic contraction and bank failure, if the banking system is operating under high NPL ratios and low levels of capital adequacy (Athukorala et al. 1997).

From the foregoing analysis it becomes obvious that the inflow of capital, in the wake of financial liberalization and capital account convertibility in Southeast Asia, including Malaysia, directly and indirectly contributed to the weakening of macroeconomic fundamentals via a rise in debt–reserve ratio, appreciation of real exchange rate, decline in export, increase in current account deficits, and the like, through expansionary effects, higher interest rate effect, unfavourable banking effect and panic effect. All these effects interacted with and reinforced one another in various ways, which have been explained above.

The hypothesis that weak macroeconomic fundamentals were the basic causes of the financial crisis of 1997 has been explained through a two-way data-based testing procedure by invoking the method of double agreement or joint method of agreement and difference.[5] This implies that when the values of some macro variables such as short-term debt–reserve ratio, the value of real exchange rate and current account deficits are going up, a crisis is created (as in Malaysia), but when their values are going down, these are no longer associated with crisis (as in India). This is shown in Table 10.4.

A number of other variables can also be added to the list of affected macrovariables. However, for the present purpose a few crucial variables may be taken as the indicators. The point to be noted here is that

Table 10.4 Macro variables and crisis

Agreement			Difference		
Macroeconomic variables	*Values*	*Association with crisis*	*Macroeconomic variables*	*Values*	*Association with crisis*
Short-term debt–reserve ratio	High	Yes	Short-term debt–reserve ratio	Low	No
Real exchange ratio	High	Yes	Real exchange rate	Low	No
Export growth	Low	Yes	Export growth	High	No
Current account deficit	High	Yes	Current account deficit	Low	No
Incremental capital output ratio	High	Yes	Incremental capital output ratio	Low	No
Ratio of private sector credit to GDP	High	Yes	Ratio of private sector credit to GDP	Low	No
NPL	High	Yes	NPL	Low	No
Short capital as % of long-term capital	High	Yes	Short capital as % of long-term capital	Low	No

these macro vulnerabilities were responsible for the financial crisis in Malaysia, as in other neighbouring countries, during the period of high economic growth in these highly globalized economies. The experience of these countries clearly reveals that financial crisis can very well occur despite a high rate of economic growth.

Policy responses

One of the reasons why the financial crisis in a country like Malaysia was so egregious in its impact is perhaps the fact that a larger proportion of capital inflow constituted short-term capital. In the case of Malaysia it went from 47.81 per cent in 1990 to an alarming 1553 per cent in 1996, the year that preceded the crisis (see Table 10.3). In the Asian countries capital inflow has not been an unmixed blessing. It has been responsible for unnecessary and unproductive expansion detrimental to the economy in the long run. Obviously these economies are too inexperienced to use the correct stabilization procedure to neutralize the harmful effects of capital inflow and to use it for advantage. Had there been any mechanism or guidelines to use the capital inflow avoiding its deleterious effects, the impact of the financial crisis in the Asian economies would not have been so strong.

Since 1990 capital inflows continuously increased in Malaysia (Table 10.3). A policy response of sterilization intervention was undertaken by Malaysia through various measures including open market operations, increase in statuary reserve requirements of the commercial banks and the transfer of government banking deposits to the central bank. But since there were no broad and diversified capital markets and no adequacy of instruments in Malaysia, the open market operations were not successful. The central bank's open market operations using market-based instruments were inadequate for the task of sterilizing the accelerated volume of capital inflow (Doraisamy 2001).[6] As adumbrated earlier, the Mundell–Fleming model becomes inapplicable in many ways in the case of Malaysia. First, as a result of capital inflow, the rate of interest did not come down until the time of crisis in 1997, except for 1994 when the net capital inflow plummeted substantially (Table 10.3). The growth of domestic credit and money supply continuously increased, showing the inefficacy of the control and sterilization measures. Second, as the capital inflow went on increasing, so did the domestic interest rate. This trend was noticeable from 1988 to 1993, and again from 1994 to 1996. The interest mechanism did not behave the way the Mundell–Fleming model envisaged. The sustained high interest regime was not, however, in response to a high rate of inflation for actual inflation rate was not officially shown to be high in Malaysia.

The meat of the matter is that, after all, the domestic monetary policy must be consistent with the exchange rate policy. Rapid growth of money supply consequent on rapid capital inflows in the regime of fixed exchange rate led to a fall in reserves, and the cumulative effect resulted in financial crisis. The Malaysian case, as in some other countries, proves that a country cannot have a fixed exchange rate, an independent monetary policy and complete capital mobility all at the same time – *an impossible trinity*. In view of the ineffective monetary policy, even in spite of increased money supply, a rise in the interest rate led to more and more capital inflow in Malaysia.

The dependency model of development that the Southeast Asian economies followed during the period of globalization contributed a great deal to the genesis of the crisis. Dependency leads to many types of moral hazards and reckless macroeconomic behaviour (say, investment overtaking savings) that make overheating possible, which is a prelude to crisis. In the case of Malaysia both monetary and fiscal policy had remained unreasonably expansionary to carry through projects that were economically unproductive but fulfilled the personal desires of political leaders. Over the past decade Asian countries have followed an export-led strategy of growth that needed massive resources to continuously upgrade their technology and skills to remain competitive. Exporting firms needed to borrow heavily from abroad, and this was possible in a system of global financial liberalization, creating high leverage (debt–equity ratio). The financial deregulation of 1990s boosted foreign borrowings by the corporate sector in the midst of an underdeveloped domestic capital market and inadequately supervised banking system.

The unwarranted expansion of crony capitalism was part and parcel of the development process in Southeast Asia, as more development meant extraction of more surpluses. It was no wonder, therefore, that these economies followed the strategy of growth and expansion up to the hilt, quite oblivious of the truth that a quantitatively high growth rate is not necessarily the optimum or the most desirable. However, in a bid to expand the economies in pursuance of crony capitalism, a number of mega projects were taken up both by the public and the private sectors, and the political bosses did not care to pay much heed to the symptoms of overheating. These projects were mostly financed by foreign sources, and for which the dictates of economic efficiency were relegated to the background.

The policy of too much economic growth within too short a period proved to be counter-productive in the long run. The phenomenology of the Asian crisis indicates that in an open and fully liberalized capitalist economy with a weak and underdeveloped financial market, growth and cycles become interactive in many ways, particularly if the policy responses are inappropriate and macroeconomic fundamentals are debilitated. In fact, the macro vulnerability theory of the Asian financial crisis that I have developed elsewhere (Ghosh 2001) is indeed a serious contesting theory often overlooked.

Concluding observations

In the dependency type of model that the Southeast Asian economies followed for their growth and development, capital inflow plays a very significant role. But all types and components of capital inflow do not have the same salutary impact. Whereas long-term capital and direct foreign investment have many beneficial growth-inducing effects, the short-term capital (the hot money) has a destabilizing, growth-retarding impact. A large part of capital inflow in Malaysia, as in other Southeast Asian economies, was directed to the property sector, real estate business and other speculative activities where the rate of profit is excessively high and such capital left the host country within a short-period of time immediately after reaping the gains.

The Southeast Asian economies did not really have any foolproof mechanism to safely utilize this capital for optimum benefits. In the absence of proper mechanism and management/control tools, the capital inflow could not be correctly sterilized. As an offshoot such capital inflows led to macroeconomic vulnerabilities such as high short-term debt–reserve ratio, unnecessary expansion in credit, appreciation of the real exchange rate, decline in export growth, current account deficit, decline in equity prices, and so on, which ultimately pushed the economy into the vortex of crisis. The development of macro vulnerabilities, however, is partly the manifestation of the symptom of policy failure. The policy of attaining and maintaining a very high rate of growth, which is not warranted given the limited domestic capital endowments, resources, technology and skill, is perhaps the root cause of these economies developing crisis sooner or later. The attempt to over-expand the economy, even in spite of the signal of overheating, as in the case of Malaysia, shows a lack of appropriate policy response. It can also alternatively be interpreted as an attempt to accumulate more and more surplus for the expanding empire of crony capitalism.

The rest-of-the-world sector in many ways can be said to be responsible for bringing about macroeconomic vulnerabilities to some of the open Asian economies. The appreciation of real exchange rate, for instance, is invariably related to the capital inflows that the open economies of Southeast Asia had been experiencing for quite some time before the financial crisis of 1997. In the case of these countries the misalignment of the real exchange rate was brought about by weak macroeconomic fundamentals. The crisis has proved that the competitive benefit from an exchange rate is only transitory. What is more significant is the strong macroeconomic fundamentals brought about by enhanced total factor productivity.

But one cannot expect strong macro fundamentals in the face of exorbitant amounts of hot money entering into the non-traded sector. There is an element of policy failure in not discouraging the entry of such volatile money into the economy. As a matter of fact one of the lessons of the Asian financial crisis is that for countries whose financial sector is not developed and disciplined it is indeed precarious to go the whole way with financial liberalization and fully-fledged capital account convertibility.

Capital inflow did work as a saviour to these nascent market economies; but it also contributed indirectly to the generation of financial crisis. International capital mobility has led to the fragility of the pegged exchange rate system, and there is no doubt that the inflow of short-term capital has resulted in conflict between the domestic macroeconomic policy and the exchange rate system. Be that as it may, in the days of globalization, international capital mobility is to continue, and therefore it is imperative to make the domestic financial sector strong and resilient, to discriminate against the inflow of hot money, to create financial safety nets and the necessary institutional framework to resolve the problems of poor policy responses, moral hazards and information asymmetry.

Notes

1. In the Schumpeterian model entrepreneurs occupy the central position and the innovation is the principal force behind all progress. Investments and innovations are financed by banks. Business cycles are the natural outgrowth of economic progress: the forces that create instability are also the forces that are responsible for economic progress (Schumpeter 1911).
2. Crony capitalism aims at improving the economic conditions not only for political bosses but also for their friends, relatives and close associates through state policies and actions. In such a case the government gives guarantees

to commercial banks to borrow and lend particularly to its cronies. Such guarantees create moral hazard problems and may ultimately lead to a banking crisis (see, Eichengreen 1999, 138–40).

3. Moral hazard refers to distortions of incentives. For instance, when banks are guaranteed by the government, they go on lending indiscriminately without much bothering about the risk involved, which would not have been so in the case of no guarantee from government.

4. Adverse selection occurs when the actual selection is different and not as good as the desired selection. For instance, a bank always wants to lend money to a sound and solvent party; but in the case of implicit government guarantee the loan is often sanctioned to cronies who may not be financially sound.

5. The joint method of agreement and difference, also called the method of double agreement, was originally proposed by John Stuart Mill as a method of experimental enquiry. According to this method there are two sets of instances. In one case the high values of some antecedents (variables) are followed by the presence of the consequence (the phenomenon) and in another case, the low values of these antecedents lead to the absence of the said consequence (the phenomenon such as crisis). In the case of financial crisis, the high values of some variables lead to the occurrence of the crisis but low values of the same variables lead to an absence of crisis.

6. Doraisamy has explained many components of the procedure of sterlization that were followed in Malaysia and the subsequent policy responses to the problems created by capital inflow (Doraisamy 2001).

References

Athukorala, Prem-Chandra et al. (1997), 'Vulnerability to a currency crisis: Lessons from the Asian experience', unpublished paper.

Basu, Kaushik (1991), 'The International Debt Problem, Credit Rationing and Loan Pushing: Theory and Evidence', *Princeton Studies in International Finance*, 70.

Cailloux, J. and S. Griffith-Jones (1997), 'International capital flows: What do we know about their volatility?' mimeo, Institute of Development Studies, University of Sussex, UK.

Calvo, G., L. Leiderman, and C. Reinhart (1993), 'Capital inflows and real exchange rate appreciation in Latin America', *IMF Staff Papers*, 40(1), March.

Chuhan, P., S. Claessens, and N. Mawingi, (1993), 'Equity and bond flows to Asia and Latin America: The role of global and country factors', *World Bank Working Paper*, No. 1160, Washington, D.C.: World Bank.

Corbo, V. and M. Hernandez (1996) 'Macroeconomic adjustment to capital flows: Lessons from Latin America and East Asian experience', *World Bank Research Observer*, 11(1), February.

Devlin, R., R. French Davies and S. Griffith-Jones (1995), 'Surges in capital flows and development: An overview of policy issues', in R. French Davies and S. Griffith-Jones, S. (eds), *Coping with Capital Surges: The Return of Finance to Latin America*, Boulder, Colorado: Lynne Reinner.

Doraisamy, Anita (2001) 'The Malaysian currency crisis: Capital flows, policy response and macroeconomic vulnerability', in B.N. Ghosh (ed.), op.cit., ch. 6.

Eichengreen, Barry (1999), *Toward a New International Financial Architecture*, Washington, D.C.: Institute for International Economics.

Fleming, J.M. (1962.), 'Domestic financial policies under fixed and under flexible exchange rates', *IMF Staff Papers*, 9(3).

Frankel, A. Jaffrey and Andrew K. Rose (1996), 'Currency crashes in emerging markets: An empirical treatment', *Journal of International Economics*, **41**.

Ghosh, B.N. (2000), 'Financial crisis in the MIT countries: Myths and realities', *Economia Internazionale*, Vol. 53(1).

Ghosh, B.N. (ed.) (2001), *Global Financial Crises and Reforms: Cases and Caveats*, London and New York: Routledge.

Government of Malaysia (1994–95), *Economic Reports*, Kuala Lumpur: Ministry of Finance.

Griffith-Jones, S. (1998) *Global Capital Flows: Should They be Regulated?*, New York: St Martin's Press.

Hussain, Mumtaz and Steven Radelet (1999) 'Export and Asia's recovery', in World Economic Forum, *The Asia Competitiveness Report*, Geneva.

IMF (1999–200), International Financial Statistics, Government of India, Economic Survey.

Kaminsky, G.L. and M. Reinhart Carmen (2001), 'The twin crisis: The causes of banking and balance of payments problems', in B.N. Ghosh, op. cit. (ed.).

Krugman, Paul (1979), 'A model of balance of payments crisis', *Journal of Money, Credit and Banking*, **11**, August.

Minsky, H.P. (1986), *Stabilizing an Unstable Economy*, New Haven: Yale University Press.

Mundell, R.A. (1963). 'Capital mobility and stabilization policy under fixed and flexible exchange rates', *Canadian Journal of Economics and Political Science*, **29**.

Radelet, Steven and Jeffrey Sachs (1998) 'The East Asian financial crisis: Diagnosis, remedies and prospects', *Brookings Papers on Economic Activity*, No. 2.

Schumpter, Joseph (1911), *The Theory of Economic Development: An Inquiry into Profits, Capital, Credit, Interest and the Business Cycle*, New York: Oxford University Press.

11

Globalization and Incomplete Technology Transfer to Developing Countries

Franco Praussello

As a matter of fact the growing liberalization of product and factors of production markets in which consists one of the main structural feature of globalization (another being the emergence of a world economy transcending the old national economic spaces) is associated with increased capital flows both between countries belonging to the core of the world economy and between the latter and the periphery. Foreign direct investment (FDI) is commonly considered to be the most dynamic component of foreign capital flows, being the channel through which technology in the form of codified and tacit technical knowledge is transferred among different countries. Yet the amount and effects of technology transfer generated by FDI can be quite dissimilar, depending among other things on the level of development of the countries acting as investing or recipient economy. When the development gap is sufficiently large it is well possible that technology transfers give rise to some adverse effects on the host economy, while at the same time transmitting only partial or outdated knowledge. But this can happen for other reasons too, as we shall see. The transmission of partial or older technical knowledge is commonly referred to as the incomplete or unbalanced technology transfer between advanced and less developed countries (LDCs). This chapter is devoted mainly to the illustration of such an argument, with its determinants and consequences, using however as a starting point a brief description of some adverse effects of FDI for LDCs, not least owing to the interdependence of the two subjects.

The chapter is organized as follows. In the following section we set the general background of the chapter by asking whether FDI is always beneficial to LDCs, and highlighting some of the many cases in which foreign investment can be detrimental to the recipient economy. The third section is assigned to the central topic of the chapter, that is, an analysis of incomplete technology transfer, in its main aspects, whereas the fourth section is focused on the unavoidable conflict of interests aroused by the unbalanced or unequal technology transfer in the relationship between multinational corporations (MNCs) and their home countries, on the one hand, and host countries of FDI, on the other. The penultimate section gives a number of examples of incomplete transfer in the form of country case studies, while the final section contains some concluding remarks.

Adverse effects of FDI towards LDCs

FDI as a main tool for transferring technological knowledge from developed to LDCs in the framework of globalization, that is, in the absence of major impediments to international financial flows typically activated by MNCs, is commonly supposed to be welfare enhancing for the recipient countries. Nevertheless, in view of setting up the stage against which the issue of the limited technology transfer by MNCs to LDCs has to be treated, a preliminary question is worth raising: are we sure that FDI promotes always growth?

According to conventional wisdom FDI produces positive direct and indirect effects through technology transfer, which foster economic expansion. In fact FDI on the one hand can close the gap between domestic savings and investment, whereas on the other can give rise to positive externalities, channelling notably new technologies from abroad by demonstrating effects, technological assistance and training, among others. Furthermore, the presence of foreign capital can improve competition in local markets. Since MNCs cannot extract the full value of such alleged positive consequences, in literature the latter are often described as forming the spillover effect (Kokko 1994). Availability of foreign capital and spillover effect explain why LDC governments, as a rule, try to compete in order to attract as much FDI as possible.

Yet in principle FDI as a channel for technology transfer can be considered as a substitute for developing local, autonomous technical capabilities. Important gains from FDI have been more affirmed than confirmed by empirical studies. The evidence is indeed mixed: whereas some studies show that FDI is positively associated to growth in LDCs, others point to different results and find no significant link between the two variables (Evenson and Westphal 2002). In particular Helleiner (1989) quotes a first list of FDI projects having reduced the host country's national product; whereas, more recently, Saltz (1992) and Mencinger (2003) find negative correlations between FDI and growth, respectively in a number of developing and east European countries in years stretching from 1970–80 to 1994–2001, whereas Görg and Greenaway (2003) indicate that negative productivity spillovers at firm level were recently reported in five out of six papers focusing on transition countries. In general, despite 'circumstantial evidence' of spillover presence, investigations on different aspects of FDI in many countries and industries trace no concrete proof of positive spillover effects. Even though some studies reveal for instance the existence of external effects in the linkage between MNCs and their suppliers and subcontractors in the form of market access or productivity spillovers, then they fail to show how significant such spillovers are and if they can be generalized (Blomström and Kokko 2003).

In addition, it has been shown that spillovers from FDI depend on the foreign ownership share in a host country's investment. In short, MNCs seem to be scarcely willing to transfer technology through FDI giving rise to positive externalities, in the absence of strong institutional warranties as to the protection of their competitive advantages. In general terms, indeed, technology transfer is linked to the ownership structure of critical resources (Namazie 2003), with the caveat that in order to control the host country firms, foreign corporations do not need necessarily to be majority partners but can also have a strong minority position, when endowed with a high technology advantage (Kasuga 2003). The critical resources include in particular non-financial contributions or proprietary intangible assets as skills, knowledge, know-how, in a word sophisticated technologies, alongside strategic materials, which are in the command of the MNC. The protection of proprietary knowledge does not require inevitably full ownership, since the parent firm displaying a strong technological advantage can become the controlling shareholder even with minority stakes in a joint venture, as shown by the approach followed by Japan's NTT DoCoMo in the field of the telecommunication industry and its strategy of mergers and acquisitions for investing in the third generation of mobile phones. But in any case technology transfers are limited to the degree that the distribution of ownership does not result in the dissipation of the MNC's core advantage.

Concerning the relevance of ownership structure, a number of empirical studies (Javorick and Spatareanu 2003) give the following evidence: positive intra-sectoral spillovers exist for fully-owned foreign affiliates but not for joint ventures, where foreign capital is associated to local funds; by contrast, the former have negative effects on domestic firm upstream industries, while the opposite is true for the latter. Positive intra-sectoral or horizontal externalities are possibly due to the presence of wholly-owned projects and to the will of MNCs to protect their proprietary technology, hampering knowledge transfer and leakages through partially-owned joint ventures (Ramacharandran 1993; Mansfield and Romero 1980). In fact MNCs have an incentive to upgrade technologies in foreign affiliates only if they can have a larger share of the latter (Lin and Saggi 2004). Negative vertical externalities on upstream local industries can be explained by the limited availability by MNCs to source locally. Indeed MNCs establishing fully-owned foreign subsidiaries managing greenfield projects in host countries are less likely to rely on local suppliers, creating a greater reliance on more sophisticated imported inputs. In addition, after full acquisition of a local firm, MNCs often reduce links and purchases with domestic suppliers.

Evanescent positive FDI externalities and findings concerning possible adverse spillovers point to the fact that not always do foreign investments improve host country welfare. Together with pro-growth effects, literature has been stressing for long a large number of negative effects of FDI, which go well beyond those identified by the traditional dependency theory (Fan 2002). In its different approaches, the latter stressed above all the distortions due to the world division of labour imposed by MNCs to LDCs in terms of under-development and increased income inequality.

Among the possible modern bads of FDI, we can list adverse terms of trade changes, when prices of exportables decline, along with possible price increases for non-tradable goods, with the ensuing Dutch disease. Indeed, the first effect can arise when foreign investment is directed to firms having a monopolistic position in world markets, by expanding outputs that can be sold only at a lower price, whereas the second one is due to shifts of resources from traded to non-traded goods and services following a price increase in the sector of non-tradables and a fall in exports, worsening balance of payment conditions. In addition, when capital inflows are channelled towards primary commodity exports, as often it is the case, besides adverse terms of trade effects, scarce or no spillovers at all to other industries of host countries are generated, reinforcing the dualism of the development model adopted. Not to speak of possible damages inflicted to environment by excessive rates of extraction of natural resources, resulting in a worsening of sustainable development conditions (Brooks et al. 2003).

Moreover different kinds of workers (e.g. unskilled workers) can be adversely affected by foreign investment. Possible explanations of the following income inequality relate to the finding that FDI is likely to favour in a number of ways skilled workers employed in technology intensive industries where FDI is flowing in, both by improving their wage-bargaining power and by providing them with more training compared with unskilled workers. Evidence on this point shows that, as in the case of Latin America, at a minimum FDI tends to perpetuate income disparities (Te Velde 2002). When, for instance, the favoured local group is placed in an intermediate position between lower and higher income groups, an improvement in its relative and absolute conditions due to the FDI-induced technological change translates into a widening of income inequality.

Above all, the protection of technology in parent firms by MNCs results in restricting technology transfer to host countries, thus lowering the rate of change of local systems and locking them in a low technology trap. In this case local affiliates produce only low value-added goods, subduing the prospects for technological upgrading of the host country industrial base. In addition, MNCs may crowd out local producers and limit vertical integration, by directing their purchases only to foreign firms. The superior market power of the MNC can lead in some cases to eliminate competition by local firms, while, as already said, vertical integration with host country producers can be damaged by the MNCs' policy to rely on foreign suppliers for their inputs (Brooks et al. 2003). Occasional empirical evidence shows that foreign investment has been the basis of a number of success stories for developing countries (Conceiçao et al. 2001). But more often than not, these are exceptions and not the rule (Archibugi and Pietrobelli 2003). It should be added that, in general, new technology per se may have potential negative implications for developing countries. That is notably true for the use of the Internet, for which least developed countries do not have the prerequisites necessary to fully exploit its opportunities, such as an appropriate provision of human and physical capital, together with a favourable institutional setting. And indeed for this kind of country there exists an empirical evidence showing the limited impact of past information revolutions (Kenny 2003).

Furthermore it is still an open question if importing consumption models derived from tastes prevailing in developed countries is compatible with the necessity for LDCs to take care of the needs experienced by low- and middle-income country consumers and producers. By definition technology transfer implies absorption and imitation of old generations of innovating products, which were originally devised and produced in countries where large amounts of capital were available for satisfying representative demands by high-income consumers; with the caveat that the latter are expressing their preferences for complex and sophisticated varieties of goods, obtained as a rule by capital and R&D intensive technologies.

Under these circumstances, as highlighted by revamped versions of the traditional dependency theories (Ghosh 2001), adopting distorted consumption models and a specialization based on a permanent catching-up with such kind of technologies could make recipient countries worse off. Western-style consumption patterns can reduce the long-term investment rate of countries that badly need to improve it, producing moreover as by-effects possible damages to health and food safety of the local population (French 1998). As to the unending attempt to close the gap with advanced countries, while imitating at the same time their outdated technology, it is clear that the exercise is too similar to the labour of Sisyphus.

Unbalanced technology transfer

Literature has emphasized the fact that FDI means geographical diffusion of technology, but does not mean always a transfer of it outside the MNC's control. Indeed, by setting up a foreign affiliate, MNCs internalize the use of core technology (Blomström and Kokko 2003), therefore reducing the risk of leaking their advantage deriving from Dunning's (1988, 1995) proprietary advanced technologies and exploiting at best their second group of advantages derived from synergies such as horizontal and vertical integration, along with economies of scale. Nevertheless, despite all possible efforts, even employing FDI as the best alternative means of transmission, technology can leak out to local firms. That is why incomplete technology transfer can arise.

In a Schumpeterian framework in which they are bound incessantly to produce innovations, the fear to dissipate their competitive advantages induces MNCs to avoid transmitting technical knowledge lying at the technological frontier, endowing thus foreign affiliates in LDCs only with former generations of technical knowledge, that is, second best or even outdated technologies. Indeed, MNCs can be prevented from investing or may be pushed to bring low quality technologies to affiliates in developing countries by the fear of dissipation of the value of knowledge embodied in their high-level investments (Blomström and Sjöholm 1999). When, for instance, MNCs decide to set up joint ventures with local partners, which have a comparative advantage in terms of better knowledge of domestic market characteristics, the latter can have access to MNCs' core technologies that are therefore in danger of dissipation (Ikiara 2003). The value of their superior technical knowledge can be dissipated, in particular, when local partners have an insufficient incentive to protect the MNC reputation (Horstmann and Markusen 1987) or when competition increases as a consequence of the technology transfer (Saggi 1999).

As to the main determinants of technology transfer restriction by MNCs, the basic explanation lies clearly in the finding that foreign investors tend to shield their most advanced innovations from imitation process, that risks putting in jeopardy their temporary monopolistic position, reducing their prospective profits. Put another way, incomplete transfer of technologies in the form of transfer of older or outdated knowledge is essentially due to the danger for MNCs of losing their knowledge capital investment. That is possibly why higher levels of country risk have been found linked to more limited technology transfer (Fosfuri 2002); or in a number of instances a MNC refuses to accept licence arrangements, fearing the loss of control over its core technology (Black 2003). In the first case empirical evidence exists showing that country risk reduces technology transfer in all its shapes (wholly-owned operations, joint ventures and licensing), whereas in the second one the case study of the strategy followed by the Behr group, a large German multinational in the automotive sector, revealed that the MNC's best choice in operating in South Africa was to purchase an existing firm, thus avoiding having to resort to licence agreements, for fear of losing control of its core technology.

The conservative policy followed by MNCs with the aim of protecting their most valuable intangible assets in the form of advanced technologies implies two strictly interwoven consequences. On the one hand, technical knowledge is channelled preferably by FDI and, on the other, technology transferred is not the most updated at their disposal. As highlighted by the knowledge capital model by Markusen and Maskus (1999), MNCs display a preference for internalizing technology through FDI, despite other possible alternative channels, owing to the public good nature of knowledge. On the other hand, because of their inescapable destiny to be imitated sooner or later by competitors, technologies transferred cannot belong to the most advanced ones, since in such a case the perceived danger by the MNCs of a prompt imitation would be too high.

In sum, MNCs choose to transfer by FDI only second-best technical knowledge because they have an incentive to minimize technology leakages to possible competitors, trying to extend the time span in which they enjoy the temporary monopolistic advantage stemming from their last generations of proprietary knowledge (Javorcik 2004a).

In any case, the transfer of knowledge is perceived as a potential cost, which reduces the competitive advantage of the transferring company by an amount that is linked to the value of knowledge (Allen 1984). In fact, if knowledge is transmitted to a possible competitor, the expected rents derived from a particular piece of information will be negatively affected.

Among the means employed to preserve the proprietary technology value, one can quote setting up formal protection of intellectual properties through patent and international agreements such as the TRIPS system, trade secrets, paying higher salaries in order to hinder labour turnover, or investing in less advanced countries where firms have lower imitation skills (Javorcik 2004a). Indeed, the fact that as a rule MNCs pay higher wages than host country firms can be interpreted as a means of retaining workers who could spread high-level technologies outside their control if they had an incentive to enter the staff of competitors (Girma et al. 2001). In such a case their specific human capital acquired through on-the-job training in MNCs could be used in favour of the latter, helping to destroy the MNCs' competitive edge. In addition MNCs have been shown to be influenced by the level of protection of intellectual property rights (Javorcik 2004b).

As a matter of fact, international protection of intellectual property rights ensured by TRIPS arrangement, despite Article 66.2 on the encouragement of technology transfer to least developed countries, has played a negative role in hampering a standing improvement of developing economies (Unctad 2004). On the one hand, the impact of Article 66.2 has been assessed as having been very limited (Maskus 2000), while on the other TRIPS agreement as such was devised as a tool to strengthen the control by proprietors on protected technical knowledge and not as a means of fostering technology transfer to LDCs.

Extreme forms of knowledge monopoly are represented by embargoes through political means, as in the case of traditional US bans on strategic equipment export (Nicholson and Sahay 2003), or the US's policy of discouraging technology transfer in the aftermath of September 11 (Levin and Williams 2003), or by creation of terminator technologies that do not allow the use of old seed for new plantations, as in the case of some genetically modified crops (Saruchera and Matsungo 2003).

Temporary monopolies allowing MNCs to extract extra rents by restricting technology transfer and protecting them from the effects of the public good nature of technological innovation pertain to the class of market failures. Thus, other kinds of market failures, such as information asymmetries (Sattin 2003), or the inability of private markets to produce socially optimal R&D, result similarly in under-provision of high-level technologies in the relationship between foreign MNCs and host countries (Tripp 2003). In all these cases higher transaction costs and possible opportunistic behaviours lead to restrictions by MNCs in transferring technological knowledge.

Another explanation of restricted transfer has to do with limited absorption capacity by the host countries, which in turn is a positive function of technological gaps, since too large a technological distance hampers LDCs in acquiring useful information from advanced countries (Damijan et al. 2003). Only host countries having high learning capabilities necessary to identify and decode advanced technologies can assimilate and exploit knowledge coming from abroad. In other words, recipient countries have to be endowed with a suitable conceptualization framework of intra-firm technological learning, as highlighted by the technological capability approach (Caniëls and Romijn 2002) and the evolutionary theories of technological change (Dosi 1988).

On this point one should note the caveat that in order to absorb foreign high-level technology host countries have to be endowed with a satisfactory provision of human capital and have to engage in training local staff (Blomström and Kokko 2003). Thus, developing countries exhibiting large technological gaps or with a limited supply of human capital are not in a position to imitate high-level technologies and FDI directed to them channels only low-quality knowledge (Görg and Greenaway 2003). Learning efforts by host country firms can increase the rate of technology transfer, but the average age of technologies transferred in developing countries is higher than in the case of those directed to developed ones (Blomström and Wang 1989).

Also, tacitness of knowledge can be considered as a powerful barrier to technology transfer (Caniëls and Romijn 2002), whereas explicitness of knowledge improves technology transmission (Chen 2004). Indeed, while the former requires an additional effort by the foreign provider (for instance in the form of personal contacts) in order to be successfully transferred, the latter can be formalized and hence communicated in an easier way.

Other forms of obstacles reducing technology transfers are institutional in nature and range from national cultural and institutional differences (Depner and Bathelt 2003), to lobbying by corporations on states in the implementation of multilateral environmental agreements as in the case of 'ISO 14000 series', which discriminates against developing countries (Falkner 2003).

Conflicting interests

Unbalanced technology transfer reflects a strong conflict of interest between MNCs and host economies in LDCs, mainly concerning the choice of technological trajectories and the transmission of advanced vintages of technologies within the latter.

As noted above, MNCs have an absolute and vital interest in protecting their competitive advantage, hampering the transfer of their more advanced technologies placed along the knowledge frontier. In order to avoid the dissipation of their value and to maintain full control on proprietor technological competitive advantages, they limit the transfer of technical knowledge, both in the forms of codified and tacit knowledge, to local partners by means of FDI channelling only their low value-added or outdated technologies. At the same time they retain their R&D and innovative activities in their home countries (Archibugi and Pietrobelli 2003). As a result, LDCs risk being steadily locked in a low technology trap, simply imitating older technologies imported from MNC home countries and perpetuating a condition of technological dependence or backwardness.

From the opposite view, domestic firms and governments in host countries have an interest in building up an independent technological capability by upgrading local technology levels and trying through a number of means, ranging from reverse engineering to shared ownership, to absorb more sophisticated technologies from foreign investors. In addition, they need to invest in high-skill human capital in order to improve their absorptive capacity. Their main aim, in a development perspective both at firm and national economy levels, consists not simply of producing minor adaptations of MNC transferred technologies, leaving their core unaffected, but introducing inventive adaptations, requiring generally some kinds of local R&D efforts. In the first case they merely change the technique received, while in the second they make use of the core knowledge that underlies them, using it as an inventive germplasm (Evenson and Westphal 2002).

With the view to upgrade the technical knowledge transmitted by MNCs mainly through FDI and to adapt it in an inventive way, host countries try to extract with different means all possible information related to the MNC proprietary knowledge. In particular, local governments tend to limit the degree of foreign capital permitted in firms operating in their country in order to foster spillovers. All this gives rise to tensions and conflicts between the two parties, in forms that are peculiar to each country. And even when tensions are provisionally reconciled thanks to an initial bargain struck between MNCs and host governments, subsequently the stability of the agreement can be put in jeopardy by new developments. *Ex post*, real terms of interaction may diverge from what was initially agreed upon and sanctions against pact breaches are as a rule difficult to enforce. In may instances formal agreements are therefore broken in a subsequent phase, both by foreign firms and by governments, revamping disputes (Helleiner 1989).

Among the several sources of conflicts between partner firms one can quote crucial choices on input levels and profit shares, decisions on company names, composition of the board of directors, locations of headquartes and so on (Kasuga 2003). This state of affairs can be considered to be the rule when partner firms have established a joint venture, whose control is coveted by both of them. A formal contract between the local firm and the MNC before the start of operations can reduce but not eliminate conflicts. Indeed, contracts are in practice always incomplete and the controlling shareholder who has the residual rights of control, beyond the written and explicit terms of the contract (Grossman and Hart 1986), can find it difficult to impose its full command on the joint venture when unforeseen states of the world occur, provoking possible reactions by the local partner.

Besides this, conflicts affecting the transfer of knowledge can be fuelled by organizational differences such as structural, cultural and bureaucratic discrepancies (Chen 2004). An outstanding example of this is the resistance in East Asia to the emergence of a hegemonic complex formed by the global information infrastructure and the extended protection of intellectual property rights through the TRIPS agreement. Resistance took the shape of public initiatives at a regional level (*e.g.* by APEC and national governments), state strategic support for the Linux movement, along with everyday individual response of software piracy (Sum 2003). In particular, the Chinese government is trying to contrast the dominant position of Microsoft's standards by purchasing local Linux-based systems. It should be added that in LDCs piracy is not only a reaction, but an economic necessity too. One century after the period in which the US was the worst robber of other countries' intellectual property, people in LDCs resort to cheap software copies because they are poor and cannot afford the cost of the original product, often amounting to many months' wages. For them, such a behaviour represents simply a rational economic choice.

In any case, at a more general level, evidence exists suggesting that conflicts between domestic and international partners involving developing countries have a curvilinear effect on technology transfer performance (Chen 2004). In other words, low and high levels of conflict strongly reduce both the quantity and the quality of the technical knowledge transferred. Thus, conflicts ignited by unbalanced technology transfer translate to even worse transfer performance, with a loop effect. At the same time, political scientists argue that conflicts between countries may be generated by the political command of scarce factors of production, among which high-level technology is included (Rosecrance and Thompson 2003).

It should be added that in some cases the conflicts of interest between MNCs and LDCs considered as a whole stem from the sometimes thieving policy by the former to use local specific resources of the latter as an input for patent-protected products marketed world-wide. Here, in a sense the technology transfer path is reversed, since MNCs take advantage of highly valued tangible and intangible assets originally located in LDCs that are transferred without any hindrance to their R&D departments. The most emblematic case in point of this kind of unbalanced technology transfer is possibly the commercial exploitation by pharmaceutical MNCs of LDCs' biological resources and traditional knowledge, which according to the United Nations convention on biological diversity should not be subtracted from the control of indigenous communities.

Country case studies

The bulk of previous findings, if not all, have been confirmed by studies on single country case experiences. That is true in particular for China, East Asian countries such as Korea, Malaysia, and other countries including Iran and Morocco.

Concerning China, a number of empirical works highlight the fact that in many cases foreign affiliates are locked in low value-added productions, having scarce backward and forward linkages and experiencing restricted transfer of high technologies (Lemoine and Ünual-Kesenci 2004). For example, many instances of limited transfer of innovation skills were found in Dalian city. This was due above all to the reluctance of foreign partners to provide the operational documents incorporating high-knowledge skills and to inform the Chinese partner on the relevant technological developments, even when a contractual obligation to do so existed. As a consequence, misunderstandings and tensions between the partners broke out frequently, downgrading the management quality of local firms. But the area where the technology transfer was most worrying was that of software skill, the most advanced form of knowledge competence, and the only one capable of enhancing the contents of the technology base by means of innovations. Both the production and the organization skill inflows were quite limited, denouncing the deliberate will of foreign investors to hold back a possible loss of command over their competitive lead (Lan and Young 1996). Similarly, a limited technology transfer from hi-tech MNCs to the Chinese party has been observed in Shenzen city (Wang and Meng 2004). Moreover, it has been confirmed that spillover effects of FDI are larger for Chinese industries with a low technology gap than for industries recording a wider gap (Chuang and Hsu 2004).

Observation in another Far East area brought to the fore similar findings. A criticism of the flying geese model, related to technology transfer activated by Japanese MNCs by means of FDI to Pacific Asia (Hayter and Edgington 2004) showed, mainly in Malaysia, that in the most advanced stage of technology transfer in form of R&D, the motivations of the two parties were in direct conflict. Whereas the host country needed to upgrade its technological capabilities, the transfer of high-level skills and expertise posed a threat to the proprietor competitive advantage of Japanese MNCs. As a result high-level knowledge transfers tended to be strictly controlled by the foreign partner, or restricted or even bluntly prohibited.

Concerning further country cases, it has to be stressed that also Korea imported second-best technologies, owing to the reluctance of MNCs from industrialized countries to transfer more advanced technological knowledge (Narula 2004). Similarly, country case studies focusing on Morocco and Iran find that there were no salient transfers of modern technologies in the former (Blomström and Kokko 2003), and that sociocultural differences could inhibit the transferability of human resources practices in the latter (Namazie 2003).

Concluding remarks: A never-ending technology divide

This chapter has focused on different aspects of the incomplete or unbalanced technology transfer to LDCs, mainly through FDI activated by MNCs, in the absence of significant controls due to the ever-increasing liberalization of product and production factor markets within the framework of globalization. At the end of our analysis it is possible to state that the kind of technological knowledge that MNCs have an incentive to transmit to host country firms without putting in danger of dissipation their proprietary intangible assets gives rise to a standing feature of the relationship between the core and the periphery of the world economy, that can possibly be considered an unequal technology transfer.

For LDCs technology transfer in the framework of globalization involves indeed a number of adverse effects, ranging from negative terms of trade changes, to adoption of distorted specialization models based on a permanent catching-up process with technologies devised and produced by MNCs for the needs of developed countries. The clash of interests between MNCs and foreign investment host countries is inevitable and concerns above all the choice of technology trajectories alongside the transfer of high-level technologies within the latter. On the one hand, MNCs need to have full control of their proprietor technological competitive advantage, in many ways restricting technology transfers and maintaining LDCs in a low technology trap, simply imitating outdated technologies. On the other hand, domestic firms and governments in host countries have an interest in building up an independent technological capability, at the same time raising the quality of their human capital stock as a prerequisite for it. In addition, they need to upgrade local technology levels by absorbing more sophisticated technologies from foreign investors through a number of means, ranging from reverse engineering to shared ownership. Other sources of conflicts between MNCs and partner firms include choices on input levels and profit shares, decisions on company names, composition of the board of directors, locations of headquarter's, and so on.

The model of incomplete technology transfer channelled to LDCs by globalized FDI flows does not allow the bridging of the technology divide. Technological convergence cannot occur owing to the overwhelming role played by MNCs, which hamper the building up of an autonomous technological base in LDCs and hinder their process of learning by doing. Also, without independent technological choices and skills absorptive capability is low and so too is the effective technology transfer.

In a model where LDCs are condemned to imitate MNC technologies without being able to innovate them, the catching-up will never end, as the latter will always be at least one stage ahead on the technology frontier. The brilliant metaphor employed by Krugman (1979) is his well-known North–South model of innovation and imitation between countries at different levels of development, where the North, in the form of the Red Queen of Alice's tale, had to keep running in order to stay always in the same place, has in fact a reverse side, in that the South is obliged at the same time endlessly to follow the Queen, without a hope of catching her.

References

Allen, J. (1984), *Managing the Flow of Technology: Technology Transfer and the Dissemination of Technological Information within the R&D Organization*, Cambridge, MA: MIT Press.

Archibugi, D. and Pietrobelli C. (2003), 'The globalisation of technology and its implications for developing countries: Window of opportunity or further burden?', *Technological Forecasting and Social Change*, 70, 861–83.

Black, A. (2003), 'Case studies of foreign direct investment in South Africa', *DRC Working Papers*, No. 9, March.

Blomström, M. and A. Kokko (2003), 'Human capital and inward FDI', *Working Papers CEPR*, No. 167, January.

Blomström, M. and F. Sjöholm (1999), 'Technology transfer and spillovers: Does local participation with multinationals matter?', *European Economic Review*, 43, 915–23.

Blomström, M. and J. Wang (1989), 'Foreign investment and technology transfer: A simple model', *NBER Working Papers*, No. 2958, May.

Brooks, D., E. Fan and L. Sumulong (2003), 'Foreign direct investment in developing Asia: Trends, effects, and likely issues for the WTO negotiations', *ERD Working Papers*, No. 38, April.

Caniëls, M. and H. Romijn (2002), 'Firm-level knowledge accumulation and regional dynamics, *Eidenhoven Centre for Innovation Studies Working Papers*, No. 2, May.

Chen, C. (2004), 'The effects of knowledge attribute, alliance characteristics, and absorptive capacity on knowledge transfer performance', *R&D Management*, 34, 311–21.

Chuang, Y. and P. Hsu (2004), 'FDI, trade, and spillover efficiency: Evidence from China's manufacturing sector', *Applied Economics*, 36, 1103–15.

Conceiçao, P., D. Gibons, M. Heitor and D. Sirilli (eds) (2001), 'Technology policy and innovation', *Technological Forecasting and Social Change*, 66, 1–128.

Damijan, J., M. Knell, B. Majcen and M. Rojec (2003), 'Technology transfer through FDI in top-10 transition countries: How important are direct effects, horizontal and vertical spillovers?', *William Davidson Institute Working Papers*, No. 549, February.

Depner, H. and H. Bathelt (2003), 'Cluster growth and institutional barriers: The development of the automobile industry cluster in Shanghai, P.R. China', *Spaces*, Phillips–University of Marburg, Germany, No. 09.

Dosi, G. (1988), *The Nature of the Innovative Process*, in G. Dosi, C. Freeman, R. Nelson, G. Silverberg and L. Soete (eds), *Technical Change and Economic Theory*, London and New York: Pinter.

Dunning, J. (1988), 'The eclectic paradigm of international production: A restatement and some possible extensions', *Journal of International Business Studies*, 19, 1–31.

Dunning, J. (1995), 'Reappraising the eclectic paradigm in an age of alliance capitalism', *Journal of International Business Studies*, 26, 461–91.

Evenson, R. and L. Westphal (2002), *Technological Change and Technology Strategy*, in J. Behrman and T. Srinivasan (eds), *Handbook of Development Economics*, vol. 3, second impression, Amsterdam, New York: North Holland.

Falkner, R. (2003), 'Private environmental governance and international relations: Exploring the links', *Global Environmental Politics*, 3, 72–87.

Fan, E. (2002), 'Technological spillovers from foreign investment: A survey', *ERD Working Papers*, No. 33, December.

Fosfuri, A. (2002), 'Country risk and the international flows of technology: Evidence from the chemical industry', *Departamento de Economia de la Empresa Working Papers*, No. 25, Universidad Carlos III de Madrid, June.

French, H. (1998), 'Capital flows and environment', *Foreign Policy in Focus*, 3, 1–4.

Ghosh, B.N. (2001), *Dependency Theory Revisited*, London: Ashgate.

Girma, S., D. Greenaway and K. Wakelin (2001), 'Who benefits from foreign direct investment in the UK?', *Scottish Journal of Political Economy*, 48, 119–33.

Görg, H. and D. Greenaway (2003), 'Much ado about nothing? Do domestic firms really benefit from foreign investment?', *IZA Discussion Papers*, No. 944, November.

Grossman, S. and O. Hart (1986), 'The costs and benefits of ownership: A theory of vertical and lateral integration', *Journal of Political Economy*, 94, 691–719.

Hayter, R. and D. Edgington (2004), 'Flying geese in Asia: The impacts of Japanese MNCs as a source of industrial learning', *Tijdschrift voor Ekonomische en Sociale Geografie*, 95, 3–26.

Helleiner, G. (1989), *Transnational Corporations and Direct Foreign Investment*, in H. Chenery and T. Srinivasan (eds), *Handbook of Development Economics*, vol. 2, Amsterdam, New York: North Holland.

Horstmann, I. and J. Markusen (1987), 'Strategic Investments and the Development of Multinationals', *International Economic Review*, 28, 109–21.

Ikiara, M. (2003), 'FDI, technology transfer and poverty alleviation: Africa's hopes and dilemma', *ATPS Special Paper Series*, No. 16.

Javorcik, B. (2004a), 'Does Foreign Direct Investment increase the productivity of domestic firms? In search of spillovers through backward linkages', *American Economic Review*, 94, 605–27.

Javorcik, B. (2004b) 'The composition of Foreign Direct Investment and protection of intellectual property rights: Evidence from transition economies', *European Economic Review*, 48, 39–62.

Javorick, B. and M. Spatareanu (2003), 'To share or not to share: Does local participation matter for spillovers from Foreign Direct Investment?', *World Bank Policy Research WP*, No. 3118, August.

Kasuga, H. (2003), 'Capital market imperfections and forms of foreign operations', mimeo, Tohoku University, February.

Kenny, C. (2003), 'The Internet and economic growth in less-developed countries: A case of managing expectations', *Oxford Development Studies*, 31, 99–113 .

Kokko, A. (1994), 'Technology, market characteristics, and spillovers', *Journal of Development Economics*, 43, 279–93.

Krugman, P. (1979), 'A model of innovation, technology transfer and the world distribution of income', *Journal of Political Economy*, 87, 253–66.

Lan, P. and S. Young (1996), 'International technology transfer examined at technology component level: A case study in China', *Technovation*, 16, 277–86.

Lemoine, F. and D. Ünual-Kesenci (2004), 'Assembly trade and technology transfer: The case of China', *World Development*, 32, 829–50.

Levin, M. and R. Williams (2003), 'Forum on rethinking technology in the aftermath of September 11', *History and Technology*, 19, 29–83.

Lin, P. and K. Saggi (2004), 'Ownership structure and technological upgrading in international joint ventures', *Review of Development Economics*, 8, 279–94.

Mansfield, E. and A. Romero (1980), 'Technology transfer to overseas subsidiaries by US-based firms', *Quarterly Journal of Economics*, 95, 737–50.

Markusen, J. and K. Maskus (1999), 'Discriminating against alternative theories of multinational enterprises', *NBER Working Papers*, No. 7164, June.

Maskus, K. (2000), *Intellectual Property Rights in the Global Economy*, Washington DC: Institute for International Economics.

Mencinger, J. (2003), 'Does Foreign Direct Investment always enhance economic growth?', *Kyklos*, 56, 491–508.

Namazie, P. (2003), 'Factors affecting the transferability of HRM practices in joint ventures based in Iran', *Career Development International*, 8, 357–66.

Narula, R. (2004), 'Understanding absorptive capacities in an "Innovation Systems" context: Consequences for economics and employment growth', *MERIT-Infonomics Research Memorandum Series*, 2004–003.

Nicholson, B. and S. Sahay (2003), 'Building Iran's software industry: An assessment of plans and prospects', *Electronic Journal of Information Systems in Developing Countries*, 13, 1–19.

Ramacharandran, V. (1993), 'Technology transfer, firm ownership, and investment in human capital', *Review of Economic and Statistics*, 75, 664–70.

Rosecrance, R. and P. Thompson (2003), 'Trade, foreign investment, and security', *Annual Review of Political Science*, 6, 377–98.

Saggi, K. (1999), 'Foreign Direct Investment, licensing, and incentives for innovation', *Review of International Economics*, 7, 699–714.

Saltz, I. (1992), 'The negative correlation between FDI and economic growth in the Third World: Theory and evidence', *Rivista Internazionale di Scienze Economiche e Commerciali*, 39, 617–33.

Saruchera, M. and O. Matsungo (2003), 'Understanding local perspective: Participation of resource poor farmers in biotechnology: The case of Weda District of Zimbabwe', background paper, Brighton: Institute of Development Studies, University of Sussex.

Sattin, J. (2003), 'Institutional framework, contractual design and survival of technology licensing agreements', *Working Papers ATOM*, University of Paris 1, May.

Sum, N. (2003), 'Informational capitalism and US economic hegemony: Resistance and adaptations in East Asia', *Critical Asian Studies*, 35, 373–98.

Te Velde, D. (2002), 'Foreign Direct Investment and income inequality in Latin America', mimeo, London: Overseas Development Institute.

Tripp, R. (2003), 'Strengthening the enabling environment for agricultural technology development in Sub-Saharan Africa', *Working Papers ODI*, No. 212, March.

Unctad (2004), *International and Technical Cooperation and Transfer of Technology*, New York and Geneva: United Nations.

Wang, M. and X. Meng (2004), 'Global–local initiatives in FDI: The experience of Shenzhen, China', *Asia Pacific Viewpoint*, 45, 181–96.

Part IV

Trade Liberalization and Unequal Competition

12
WTO and the South: Past, Present and Future

*Raj Kumar Sen**

This chapter attempts to deliberate on the origin and working of the World Trade Organization (WTO) from the viewpoint of the developing South and the agenda for the future. It appears that after 10 years of WTO existence, the expectations of developing countries have been largely failed and the apprehensions expressed by many experts during its formation have become mostly true. To help refresh the memory of the current generation of readers, the first section briefly discusses the origin and formation of the WTO, while the next section depicts the present scenario with an assessment of its working in its first decade with special reference to its impact on the major developing countries such as India. The last section formulates a future action plan for such countries if they are to meet the challenge of an adverse situation created by the present global scenario.

The past

More than 60 years after the Bretton Woods Conference in 1944, many have perhaps forgotten that this conference recommended the establishment of three, not two, international organizations, namely, the International Monetary Fund (IMF), the World Bank (WB) and the International Trade Organization (ITO) (Sen 1994). The initial objectives of their establishment were to deal with the problems of the balance of payments (BOP), reconstruction and development, and international trade respectively. While the first two organizations came into existence in 1945, where India was a founder member, the third could not see a clear purpose because of the lack of unanimity among the countries. Consequently, as an interim organization, the General Agreement on Tariffs and Trade (GATT) was established in 1947 especially on the initiative of the USA and UK. India was also a founder member of GATT. Although after a few years there was a move to set up the ITO as recommended by the Havana Conference, it could not yet be set up as it was not ratified by the US Congress and hence the GATT continued for nearly five decades when it was substituted by the present WTO. All three bodies, viz., the IMF, WB and GATT were dominated by the US for financial reasons. In particular, the high-income countries (HICs) were the main participants in the GATT partly due to its nature and partly due to the policies of the low-income economies (LIEs) (Cohm 2005). The GATT's bias in favour of the HICs, led to its being called informally the 'rich men's club'.

The period of transformation of GATT into WTO can be divided into four periods: up to the early 1960s, up to the early 1970s, up to 1980 and up to 1995 when the WTO was formed. In the first phase the LIEs had only limited involvement in the GATT because of their limited number, their protectionist trade policies and GATT's neglect of their development problems. Influenced by the arguments of Raul Prebisch, the LIEs focused on inward-looking policies. The GATT also contained only one Article (25) dealing with the trade problems of the developing South, which gave the LIEs some facilities to protect their infant industries and to solve the BOP problems. The Southern countries wanted to obtain special and differentiated treatment, but their influence was too insignificant in this phase.

In the second period the South's bargaining power increased because of decolonization. The UN declared the 1960s as the Development Decade and as an alternative to the demand of the LIEs to set up the ITO, the United Nations Conference on Trade and Development (UNCTAD) came into existence in 1964. In this period the G-77 group of developing countries was formed to express their economic interests vis-à-vis the North which was led by the G-7 group of HICs. Initially several HICs including the Scandinavian countries were sympathetic to G-77, but the situation changed later as a consequence of extreme positions taken by some newly independent countries. Of course UNCTAD never posed any serious challenge to the GATT, but it could influence it in giving more attention to the Southern issues. Here again some of the new policies favouring the South were only symbolic in character, while others helped the newly industrialized economies (NIEs) excluding the poorer LIEs.

The third period was one of increased North–South confrontations, when the South demanded the formation of a New International Economic Order (NIEO) in the UN following OPEC's success in increasing oil prices in 1973–74. This was expressed in the form of a wide range of concessions from the North. Of course the South also participated in the 1973–79 GATT Tokyo Round, which approved the 'enabling clause' establishing a legal basis in trade relations for preferences in favour of the developing economies. However, neither the South nor the North were satisfied with these developments and pressed for further amendments of the GATT leading to the beginning of the Uruguay Round in the next period.

The last period marked the active participation of the South in the Uruguay Round which began in 1986 as the North agreed to include some issues in which the South was interested, though the South was dissatisfied with the unequal world trade scenario and the efforts of the North to include issues in which they had comparative advantages. Such issues included, among others, services, IPRs, investment, and so on. Besides, the South did not always function as a bloc and there were many North–South coalitions like the Cairns Group of agricultural exporters. In fact, until 1989, the core group of G-77 countries led by India and Brazil were united but then India became isolated as she agreed to some US proposals unilaterally. Further, the position of the South was weakened as it agreed to treat the Uruguay Round as a single undertaking (Dunkel Draft) though it continued to receive the special and discriminators (S&D) treatment during the Uruguay Round. This policy shift of the South was due to various economic and political factors, such as the failure of inward-looking import substituting industrialization policies and the success of export-led strategies of the East Asian countries and also the emergence of the unipolar economic world following the disintegration of the USSR. In reality it has been argued that the South was compelled to change their policies because of the shift in the lending policies of the IMF and World Bank which introduced conditionality of economic reforms in the form of liberalization, privatization and globalization (LPG) strategies, where the globalization was not real in the true sense as it did not allow free movement of labour, where the South enjoyed comparative advantages. Ultimately the Uruguay Round gave birth to the WTO which came into existence on 1 January 1995 though both the US and India had strong reservations about its present form as they considered the provisions as an infringement on their sovereignty.

Expert opinions differ about the impact of the Uruguay Round on the developing countries. Many felt that in the Uruguay Round the developing countries had to surrender their interests to a great extent. For India in particular there were strong possibilities that her desired pattern of development would be changed because of the various conditionalities imposed by the WTO. Thus the provisions regarding agriculture and intellectual property rights (IPR) and the stringent clause of cross-retaliation were considered as traps led by the HICs and their MNCs that would help neo-colonization to enter through the back-door. On the other hand, others thought that the WTO would greatly help countries like India by enlarging the world trade substantially and boosting agricultural exports leading to increased prosperity and poverty alleviation. According to them, the concessions made by the South in the areas of services trade, investment and IPRs are only short-term ones and in the long run the South will gain through liberalization. This is however denied by still others who think that the South has given up more than they have received from the Uruguay Round as it will not be able to compete effectively in the areas in which they had to make concessions and there will be a transfer of income from the poor countries to the rich.

After all, it was expected that the impact of the WTO would be quite different from its predecessors as it included new industries such as services, investment, and so on, which are only distantly related to trade. There are also attempts to include the issues of labour and environment. With these provisions and aided by already powerful bodies like the IMF and the World Bank, which are dominated by countries like the US, the principal providers of finance, it is quite likely that the WTO, currently the most powerful supranational body, will control the developing world in all economic and financial matters. During the formative stage, India prepared a detailed report on the Dunkel Draft highlighting her points of disapproval, but as it could not be placed before the deadline of 15 December 1993, nothing effective could be done afterwards. In fact, during the negotiations at the formative stage, India had to endure much because of her political instability (Sen 1996).

The present

After 10 years of WTO existence, it appears unfortunately that it has played a more or less negative role when considered from the point of view of the developing South, although it has clearly stated that it 'recognises the need for positive efforts designed to ensure that developing countries, especially the least developed ones, secure a better share of growth in international trade'. Before we embark upon an analysis of this negative role of the WTO, it may be pointed out that currently our expectations are suffering from an oversimplistic understanding of economic theories based on now unrealistic assumptions. Thus, all the conclusions are drawn from the classical and neo-classical theories of international trade, which are dependent on an idealized framework of perfect competition, free trade in goods and services, a distortionless market, and a transparent, equitable and fair information system (Panchmukhi 1999). The factor and product markets and the production process have all become highly complicated in modern times and now trade flows cannot be expected to be determined by the simple patterns of natural comparative advantage nor are the resources optimally allocated. While the WTO seeks such an idealistic framework according to its objectives, the current global scenario as well as various WTO provisions works completely against the achievement of such targets. Thus while the various rounds of trade negotiations always aimed at the gradual elimination of tariffs as barriers to trade in order to liberalize the world trade, there has been a continuous expansion of non-tariff measures and imposition of various trade restrictive rules. Attempts to introduce various new considerations (such as human rights, environmental and labour standards, social clause, etc.) have surely distorted the free play of natural forces of comparative advantage. Besides, the market imperfections are accentuated further because of the transnationalization of production and the different types of acquisitions and mergers. International prices are determined mostly as part of the global strategy of the MNCs and consequently are not free from market distortions. This is also due to the current asymmetry of information order. It is paradoxical that while there has been explosive expansion of information technologies, it is not uniformly spread over the developing world in particular. This feature has also resulted in changes in the labour market through generating excessive demand for a specially skilled type of labour only, making a large section of the work-force virtually unemployable.

Analysing the impact of the WTO on world trade, it is noted that the original expectation of an annual growth of 20 per cent due to liberalization of trade fell short of the realization of this target (5.5 per cent only during 1990–2002), especially in exports of developing countries. The World Commission on the Social Dimension of Globalization (2004) has observed that 'the trade expansion did not occur uniformly across all countries, with the industrialized countries and a group of 12 developing countries accounting for the lion's share. In contrast, the majority of the developing countries did not experience significant trade expansion. Indeed, most of the least developed countries, a group that includes most of the countries in sub-Saharan Africa, experienced a proportional decline in their share of world markets – despite the fact that these countries had implemented trade liberalization measures'. As far as the case for India is concerned, her insignificant share in world exports (0.52% in 1990) increased only marginally (0.76% in 2002). At the same time it may also be pointed out that India's growth of imports has been far greater than the increase in her exports leading to a continuous negative trade balance that hovered around 3 to 4 per cent of her GDP during 1990–91 to 2002–03 (Datt 2005). This also shows that developing countries like India could not obtain the expected advantages of market access for their products in the markets of the HICs owing to the asymmetry in implementation of the WTO provisions. Here also the HICs appear to be rather sluggish in honouring their commitments. Moreover, these countries have maintained high peak tariff rates and also high specific duties for many products the LIEs may export.

Another change in recent decades in the established linkages between the expansion of trade, economic growth, transfer of technology and employment generation, is seriously challenging the well-known theory that considers international trade an engine of growth. This has taken place since the first oil-shock of 1973, the year of the beginning of the collapse of the Bretton Woods system leading to a highly volatile exchange rate regime. As the annual average growth rate of the HICs started to decline, compared with the pre-1973 period, their share in the export of the LIEs is also shrinking and thus the declining size of the market may lead to the so-called 'fallacy of composition' resulting in a new trading system without the engine of growth distorting the crucial linkage mentioned above.

It has been further observed that the world economy has also experienced instabilities in the exchange rate and short-term capital flows in particular, while the international bodies are preaching stabilization at the national level through structural adjustment programmes. This instability has been experienced both by the HICs and the LIEs, especially in the period since 1973 compared with the period 1960–73. It is recognized that this instability has been the cause of severe crisis in the Latin American and Southeast Asian countries. Unfortunately, nothing effective was done by the world bodies to bring about stability and order. And this trend is continuing even following the formation of the WTO, and is nothing but a new strategy to accelerate globalization as defined by the IMF and World Bank.

This globalization process implemented through the WTO in the last decade has resulted in an altogether different type of growth process for developing countries which may be called simultaneously ruthless (indifferent or harsh to the weak and poor), rootless (not concerned about tradition, culture and heritage), jobless and hence futureless.

Owing to very fast technological growth at a rate developing countries are unable to assimilate, and the ever-growing labour-replacing character of such technologies, it has been noticed that the growth rates of employment were lower than the growth rate of the labour force in both developed and developing countries. Thus there has been a drift away from the long-coveted goal of achieving full employment. In the HICs it is argued that one of the main reasons of this type of jobless growth is the increase of imported goods from the LIEs produced with the help of cheap labour. This has also increased the new protectionist tendencies of the former group of countries leading to increasing adoption of many non-tariff barriers (NTB) and new issues in trade negotiations.

All these features are clearly observed if we look at the experiences of India. There the average annual growth rate of employment declined from 2.04 per cent during 1983–94 to only 0.98 per cent during 1994–2000 according to the 2001 Report of the Taskforce on Employment Opportunities appointed by the Planning Commission. The sectoral figures show negative rates of employment growth in agriculture, mining and quarrying, and electricity, gas and water supplies. Of these the decline in agriculture is most serious, as even now nearly 65 per cent of workers are dependent on this sector. The paradoxical situation of rising GDP (5.8% during 1990–91 to 1999–2000 compared with 5.63 per cent during 1980–81 to 1990–91) with falling employment growth, resulted in the increase of India's unemployment rate (6.03 per cent in 1993–94 to 7.32 per cent in 1999–2000). With the gradual withdrawal of the public sector and slow growth of the private sector, the share of the organized sector in employment declined from 7.93 per cent (1993) to 7.08 per cent (1999–2000). The natural consequence of this swelling of the unorganized sector has been a decline in workers' conditions in the last decade. In fact, the whole scenario of the labour market has undergone a thorough structural change in this period with the acceleration of the process of informalization. This becomes clear when we note from the National Sample Survey (NSS) data that the proportion of the casual workers increased from 28.7 per cent (1983) to 33.2 per cent (1999–2000). While we discuss the employment situation, it is not merely the number in employment, but the nature and quality of the work that is even more important. In fact it is revealed that during 1991–98, while the total employment increased by 2 per cent approximately, most of the increase was accounted for by temporary, casual, contract and other flexible and irregular categories of workers. Thus there has been feminization of labour in low-wage jobs leading to exploitation of female workers. Distortions in allocation of labour are taking place to the extreme disadvantage of the workers because of insecurity and scarcity of jobs. The social impact of this structural change is perhaps more serious than the economic effects and must not be ignored for the sake of GDP growth only. We are already observing with grave concern that in the current decade, exclusion of the poor and marginalized groups is taking place with growing inequality of income and assets not only between various income groups, but also between different countries and different regions of the same country. The present decade has been one of declining earnings of the unskilled workers, neglect of environmental norms and denial of basic rights in the work-place (e.g., violation of the norm of a daily eight hours of work) leading to more insecurity for labourers and a growing militancy of employers where there is no proper social security against unemployment.

Let us now turn to a few more direct issues about the impact of the WTO on the South in the last 10 years, which will show that the WTO, formed as the organization of the multilateral trading system, has in reality become the main instrument of the HICs for enforcing a global economic governance in consonance with the unipolar world economic order (Khor 2001). To comply with the provisions of the WTO, the developing countries had to change their national laws and policies in a wide range of areas, occasionally leading to further drainage of their economic resources. Such changes are also binding on the future governments of such countries. In the Uruguay Round, as these countries had to make major concessions in favour of the HICs (without obtaining in exchange satisfactory conditions of market access) because of the massive gap in economic and political strength existing between these two groups of countries, it is likely that the industrialized countries, constituting only 20 per cent of the WTO membership, will appropriate 70 per cent of the additional income generated out of this trading arrangement leading in a way to unbalanced and inequitable outcomes.

It should be also borne in mind that WTO provisions are actually a combination of measures leading to both liberalization and protectionism mainly formulated to the benefit of the North. Thus free movement of labour, which is advantageous to the South, was not allowed and in the areas of technology and IPRs, protectionism was practised for the benefit of the North. On the other hand, the North pressed for the opening up of new markets such as that in services or the liberalization of investments, and negotiated for trade-related investment measures (TRIMs) so that the South may not restrict the entry of the MNCs yet at the same time the transfer of technology was restricted for the South through the introduction of trade-related IPRs (TRIPs). In other words, the so-called ideal of free trade was actually meant for the free operation of the MNCs, most of which are operated from the industrialized countries. Such big companies are observed to be the principal gainers in the present WTO where initial opposition from developing countries could not prevent the inclusion of new issues putting the developing countries in a disadvantageous position.

Of course this does not mean that the developing countries are always the losers under the present situation. In fact, those countries with capacity to export manufacturing goods, textiles and agricultural products can be gainers from the lowering of industrial tariffs and agricultural subsidies by the North and by the phasing out of the Multi Fibre Agreement (MFA). But it was pointed out at the UNCTAD meeting in 1996 that the opportunities of the LIEs in the WTO are indirect and may materialize in the long run. But the challenges faced by them are more immediate in nature. In reality these countries are not well-placed to gain from the opportunities because of erosion of preferences, limited number of exportable items, higher prices for import of food, pharmaceuticals and capital goods, and finally for increased administrative cost of compliance with the WTO obligations. But this is the story of the developing countries with export capacity. For others, the situation is bleak with possibilities of certain loss. This is true especially for food importers (about a hundred countries) where food security may be in danger as a result of the rise in food prices following agricultural liberalization.

The LIEs' prospect of indigenous technological development is also in danger due to the IPR laws introduced under TRIPs agreements. As everything is now under IPR, it is likely that the MNCs will be able to obtain patents on many items in LIEs that are as yet outside the scope of national patent laws. The scope for patenting the life-forms is considered as detrimental to the global environment through biodiversity loss and threats to the eco-systems. Under the TRIMs, the national policies relating to foreign investments are now within the ambit of the WTO system and there is pressure from the North to establish a multi-lateral investment guarantee agreement (MIGA) in it. There are also attempts to link trade with labour and environmental standards and in future issues such as human rights and others may also be linked to trade measures. The proliferation of trade-related issues is really designed to further open up the LIEs and to reduce their competitiveness in the global trading system.

We should not forget also about the unfair distribution of FDI (which is another aspect of the multi-dimensional impact of the WTO's globalization process) that took place in the last decade. From the World Investment Report (2004) it is observed that in 2003 65.5 per cent of total FDI inflows went to the HICs and only 30.7 per cent went to developing countries. The share of India was only 0.8 per cent. Only 12 developing countries (India is not included in this group) accounted for 74.7 per cent of the total FDI in the 1990s. FDI inflows are not always growth promoting as claimed by their advocates and they often destroy the comparative advantage of host countries.

India is not only a founder member of the GATT and WTO, but is also scrupulously following WTO rules. It has been observed that due to the reduction of import duties Indian industry had to face increasing competition from foreign goods. Imports of finished products have become an important cause of recession in the industrial sector. In particular, the import of second-hand cars, near dumping of cheap Chinese goods and similar other activities have caused serious repercussions in the industrial scene in India.

Of course, since the very beginning, the WTO has been subjected to widespread criticisms and protests (Stiglitz 2002). Mention may be made of the enormous turn-out of protestors during the third WTO ministerial meeting in Seattle in 1999, the demonstration in Costa Rica in 2000, protests at the G-8 meeting at Genoa in 2001, and the demonstration during the fourth WTO ministerial meeting in Cancun in 2003, in addition to the large number of protest rallies throughout the world. In Seattle various groups of protestors wanted fairer trade with less exploitation and argued against the current pattern of corporate-led free trade. The demonstration in Costa Rica was against the privatization proposals of the IMF. Here one protestor died as a result of police firing. In Genoa also, owing to police atrocities, one protestor named Carlo Giuliani was killed and he is considered the first martyr in the fight against globalization. The protestors at Cancun opposed the imperialistic design of the US and EU to capture the world markets. One South Korean peasant leader, Li Kiyung-He, stabbed himself to death before the police barricade with a poster around his neck bearing the words 'WTO killing the farmers'. It may be mentioned that the WTO website does not mention any death during the demonstrations. An alternative to the World Economic Forum called World Social Forum arranged organized meetings against the present world economic order. Of course it should be mentioned that at Cancun the developing countries united to place their demands before the leadership of countries such as India, China and Brazil, known as the G-20 group, which could frustrate the North's design to implement the controversial Singapore issues.

Finally it should be highlighted that the system of one vote for one country in the WTO sounds highly democratic in comparison with other world bodies with quota-based voting system, but in reality this is a myth as no decision is taken by majority vote. All decisions are taken by the so-called consensus, which ultimately means the agreement of others to the decisions adopted by the major economic powers. This situation is enhanced by the WTO working in close cooperation with the World Bank and IMF through the cross-retaliation clause. In the Singapore ministerial meeting most developing countries were never invited to the crucial discussions on debatable issues, which took place in informal groups where the HICs comprised the majority. This lack of transparency in the working of the WTO has made, in fact, its agreements illegitimate and no institution lacking legitimacy can command or expect obedience or acceptance in civil society. This is one of the reasons why the LIEs are gradually becoming frustrated at the outcome and working of the WTO.

The future

In the light of the above discussion about the experience of the working of the WTO in the last decade, the South in general and India in partic-ular must seriously decide about the future course of action to protect their interests in the WTO, which was nicknamed by P.R. Brahmananda as the 'World Terrorist Organisation' when viewed from the standpoint of the South. Briefly speaking, the joint demands of the South (Sen 2005) in the present perspective should be:

(a) To form effective viable economic blocks as countries individually are too weak to negotiate with the rich North. There are already suggestions to form an Asian Economic Union on the lines of the EU (Agarwala 2003).
(b) To demand a decadal review of WTO rules, which are biased against South (e.g., articles 6, 20 and 24 in particular) and to introduce trans-parency in its operations by following the majority rule instead of Greenroom closed-door meetings of the selected powerful countries.
(c) To prevent entry of new issues in the WTO at least until the imple-mentation of the existing agenda. It may be pointed out that there is the ILO to look after labour issues and the WTO already contains a number of environmental norms (Sen 2003). It is also not possible to prescribe uniform environmental norms for different regions. Besides, the WTO needs to confine itself to purely trade-related matters only in the strict sense.

(d) To strengthen their own patenting system to protect their own resources from patenting by the MNCs and to demand for patenting on the basis of geographical indicators throughout the world. This is vital for mega bio-diversity countries like India. Under present patent rules the accused country has to prove its innocence going against the age-old system of jurisprudence where the onus of proving wrong lies with the accuser. This should be removed (Sen 2006).

(e) To develop their indigenous technologies to meet the challenges of the MNCs as far as possible, though it is quite difficult in the present situation when the LIEs are unable to spend adequately on R&D. However, this is particularly important as at present knowledge and information play a crucial role as determinants of comparative advantage.

(f) To place demand on the HICs to reduce their peak tariffs and to eliminate the NTBs to provide effective market access for their exportable products according to the commitment under the WTO rules.

(g) To develop knowledge and information industries as these are now becoming the prime movers of the patterns of comparative advantage and production. India is quite well placed in this matter and she should take advantage of her position in the near future.

(h) To demand the abolition of the US Trade Act and Buy America Act which violate the basic principles of the WTO and to decentralize the WTO Dispute Settlement Body in LIEs also considering its prohibitive costs.

(i) To demand the completion of the globalization process by allowing free mobility of labour for the sake of an equitable world order. This is also important as human resources account for 64 per cent of the world resources, according to a World Bank study.

After 10 years of experiencing WTO activities, the developing countries should no longer expect to gain substantially from global trade in the near future if the present structure and type of its functioning remain unchanged in the coming decades. In the present international economic and political situation of unipolar world, it is also not advisable that they should withdraw from the WTO as their interest is not properly protected. What is necessary is to derive appropriate country-specific strategies to meet the challenges and to make the best of a bad bargain. As a country of continental dimension India's appropriate strategies should be region-specific depending on individual regional characteristics. Redefining the proper role of the state in this market-dominated world is also necessary to control the market in the interests of society and especially to protect weaker sections of the population for whom the market has failed. Since the WTO is nothing but an adjunct to the current phase of truncated globalization, all steps necessary to protect people and the economy from undesirable consequences of the process need to be adopted judiciously as far as possible. In particular, remedial measures are urgently needed to correct the income inequalities and inter-regional and international disparities, which have grown very rapidly in recent years to beyond tolerable limits. We should remember that Gandhi's famous saying is still very much relevant even today, that is, one should open the windows of the room to allow outside wind to blow in but one must keep the feet firmly on the ground so that they are not uprooted by it. But nothing fruitful is possible in this WTO regime unless the South is united and also keeps united in the face of pressures and temptations from the North. Of course it is very difficult to achieve, but perhaps here only lies the future for the South until the WTO itself is changed, modified and becomes truly friendly to all parts of the world, or alternatively, is dissolved altogether.

Note

* I am grateful to Anathbandhu Mukherjee and Fr. Felix Raj for their help in the preparation of this chapter.

References

Agarwala, R. (2003), 'Towards a multipolar world of international finance', *Indian Economic Journal*, 51(2).

Cohm, Theodore H. (2005), *Global Political Economy: Theory and Practice*, New York: Pearson Longman.

Datt, Ruddar (2004), 'Globalisation, the WTO and its impact on India: A developing country perspective', Clem Tisdell and Raj Kumar Sen (eds), *Economic Globalisation*, Cheltenham: Edward Elgar.

Datt, Ruddar (2005), 'From unfair to fair globalisation'. in L.L. Achha, (ed.) *New Dimensions in India's Economic Growth and Social Change*, New Delhi: Centre for Indian Economy and Business Studies.

Dubey, M. (1996), *An Unequal Treaty. World Trading Order after GATT*, New Delhi: New Age International Ltd.

Jomo, K.S. (2001), 'Implications of the GATT Uruguay Round of development: The Malaysian Case', in K.S. Jomo and S. Nagaraj (eds), *Globalisation Versus Development*, London and New York: Palgrave Macmillan.

Khor, Martin (2001), 'The World Trade Organization and the South: Implications of the emerging global economic governance for development', in K.S. Jomo and S. Nagaraj (eds), *Globalisation Versus Development*, London and New York: Palgrave Macmillan.

Panchamukhi, V.R. (1999), 'Trade, technology and employment – A profile of systemic dilemmas and paradoxes', *Indian Journal of Labour Economics*, Conference number.

Ray, Kalyan (2005), *Globalisation or Colonisation*, New Delhi: Deep and Deep Publications.

Sen, Raj Kumar (1996), 'The inherent contradictions of NEP in India', in B. Ghosh (ed.) *Socio-Economic Transformation in India*, Vol 2, New Delhi: Kaniska Publishers.

Sen, Raj Kumar (2003), 'WTO, environment and developing countries', in M. Jahagirdar and S. Desmukh (eds), *Post Economic Reforms Scenario of Indian Economy*, Amravati, Maharashtra: Centre for Economic and Social Studies.

Sen, Raj Kumar (2005), 'The Indian economy and current globalisation', in Clem Tisdell (ed.) *Globalisation and World Economic Policies*, Vol 2, New Delhi: Serials Publications.

Sen, Raj Kumar (2006), 'WTO after ten years and large developing countries like India', in Raj Kumar Sen and John Felix Raj (eds), *Ten Years of WTO and Towards an Asian Union*, New Delhi: Deep and Deep Publications (forthcoming).

Sen, S.R. (1944), 'From GATT to WTO', *Economic and Political Weekly*, 22 October.

Stiglitz, Joseph E. (2002), *Globalisation and its Discontents*, New York: W.W. Norton.

Tisdell, Clem (2000), 'Globalisation, WTO and Sustainable Development', Working Paper No. 46. University of Queensland, Australia.

Tisdell, Clem (2000), Globalisation and the WTO: Attitudes expressed by pressure groups and by less developed countries', Working Paper No. 40. University of Queensland, Australia.

13
Globalization, Trade Liberalization and Conflict: A Southern Perspective

Amitava Krishna Dutt

The phenomenon of economic globalization – reflecting increased trade, capital flows and technology transfers between countries – has received widespread attention in recent years. While many see it as a panacea for almost all the world's ills, some see it as a font of problems, one of which is the exacerbation of the conflict between rich and poor countries, or the North and the South.

The purpose of this chapter is to examine the implications of economic globalization for North–South conflict, focusing on the South, and concentrating on one major aspect of the process, trade liberalization and the expansion of international trade. Especially since the late 1980s and 1990s, quantitative restrictions on trade have been reduced around the globe and rates of import duties have been reduced even in previously highly-protectionist countries, and this has led to a significant increase in world trade in relation to GDP.[1]

To start with some definitional issues, the term 'trade liberalization' has different meanings in the literature (see Greenaway et al. 1997). It sometimes refers to policy changes that reduce the gap between the *relative* prices of exports and imports domestically and internationally, which amounts to reducing the anti-export bias without necessarily reducing tariffs and subsidies. Alternatively, it refers to replacing the arguably more distortionary methods of protection, such as import quotas, by tariffs. A third meaning, the one on which we will concentrate, is the reduction of import tariffs and export subsidies, thereby reducing the gap between domestic and international prices of goods and services.

We interpret 'conflict' to refer both to conflicting interests and to actual conflict – expressed, for instance, at the World Trade Organization (WTO) – between the North and the South. A long tradition, exemplified in the writings of the dependency school, sees the inter-action between the North and the South as widening the gap – and hence exacerbating conflict – between them, and recent empirical work finds that gap continues to grow in the era of globalization. However, the strong performance of some Southern countries, especially China, has led some to argue that globalization is actually good for the South. It is claimed, in fact, that globalization hurts rich countries as their indus-tries lose to 'unfair' competition from poor countries with cheap and under-age labor, and Northern policies are adjusted to result in a 'race to the bottom'. There have been calls for protectionism in the North, and for putting pressure on the South through the WTO and elsewhere to 'level the playing field' by the forcible adoption of labor and envir-onmental standards in the South. In this chapter, however, we focus on the South.

The rest of this chapter proceeds as follows. The following section briefly reviews some theory regarding trade liberalization. The next one discusses some of the empirical evidence concerning the South and international inequality. The fourth section turns to some historical issues and relates them to the current situation with the fifth section discussing the role of international institutions and the last section ends with some concluding comments. Space limitations force us to confine our discussion to a few key issues.

Theory

Despite the emergence of other approaches to international trade theory, the standard method for examining the implications of trade liberaliz-ation remains the Heckscher–Ohlin–Samuelson (HOS) approach. In its simplest form this assumes 'perfect' markets with the full employment of all resources, constant returns to scale, no 'distortions' in production and consumption, and given international terms of trade. It implies that trade liberalization – for instance, a reduction of import taxes – results in an unequivocal gain for the liberalizing economy due to a shift of resources to sectors in which it enjoys a comparative advantage, and to a reduction in the distortion in consumption created by the import tax, capturing the ideas that trade liberalization leads to a more efficient allocation of resources, promotes exports, and results in lower prices for consumers.

Some modifications of this approach strengthen these positive effects. For instance, with domestic monopolies, trade liberalization can reduce the inefficiency due to this distortion. It can also lead to greater productive – as distinct from allocative – efficiency by exerting competitive pressures that reduce X-inefficiency and lead to the adoption of better technology, and by facilitating scale economies. Moreover, it can reduce rent-seeking and other directly unproductive activities that are alleged to result from import restrictions, reallocating resources to productive activities.

Modifications of the simple framework, however, can overturn these results. It is convenient to classify these modifications in terms of how they depart from the HOS approach. For each departure we discuss how it can lead to losses from trade liberalization, especially for Southern economies, and the debates about their relevance.

First, even maintaining all the HOS assumptions, trade liberalization can hurt some groups. The Stolper–Samuelson theorem states that trade liberalization will increase (reduce) the return to relatively abundant (scarce) factors. For countries in the North this has been taken to imply that trade liberalization will reduce the wage (if, in comparison to the South, labor is taken to be the scarce factor and capital the abundant factor) and hence change the distribution of income away from labor, or reduce the wage of unskilled labor and raise the wage of skilled labor (if skilled labor is taken to be the abundant factor and unskilled labor the scarce factor). Trade liberalizers often argue that losses such as these affect special-interest groups that hold society as a whole hostage to their own selfish interests, and fail to see the general benefits of lower prices. Such arguments are little consolation to large segments of society, such as unskilled labor, who can lose in real terms (taking into account lower product prices due to trade liberalization) without actually getting compensated by the gainers, and who cannot easily transform themselves into skilled workers or capital owners. It is another matter, of course, how much of the erosion of unskilled labor real wages in the North has been due to trade liberalization, as opposed to technological change (see Bhagwati 2004, for a recent review), and whether the theory is valid for Southern countries where in more countries than not, income distribution has worsened.

Second, it can be argued that the HOS approach may well capture long-term tendencies, but not short-term effects. For instance, in the short run wages may be rigid, and factors – especially capital – may be immobile across sectors. Labor skill requirements may also vary across sectors, and those laid off from some sectors may not be employable in other sectors. While proponents of trade liberalization sometimes recognize these losses, they argue that they are better dealt with through social policies rather than protectionism, ignoring the rolling back of social programs in the North which can afford them, let alone in the poor South.

Third, it is well known that the HOS results can be overturned by various kinds of 'distortions', including rigid wages, externalities in production and consumption, and the possibility that economies may be large enough to affect their terms of trade. Proponents of trade liberalization, including those who have examined the effects of these distortions extensively (see Bhagwati and Srinivasan 1983), would argue that these distortions are 'pathologies' rather than representing 'central tendencies' of the real world (Srinivasan and Bhagwati 2001); moreover, to the extent they do exist, they are best addressed at the source (for instance, a production externality with a production tax or subsidy, rather than an import tariff). But opponents can point to the many market imperfections they observe in real economies, especially given poor Southern institutions, and argue that tariffs may often be the most feasible means of addressing these distortions for resource-strapped Southern states.

Fourth, by adopting a static framework with given technology and factor endowments, the HOS approach ignores dynamic factors. An example of a dynamic factor can be shown within a simple partial equilibrium framework in which a country with no production experience initially cannot compete with its simple technology with imports. An import tax, by allowing learning from domestic production, can allow it to switch to a new technology which results in dynamic scale economies, which can eventually allow production at a cost lower than the import price. Further learning can even allow the country to become an exporter, competing in world markets.[2] Since the switch to the new technology is non-marginal, private firms may not recognize it. Moreover, the economies may involve externalities which prevent private firms from adopting the technology without protection. In a more general equilibrium setting, the market may be unable to allocate resources into sectors in which learning opportunities are important. Such phenomena can be subsumed into the previous category as a production 'distortion', but treating them as dynamic factors is less likely to allow their dismissal as a 'pathology'. Several dynamic models of learning have been developed to show how the South can protect its skill-intensive industries against competition from the North which, for historical reasons, enjoys a static comparative advantage in them, thereby possibly stemming the tide of uneven North–South development (Krugman 1981, Dutt 1990). Trade liberalization, by preventing poor countries from developing their dynamic comparative advantage, possibly sentences them to technological backwardness.

Proponents of trade liberalization argue that it is in practice difficult to pick the 'right' industries to protect, and even if not, they can be dealt with at the source with production subsidies, or through other measures to promote technology transfers from the North. However, it is hazardous to ignore the large literature on technological change in late-industrializers (see, for instance, Amsden 2001) on the possibilities of using directed trade and industrial policy for developing domestic technological capability (which cannot just be transferred from abroad), or to downplay the difficulties of subsidizing sectors for the possibly long period of time over which learning is required to compete against Northern technology (which is not, meanwhile, standing still).

Such dynamic factors are not the only ones ignored in the HOS framework. Even extensions of the framework to incorporate the dynamics of technological change and factor accumulation using the standard Solovian neo-classical framework fail to examine the possible long-run growth effects of trade liberalization, given the assumption that the marginal product of capital – the produced factor – tends to zero as more and more capital is accumulated which usually makes growth depend on factors exogenous to the economy. New growth theory, by departing from this assumption about the marginal product of capital, allows an examination of the growth effects. Trade liberalization, by increasing (lowering) the rental rate on physical capital and the wage for skilled labor in the North (South) along Stolper–Samuelson lines, can speed up (slow down) physical and human capital augmentation in the North (South), thereby exacerbating North–South uneven development (see Stokey 1991). Moreover, rents from 'unproductive' activity may be used for capital accumulation, which could be reduced with trade liberalization.

To be sure, not all dynamic considerations imply that trade liberalization leads to losses for the South or to uneven development. For instance, trade may be a medium through which technology is transferred from rich to poor countries due to reverse engineering of imports, or through interpersonal contacts accompanying trade. A full appraisal of the dynamic effects will have to take into account these diverse mechanisms, their empirical relevance, and their relative strengths.

Finally, the HOS approach ignores macroeconomic considerations such as the role of aggregate demand (by assuming full employment) and the balance of payments (by assuming balanced trade). Aggregate demand considerations are ignored in the approach in part by ignoring 'distortions', such as fixed wages, which are often taken to represent short-run problems which disappear in the longer run (and hence can be subsumed under the second and third previous categories discussed earlier) and with the small country assumption which implies all goods not domestically in demand will find markets abroad at a given price (ignoring the fact that poor countries have less than infinite price elasticity of foreign demand). But these so-called short-run problems may last for a long time, or never completely disappear if, for instance, falling wages exacerbate aggregate demand problems and falling prices cause debt deflation, and governments are prevented from pursuing expansionary policies by international institutions forcing fiscal austerity, or with international financial markets quick to jump on budget deficits as signs of economic weaknesses.

Departing from the HOS world of full employment with balanced trade has a number of implications. First, trade liberalization increases imports, and if it does not increase exports sufficiently (through lower price of intermediate imports, and greater efficiency in general), reduces net exports. This will reduce aggregate demand and resource utilization, and as a result, slow down growth. Second, lower growth may slow down Verdoorn–Kaldor–Arrow learning by doing and productivity growth, and render the economy less competitive, exacerbating the balance of payments problem (see Ocampo and Taylor 1998). These macroeconomic effects may well overturn whatever microeconomic efficiency gains one may expect from trade liberalization. Third, it is possible for countries to pursue export promotion policies while maintaining import protection, increasing exports and reducing imports at the same time (which is impossible in a two-good full-employment model with balanced trade). Fourth, one needs to examine trade liberalization issues in conjunction with other macroeconomic issues which affect trade, including the balance of payments, exchange rate policy and capital flows.[3] For instance, to the extent that trade liberalization is accompanied by the liberalization of capital flows and the exchange rate is allowed to float, exchange appreciation due to capital inflow surges can erode whatever improvements in competitiveness that trade liberalization brought about, feed speculative booms in asset markets and after the bubbles burst, eventually lead to capital outflows and foreign exchange crises.

Empirics

The empirical analysis of the effects of trade liberalization compares what happens when trade liberalization occurs and when it does not. For individual countries the comparison is made before and after trade liberalization, while comparisons across countries contrast the experiences of countries that liberalize and those that do not. Two main methods have been used in the literature to make such explorations: formal econometric analysis, and case studies. Before providing a flavor of these contributions, it should be noted that these analyses face the problem of disentangling the effects of changes due to trade liberalization from the effects of other exogenous and policy changes. Trade liberalization often occurs with the liberalization of international capital flows and internal financial and other sectors, and it is difficult to separate out their effects. Trade liberalization often takes place in response to balance of payments crises which require macroeconomic stabilization, which makes it necessary to separate out the effects of the exogenous changes which led to the crisis and the effects of macroeconomic stabilization from those of trade liberalization.

Starting with formal econometric analysis using data from a large set of countries, some of these problems were initially side-stepped by directly examining the effects of export expansion without looking at trade liberalization at all, implicitly assuming that trade liberalization leads to export expansion.[4] These studies inserted the export–GDP ratio or the growth rate of exports into a growth equation with other variables such as the saving or investment rate, and the rate of growth of labor supply, usually following a production function approach in which the export sector has a higher productivity compared to other sectors, and has positive technological spillovers. Many studies found positive effects of exports on growth.

It is not clear, however, whether measures of outward orientation (such as the export–GDP ratio) are appropriate measures of policy regimes since they are affected by a variety of factors such as factor endowments, technology and preferences. Other studies have therefore attempted to examine the effects of trade policy and openness more directly, using a variety of techniques. Papageorgiou et al. (1991) examine a cross section of countries which underwent trade liberalization and found that liberalization increases both the growth of exports and the growth of real GDP. Sachs and Warner (1995) classify countries as being 'closed' or 'open' in 1970 using the extent of non-tariff barriers, tariff rates, exchange rate black-market premium, overall economic system (capitalist or socialist) and government intervention in the export sector, and take a country to be closed if it fails on any one of these criteria. Measuring openness with a dummy variable, they find that only among open countries did poor countries grow faster than richer countries from 1970–89. However, Greenaway et al. (1997), using a smooth transitions framework, find no systematic evidence of positive growth effects of trade reforms.

Although it would seem that several of these studies make a convincing case for trade liberalization in the South, they suffer from a number of serious problems (see Rodriguez and Rodrik 2000). In addition to sharing the general problem of cross-section studies of taking all countries to share a common structure, they are not robust with respect to the choice of independent variables. Rodriguez and Rodrik (2000) also argue that many of the measures of trade policy are problematic. For instance, statistical power of Sachs and Warner's measure comes almost entirely from the black market premium and the presence of state export monopolies, and has little to do with trade policy as such. Finally, the studies invariably equate correlation with causality. Regarding the export equations, they do not distinguish between whether export growth causes growth, or vice versa. Despite their problematic interpretation of causality, the results of Granger causality tests are instructive. For instance, Jung and Marshall (1985) find that for 62 percent of their sample, the causality tests are inconclusive, and in the rest there is an even split between cases in which exports increase growth and those in which it reduces it, and subsequent studies find little evidence of a causal link from exports to growth.[5] The same kind of problem afflicts trade policy equations: it may be that countries that followed import substituting policies successfully grew faster in consequence and then liberalized their trade regimes, while countries that did not successfully do so had a poorer growth performance (for instance, due to balance of payments problems) and did not liberalize their trade regimes.

For reasons such as these it is preferable to rely on careful case studies of the effects of trade liberalization. The early studies in this vein – such as those coordinated by Little et al. (1970) and Balassa (1971) – argued that the highly protectionist trade regimes of many LDCs created disincentives for agricultural production and exports, and that these policies reduced savings, increased unemployment and excess capacity, and worsened income distribution, but only examined import-substituting regimes. The studies directed by Krueger (1978) and Bhagwati (1978) systematically classified trade regimes and explored their implications for economic performance. They measured trade orientation in terms of the gap between the relative prices of exports and imports domestically and internationally, and this does not require removing or even reducing tariffs and subsidies. Bhagwati and Krueger found that countries that followed import substitution strategies performed much worse than outward-oriented economies, because their highly policy-distorted economies – unchecked by market constraints and the availability of funds for subsidies which restrained the latter – resulted in an inefficient allocation of resources.

These and other similar studies argue that the superior growth performance of the East Asian NICs has been due to their more liberal trade regimes. For South Korea, for instance, the story is told that trade liberalization started from the early 1960s, and this, together with aggressive export promotion measures, resulted in rapid export and economic growth. All Korea experienced rapid growth yet its government policies were hardly free-market oriented and liberal. The government allocated finance to pick winners in return for meeting performance standards. Moreover, trade barriers on imports were maintained well into the so-called liberal period in the form of quantitative restriction and import tariffs (Amsden 1989, 69–70).

More recently the experiences of China and India have been cited as evidence of the benefits of trade liberalization, both for growth and for poverty alleviation (Bhagwati 2004, 64–5). From 1978 onwards China embarked on wide-ranging economic reforms which involved opening up the economy to foreign trade and foreign direct investment (FDI) and experienced rapid export and economic growth after that. However, trade liberalization has been gradual, and government intervention in the economy has followed the East Asian pattern rather than the model of market liberalism. China began to dismantle its trade barriers only after 20 years of market-oriented reforms (Stiglitz 2002, 60), tariffs remained high in many sectors at the end of the 1990s, and there were numerous non-tariff barriers (see Nolan 2004). India underwent thoroughgoing market-oriented reforms since 1991, and has broken free of its earlier 'Hindu' rate of growth. However, the higher growth was achieved in India prior to 1991, and in fact the post-reform growth was lower in the 1990s than in the 1980s; moreover, the relation between growth and poverty reduction has become weaker, the rate of poverty reduction lower, and inequality higher after the reforms (Rao and Dutt forthcoming). Furthermore, trade liberalization was accompanied by other policy changes, including the dismantling of the Byzantine industrial licensing apparatus, so that the post-reform improvement may largely be due to internal reforms. Finally, Indian tariff rates on manufactures continue to be among the highest in the world.

Trade liberalization elsewhere in the South has not had the effects hoped for by its proponents. Most Latin American economies underwent structural economic reforms in the late 1980s and early 1990s.[6] A major component of these reforms was trade liberalization, but there was also the liberalization of restrictions on FDI, domestic financial sector reform, and the adoption macroeconomic stabilization packages after the debt crisis of the 1980s. Overall the reforms did result in a closer integration of the region to the world economy, generating rapid export growth and attracting FDI, and inflation and budget deficits were also brought under control. Despite the fact that the growth in FDI and macroeconomic stabilization could be expected to increase growth, the average growth rate was lower in 1990–97 compared to the interventionist period from 1950–80, and declined further after 1998. Ocampo (2004, 73–4) argues that the Latin American pattern of specialization, especially the South American type based on natural resource-based manufactures and extractive exports, has favored goods that do not have a dynamic role in world trade, and increasing globalization may have led to weaker technological and other links among domestic firms, as import substitution has been reversed and the demand for imported intermediate and capital goods has increased. Unemployment, the share of informal employment, and inequality have increased and the trend in poverty reduction has slowed or been reversed.

In Africa, in country after country, trade liberalization has been associated with a reduction in industrial output and employment (see Buffie 2001, 190–2). In Senegal trade liberalization in the middle and late 1980s eliminated one-third of all manufacturing jobs. In Côte d'Ivoire industries such as chemical, textiles and automobile assembly, virtually collapsed in the face of import competition when tariffs were reduced in 1986. In Sierra Leone, Zambia, Zaire, Uganda, Tanzania and the Sudan, trade liberalization in the 1980s resulted in a rapid increase in consumer goods imports and a sharp reduction in the foreign exchange for the purchase of intermediate and capital goods, resulting in sharp falls in manufacturing employment and output. World Bank calculations show that in Sub-Saharan Africa, overall income declined by more than 2 percent with trade liberalization as a result of the 1990s WTO agreements (Stiglitz 2002, 61).

The poor performance of many countries in the South may be expected to have increased the North–South development gap. Indeed, calculations of the inequality across nations using purchasing power parity (PPP) adjusted per capita real GDP employing a variety of measures show that inequality across countries has increased. For instance, the standard deviation of the log of per capita income for 110 countries increased more or less steadily between 1960 and 1990, and regressions of growth rates of per capita GDP for the 1960–90 period on the logarithm of initial level of per capita GDP show that richer countries on average grow faster (Sala-i-Martin 1996). Overall growth figures for groups of countries tell a similar story.

These findings, however, have been disputed by Bhalla (2002), among others, who points out that by treating each country as one observation, the studies do not give adequate weight to the large low income countries, China and India, which have experienced relatively high rates of growth in recent years because of their globalizing and liberalizing strategies, and giving them their due weight implies an improvement in North–South inequality. In order not to lexicographically determine the results of such investigations by the experiences of two giants, in which the growth effects of trade liberalization has been questionable to say the least, it may be preferable to deal with simple, rather than weighted averages. But divergence may not have been due to trade liberalization and associated globalization, but caused instead by factors internal to the countries. However, Dutt and Mukhopadhyay (2005) examine the relationship between global inequality as measured by the variance of the logs of per capita PPP adjusted GDP and trade and capital flows using vector auto-regression models and find that the expansion of world trade has increased inequality.

History

Five points concerning the experience of currently-developed nations with trade protection in the past sheds further light on the recent debate about trade liberalization.

First, these nations used various kinds of economic policies, including tariff protection, to promote industrialization. In the early part of the eighteenth century, when Britain was still technologically behind the Low Countries and unable to compete against Indian manufactures, the government significantly raised import taxes on manufactured goods and provided export subsidies to industries. In the US, while tariff protection was not allowed during the colonial period, it was advocated by Alexander Hamilton, who argued that the inertia of habit and foreign competition would prevent the establishment of industries in the US which could later become competitive in world markets, unless their initial losses were protected by government interventions in the form of import tariffs or, in some cases, import bans. A low tariff of 5 per cent was imposed on all imports in 1789, and with some ups and downs, continued rising to close to 50 percent in 1931. Germany also used tariff protection for industrialization as recommended by Friedrich List.

Second, although the role of tariffs on industrialization and growth of the now-advanced countries has sometimes been downplayed, it is now generally agreed that tariff protection was crucial to the development of key industries. Such was the case for textiles in the early part and iron and steel in the later part of the nineteenth century. As Bairoch (1993) notes, the US was the world's fastest growing economy and the most protectionist, and periods of high protectionism for the US were also periods of the best growth performance. Bairoch (1989) also notes that for Europe in the late nineteenth century protection went with the expansion of trade and economic growth, and liberalism went with stagnation. O'Rourke (2000) has confirmed this by estimating growth equations examining the effect of import tariffs on economic growth from 1875 to 1914 for 10 currently developed countries.[7]

Third, the advanced countries championed the cause of free trade only after they achieved technological superiority. In Britain trade liberalization was supported by the classical economists after British manufacturers started widening its technological lead over its competitors from the middle of the nineteenth century. But as Britain's supremacy came to be challenged by the US and Germany, pressures towards protection increased, and in 1932 tariffs were re-introduced. The US supported free trade after World War II, after achieving unchallenged global supremacy in manufacturing. List has written that '[a]ny nation which by means of protective duties ... has raised her manufacturing power ... to such a degree of development that no other nation can sustain free competition with her, can do nothing other than to throw away these ladders of her greatness, to preach to other nations the benefits of free trade, and to declare in penitent tones that she has hitherto wandered in the paths of error, and has now for the first time succeeded in discovering the truth.'[8]

Fourth, the imperial powers imposed free trade on their colonies and dependent countries. While protecting industries in Britain, the East India Company rulers subjected India to free trade. While colonies were denied protection, tariff rates were higher in sovereign lagging countries, not only in the US, but also in Latin America and many European countries.[9]

Finally, one can ask whether these historical trends have any relevance for the current episodes of trade liberalization given differences in conditions. One, transport and communication costs are much lower today than before. Lower transport costs imply that a given level of import taxes means lower amounts of protection than in the past, where local industries faced import protection due to high transport costs, making the current situation worse for the South. Lower costs of communication, however, may appear to make it more favorable to them since, in a more interconnected world, capital and knowledge can flow across borders more easily than in the past, allowing more rapid technology transfers to the South, so that its wage advantage is more likely to result in an overall cost advantage. It is perhaps for this reason that the North fears Southern competition. However, lower communications costs may facilitate more technology transfer, but do not necessarily bring it about. Successful technology transfer is not as different from developing new technology as previously thought, and may require the development of domestic technological capability, that may well be hurt by the change in product mix due to globalization. Three, the age of overt colonization is over, so that countries can no longer be forced into liberalizing their trade regimes by their rulers. To this last issue we now turn.

Institutions

Although the South is not colonized by countries of the North, it can be argued that trade liberalization can be imposed on it by international institutions like the International Monetary Fund (IMF), the World Bank and the WTO.

The World Bank has long imposed trade liberalization on less-developed countries (LDCs) through its structural adjustment programs when it provides development loans. The IMF imposes conditions on countries when it comes to the assistance of countries facing balance of payments problems, and these conditions have increasingly included trade liberalization. Although they do not have to seek World Bank or IMF assistance and face these conditions, LDCs in great need of development assistance, or undergoing foreign exchange crises, are in no position to refuse. These institutions represent the views of policy-makers in the North, given that voting in these institutions is in accordance with financial contributions.

Stiglitz (2002) provides an account of how LDCs are forced to liberalize their trade regimes by the Bretton Woods institutions. Bhagwati (2004) argues that the effective pressure placed by these institutions has been exaggerated by Stiglitz and others, and there is much room for LDCs not to adhere to the conditions imposed by the institutions. Bhagwati argues domestic policy-makers are often the ones pushing for trade liberalization, and to the extent that these measures are politically unpopular they find convenient scapegoats in the international institutions. While Bhagwati certainly has a point when he argues that in some countries policy-makers have some latitude, in many cases it is well documented that institutions have enforced liberalization. Furthermore, the views of the policy-makers may well have been influenced by these institutions (sometimes in the hope of lucrative employment opportunities), in addition to being affected by academic opinion in rich countries and by the pressures of domestic middle classes hungry for imported goods.

The WTO, which succeeded the General Agreement on Trade and Tariffs (GATT) from the 1990s, pushes for multilateral reductions in import barriers and export subsidies. Member countries have to follow their liberalizing timetables. Successive rounds of WTO negotiations have led to reductions in trade restrictions, and to coverage in new sectors, such as services. Despite the fact that countries of the South are allowed some time to liberalize, their ability to conduct trade and industrial policies for development objectives is seriously undermined.

But the WTO, unlike the Bretton Woods institutions, runs along formally democratic lines, each country having one vote. Since there are more countries in the South than in the North, one would expect the South to prevail. Moreover, countries are not forced into joining the WTO. So why is the WTO able to force countries of the South to work against their best interests? Regarding the functioning of the WTO, despite formal democracy, decisions are made by 'consensus'. Negotiations are pursued by representatives of small groups of countries in which the advanced countries are over-represented, as in the meetings in the so-called 'green room' which excludes many LDCs. At these meetings specific LDCs are often bullied or paid off with bilateral negotiations outside the auspices of the WTO. Resource-strapped LDCs are unable to prepare for, and in many cases, even attend all the crucial meetings they could (see Das 2003). As a result, the advanced countries, and especially the US, have been able to have their way on many issues. For instance, despite the strong opposition to the provisions of the services and intellectual property rights agreements from many countries of the South, they were included in the final Agreement. Attempts continue to include labor and environmental clauses into the WTO agreements – which many see as disguised Northern protectionism – in the face of Southern opposition. Moreover, the method adopted for many changes in the agreements is to have members accept the changes or opt out of the system as a whole. Countries of the South are prevented from leaving the WTO because they could thereby lose access to the markets of member countries, and have to enter into bilateral negotiations with countries in the North, losing the rights and guarantees offered by the multilateral system. The dispute settlement process in the WTO, moreover, is heavily biased against LDCs given the high costs of litigation, and the structure of punishments according to which only the country that has won the complaint can take retaliatory actions against the perpetrator (clearly less of a concern to rich countries like the US than to smaller countries of the South) and the fact that retaliations across issues (violations in intellectual property rights clauses which is likely to occur by only the South can result in retaliation on the trade front) are allowed. Thus, even the liberalized trade system works against the interests of the South. Indeed, the North has continued to maintain many trade restrictions, especially those on Southern products (although, as one would expect, given its technological superiority, at levels generally lower than the countries of the South).

All of this is not to imply that LDCs have *no* possibility of conducting industrial policy under the WTO. The WTO law, in fact, does allow member countries to protect themselves from two types of import competition for a duration of up to eight years, that is, competition that destabilizes their balance of payments, and competition that threatens individual industries owing to a surge in imports (temporary safeguards) or an unfair trade practice, such as dumping. Several types of subsidies are also allowed, including those to promote R&D, regional development and environmentalism. Amsden (2003, 87) argues that 'the liberal bark of the WTO appears to be worse than its bite' and that neo-development states in LDCs can continue to foster industrialization through reciprocal control mechanisms which require protected firms to satisfy performance standards, as they did in the successful NICs of East Asia. However, the exceptions to import liberalization are more stringent than earlier GATT laws which, for instance, placed no time limits on protection, and in fact allowed LDC members to use relatively high tariffs and non-tariff barriers. Subsidies on exports and for domestic, rather than imported, inputs are prohibited (other than for countries with a per capita income not exceeding $1000), and even subsidies on domestic production – if they can be shown to injure trading partners – are 'actionable'.

Conclusion

The conflict between the North and the South over the possible adverse effects of globalization on the North, and Northern protectionism, has received a great deal of attention. Adverse 'social' consequences in the

South have also been discussed. While these are important issues, arguably the most important conflict regarding trade issues between the North and the South is over the question of trade liberalization and its consequences for Southern development and North–South uneven development.

Many industrialized countries of the North developed under tariff protection. Several poor countries, especially the East Asian NICs, have in the past followed their example and been able to grow using trade and industrial policies. Echoing the earlier practice of colonial powers, countries of the North have been able to impose trade liberalization on the South through international institutions such as the World Bank, IMF and the WTO, despite the fact that economic theory does not necessarily show that it is beneficial to them; the experiences of many Southern countries suggests that it harms them, and that it very likely exacerbates North–South inequality. While it is true that many import-substituting policies in LDCs in the South were ill-conceived and counter-productive, their lesson is that excesses should be avoided and the political economic situation of all southern countries does not allow the successful implementation of trade and industrial policies, not that trade liberalization is the panacea.

Despite its restrictions on protectionism, the world trading system does give the South some room to pursue development policies. Beyond that, the system should be reformed to allow the countries of the South to achieve their development potential. It may be in the short-term interest of the North to kick away the ladder that allowed their own development, but not so in its enlightened long-term interests.

Notes

1. It has also arguably affected other aspects of the globalization process – for instance, lower trade barriers may have increased 'vertical' foreign direct investment and it may reduce tariff-jumping, 'horizontal' investments – but we concentrate primarily on the direct effects of trade flows.
2. See Ocampo and Taylor (1998).
3. See Ocampo and Taylor (1998).
4. See Edwards (1993) for a survey.
5. See Ahmad and Kwan (1991) on Africa and Hsiao (1987) on the four Asian NICs.
6. The following discussion is based on Ocampo (2004).
7. Irwin's (2002) finding of no positive correlation between growth and tariffs when one adds a number of peripheral countries can be explained by the fact that many of these countries achieved high rates of growth based on

primary production and extractive industries which did not require high rates of protection for industrialization.

8. Quoted in Chang (2002, p. 4–5).
9. This is not to say that all sovereign nations made use of protection, since its use depends on the interests of the dominant policy-makers, as the divergent experiences of the US and most Latin American countries in the nineteenth century suggest.

References

Ahmad, J. and A. Kwan (1991), 'Causality between exports and economic growth: Evidence from Africa', *Economics Letters*, 37, 243–8.

Amsden, Alice H. (1989), *Asia's Next Giant. South Korea and Late Industrialization*, New York and Oxford: Oxford University Press.

Amsden, Alice H. (2001), *The Rise of 'The Rest'*, New York and Oxford: Oxford University Press.

Amsden, Alice H. (2003), 'Industrialization under the new WTO law', in John Toye (ed.), *Trade and Development. Directions for the 21st Century*, Cheltenham: Edward Elgar.

Balassa, Bela (1971), *The Structure of Protection in Developing Countries*, Baltimore: Johns Hopkins University Press.

Bairoch, Paul (1989), 'European Trade Policy, 1815–1914', in P. Mathias and S. Pollard (eds), *The Cambridge Economic History of Europe: Vol. XIII*, Cambridge: Cambridge University Press, 55–8.

Bairoch, Paul (1993), *Economics and World History. Myths and Paradoxes*, Chicago: University of Chicago Press.

Bhagwati, Jagdish (1978), *Anatomy and Consequences of Exchange Control Regimes*, Cambridge, Mass.: Ballinger.

Bhagwati, Jagdish (2004), *In Defense of Globalization*, Oxford: Oxford University Press.

Bhagwati, Jagdish and T.N. Srinivasan (1983), *Lectures on International Trade*, Cambridge, Mass: MIT Press.

Bhalla, Surjit S. (2002), *Imagine There's No Country. Poverty, Inequality, and Growth in the Era of Globalization*, Washington, D.C.: Institute of International Economics.

Buffie, Edward (2001), *Trade Policy in Developing Countries*, Cambridge: Cambridge University Press.

Chang, Ha-Joon (2002), *Kicking Away the Ladder. Development Strategy in Historical Perspective*, London: Anthem Press.

Das, Bhagirath Lal (2003), *The WTO and the Multilateral Trading System. Past, Present and Future*. London and New York: Zed Books, Penang: Third World Network.

Dutt, Amitava Krishna (1990), *Growth, Distribution and Uneven Development*, Cambridge: Cambridge University Press.

Dutt, Amitava Krishna and Kajal Mukhopadhyay (2005), 'Globalization and the inequality among nations: a VAR approach', *Economics Letters*, 88, 295–9.

Edwards, Sebastian (1993), 'Open-ness, trade liberalization and growth in developing countries', *Journal of Economic Literature*, 31, 1358–93.

Greenaway, David, S. J. Leybourne and David Sapsford (1997), 'Modeling growth and liberalization using smooth transition analysis', *Economic Inquiry*, 35, 798–814.

Hsiao, M. (1987), 'Tests of causality and exogeneity between exports and economic growth: The case of Asian NICs', *Journal of Economic Development*, 12, 143–59.

Irwin, Douglas (2002), 'Interpreting the tariff-growth correlation in the late 19th century', *American Economic Review*, May.

Jung, Woo S. and Peyton J. Marshall (1985), 'Exports, growth and causality in developing countries', *Journal of Development Economics*, May/June, 18(2), 1–12.

Krueger, Anne O. (1978), *Foreign Trade Regimes and Economic Development: Liberalization Attempts and Consequences*, Cambridge, Mass.: Ballinger.

Krugman, Paul (1981), 'Trade, accumulation, and uneven development', *Journal of Development Economics*, 8, 149–61.

Little, Ian M.D., Tibor Scitovsky and Maurice Scott (1970), *Industry and Trade in Some Developing Countries*, Oxford and New York: Oxford University Press.

Nolan, Peter (2004), *China at the Crossroads*, Cambridge: Polity Press.

Ocampo, Jose A. and Taylor, Lance (1998), 'Trade liberalization in developing countries: modest benefits but problems with productivity growth, macro prices and income distribution', *Economic Journal*, 108, September, 1523–46.

Ocampo, Jose A. (2004), 'Latin America's growth and equity frustrations', *Journal of Economic Perspectives*, 18(2), Spring, 67–88.

O'Rourke, Kevin (2000), 'Tariffs and growth in the late 19th century', *Economic Journal*, 110, 456–83.

Papageorgiou, D., M. Michaely and A. Choski (1991), *Liberalizing Foreign Trade*, Oxford: Blackwell.

Rao, J. Mohan and Amitava Krishna Dutt (forthcoming), 'A decade of reforms: The Indian economy in the 1990s', in Lance Taylor, (ed.), *External Liberalization in Asia, Post-Socialist Europe and Brazil*, Oxford: Oxford University Press.

Rodriguez, Francisco and Dani Rodrik (2000), 'Trade policy and economic reform. A skeptic's guide to the cross-national evidence', in B. Bernanke and K. Rogoff (eds), *NBER Macroeconomics Annual 2000*, Cambridge, MA: MIT Press.

Sachs, Jeffrey D. and A. Warner (1995), 'Economic reform and the process of global integration', *Brookings Papers on Economic Activity*, 1, 1–118.

Sala-i-Martin, Xavier (1996), 'The Classical Approach to Convergence Analysis', *Economic Journal*, 106, 1019–36.

Srinivasan, T.N. and Jagdish Bhagwati (2001), 'Outward-orientation and development: Are revisionists right?' in Deepak Lal and Richard Snape (eds), *Trade, Development and Political Economy*, Basingstoke: Palgrave.

Stiglitz, Joseph E. (2002), *Globalization and its Discontents*, New York: W.W. Norton.

Stokey, Nancy J. (1991), 'Human capital, product quality and growth', *Quarterly Journal of Economics*, 106(2), May, 587–616.

14

Globalization and Agricultural Trade: the Market Access and Food Security Dilemmas of Developing Countries

Tim Anderson

Poverty reduction and debt relief programs, fixed by the big powers, have repeated the dogma of globalization through 'free trade' as a means of salvation for poor countries. The Cairns Group, an agricultural export lobby, has reinforced this message in relation to farming. Yet agriculture in developing countries is far too important to be reduced to a function of the latest export opportunity. In poor, rural-based communities there is a huge cost in abandoning subsistence production and domestic markets to the vagaries of global markets. Nevertheless, international trade remains important as a source of income and foreign exchange, and whatever their attitude to global institutions, all countries engage in agreements in pursuit of trade opportunities. The problems lie in the terms of engagement.

The disadvantage faced by developing countries in international trade agreements has been characterized as an over-emphasis on industrial trade and a failure of 'market access' arrangements for agricultural produce. An Agreement on Agriculture in the final round of the GATT and a new emphasis on agricultural 'market access' in the WTO's 'Doha Round' were said to be important means of addressing this disadvantage. These arguments were made most strongly by the grain exporting member countries of the Cairns Group, such as Australia. However, tensions within the 18-member Cairns Group have underlined some serious problems with this approach. The agricultural exporters are divided over the mechanisms of trade re-regulation, and the means towards establishing greater market access for their exports, while protecting food security and rural livelihoods.

For developing countries the two major problems with the globalization of agricultural trade and its associated liberalization ideology are the practical dilemmas of market access and food security. Trade negotiations are poorly represented by theoretical models of mutual advantage. Rather, they are exercises in power politics with new rules constructed to suit the interests of the big powers (see Jawara and Kwa 2003). Capital intensive agriculture, carried out in the wealthy countries on large tracts of land and with substantial subsidies and infrastructural support, has an enormous commercial head start on the poor farmers of the developing world. To this advantage we must add the capacity of wealthy states to stay two steps ahead of trade re-regulation, through new and non-proscribed subsides. This has been a particular feature of agricultural trade, where the wealthy countries have shifted, rather than reduced, their various forms of protection. This uneven capacity helps explain the need for the closest scrutiny of new 'market access' proposals, and their associated and usually simplistic liberalization rationale.

'Free trade' in agriculture has always been a more than usually strained concept. It took decades for the big powers (the US and the EU) to decide seriously to include agriculture in international trade agreements, with a focus on tariff reduction. Yet an increase in the range of subsidies has accompanied this tariff reduction, a shift that causes more grief for the poorer countries, which rely more on tariffs and can less afford subsidies.

Despite the expansion of global trade most people in developing countries survive through farming and have only a marginal stake in international trade. Yet the non-commercial value of their land use – as subsistence production, barter, informal employment, housing, ecological management, cultural reproduction, social security and food security – are critical factors that are poorly understood in the wealthy countries. Changes in international trade regulation force us to pay more attention to these non-commercial aspects of agricultural production (FAO 2000, Mazoyer 2001). After introducing the main elements of international trade agreements on agriculture, this chapter will discuss the dilemmas of market access and food security posed for developing countries through the globalization of agricultural trade.

The Agreement on Agriculture

Several of the trade treaties signed at the conclusion of the final round of GATT in December 1994 had important implications for agriculture. The new agreement on intellectual property (TRIPS) raised, for the first time, the prospect of corporate ownership – and therefore restricted supply and high prices – for new seed varieties. The Sanitary–Phytosanitary Agreement appeared to maintain states' capacities to regulate quarantine and public health standards; but this was subject to challenge. However, the Agreement on Agriculture (AOA) was the first real attempt to comprehensively include agriculture in the GATT liberalization schedules. The final Agreement on Agriculture forms part of the final set of GATT agreements, which were taken over and administered by a new permanent body, the World Trade Organization (WTO). The AOA is a much less developed treaty than the industrial trade agreements, but it does form a framework for future negotiations. Back in 1994 the US and the EU said they had already complied with the terms of the AOA, before it was finalized. But they had done this by changing, not eliminating, their subsidies. The Special and Differential Treatment (SDT) accorded to developing countries was almost entirely through more gradual schedules of liberalization. There are four main heads of agreement in the AOA: market access, tariff cuts, domestic support and export subsidies. 'Market access' here means that states agree to convert their protection measures into import taxes (tariffs) which can then be 'bound' (fixed) and negotiated downwards. Domestic subsidies were compiled into an Aggregate Measure of Support (AMS) and there were 'special and differential' schedules for developing countries. Schedules were set up for countries to reduce their levels of agricultural tariffs, domestic support and export subsidies (see Table 14.1). However, most schedules were set

Table 14.1 Gatt's 1994 Agreement on Agriculture

	Principle	Numerical target	Other features
'Market access'	Remove NTBs, 'tariffication', and 'bound' tariffs		Eliminate quotas, but introduce 'tariff quotas'; 'safeguard' action allowed against surging imports
Tariff cuts	Scheduled tariff reductions	Average cut (from base 1995): WC: 36% by 2000 DC: 24% by 2004	Minimum cut per product: WC: 15% DC: 10%
Domestic support	Limit trade related domestic support schemes	Total AMS cuts (from base 1986–88): WC: 20% DC: 13%	The 'boxes': green, blue and amber
Export subsidies	Prohibit export subsides unless 'specified'	Total value cuts: WC: 36% DC: 24%	Cuts in subsidized quantities: WC: 21% DC: 14%

Note: WC = wealthy countries, DC = developing countries
Source: WTO 2003

to run out in 2004 and so needed renewal if agricultural liberalization were to proceed.

There are currently many exceptions to rules within the AOA. Special measures are authorized to allow higher tariffs when prices fall or imports surge ('safeguard mechanisms'), and to protect 'sensitive products'. However, as at 2004 for example, the EU had 539 listed sensitive products to which special protection measures can be applied (Windfuhr 2002, 31–4). Many Asian countries list rice as a sensitive product but wealthy countries were clearly taking even greater advantage of protective opportunities in the agreement.

No domestic support measures for agriculture were totally prohibited. They were categorized in the WTO colour system, like traffic lights, where red is not allowed and green is allowed. The AOA has 'green', 'amber' and 'blue boxes' but no 'red' box. Green box subsidies (allowed) are those which 'must not distort trade, or at most cause minimal distortion', and must involve government funds rather than price controls. Such subsidies include government-funded research, disease control, infrastructure, food security programs, direct income support to farmers, assistance to restructure agriculture, and direct payments under conservation and regional assistance programs. In other words, a large number of agricultural subsidies have been defined as 'outside' the scope of trade regulation. Blue box subsidies (allowed, with conditions) include those which require farmers to limit production, which encourage rural development in developing countries, and which provide small scale support (5 per cent of total value in wealthy countries and 10 per cent in developing countries). Amber box subsidies (those expected to be reduced) are those which must be wound back (on the AMS measure) according to the quantitative schedules of the AOA (WTO 2003; see Table 14.1). These are measures that are said to be more closely 'trade related'.

However, tariffs and simple trade restrictions are often more convenient farm support (and therefore food security) measures for developing countries, compared to domestic subsidies. Only wealthy countries can afford to pump large fiscal subsidies into their agriculture. The US and the EU complied with the AOA by shifting their protection measures away from tariffs and export subsidies and into tens of billions of dollars of 'green boxed' domestic subsidies (e.g. European Commission 2004). In this way, they escaped regulation. On the other hand, after the AOA the applied tariff levels in many developing countries were found to be much lower than their 'bound' tariff commitments, in part because of previous 'reforms' (such as World Bank programs); yet their capacity for domestic subsidies was so low that their AMS were often 'well below the committed or permitted levels' (FAO 2000, 2–5). Economic power is thus directly related to the capacity to evade changing regulation.

Market access

The agricultural 'market access' argument suggests that trade liberalization has so far been biased, only suiting the interests of the wealthy exporters of industrial goods. Liberalization of agricultural produce, it is claimed, will begin to redress the balance and allow developing countries access to a greater share of world trade. This argument has been put most forcefully by the Cairns Group, formed in 1987. This agricultural trade lobby group had 13 original members (some wealthy, but many developing countries) but later several more joined. By 2001 there were 18 members (see Table 14.3). The Cairns Group has pointed to the massive agricultural subsidies of the EU and the US. OECD calculations put total annual subsidies to agriculture in OECD countries at US$318 billion (2002: Tangermann 2004), with subsidies comprising 18 per cent of farm income in the US, 37 per cent in the EU and 58 per cent in Japan (Way 2005, 3). These subsidies are said to unfairly distort agricultural trade and to contribute to the dumping (sale below cost) of cheap food, which damages domestic markets and production in developing countries.

The Cairns Group called for the elimination of all amber and blue box domestic subsidies, and bigger cuts to export subsidies, as part of a WTO 'development round'. An associated argument is that the removal of these huge subsidies would help raise the international prices of agricultural produce (Anderson and Tyers 1991) and thus provide a better and fairer return to poor farmers, or at least to 'non-subsidized' farmers. This is distinct from the usual argument that liberalization would reduce prices for consumers.

In support of this argument Australia, a wealthy agro-exporter that claims solidarity with developing countries, argues that 'unfair subsidies' must be removed and that this must apply to all, as 'market access reform is for everyone or for no one' (DFAT 2003). As a liberal argument, stressing mutual advantages and masking distinct interests, these assertions have caused tensions in the Cairns Group and exposed Australia to criticisms of hypocrisy. Other countries in the group have expectations that the WTO's professed 'special and differential treatment' for developing countries can be used to oppose the domestic and export subsidies of the wealthy countries, while allowing tariff protection and safeguard measures for the poorer countries.

While making its criticisms of subsidies in the US and the EU, Australia has hidden the fact that (like other wealthy countries) its own agribusiness has been constructed with the support of important public investment and subsidy. Substantial public infrastructure in the form of roads, rail, ports, finance, communications and scientific support underwrote the capacity of Australia's agro-exporters. Historical advantages accrued through the British system of imperial trade preferences (dismantled in the 1960s), internal and external protection measures (e.g. margarine quotas, to protect the milk industry), as well as the assistance of the price stabilization authorities for wheat and wool. Then there are ongoing rural industry subsidies in the form of diesel fuel rebates for the transport of rural produce (more than A$2bn per year: ATO 2003), the semi-permanent 'drought relief' packages (which encourage farming in semi-arid areas), well-funded industry restructuring packages (e.g. to help consolidate the sugar and milk industries), and remediation programs for the environmental damage caused by farming (e.g. salination). The fact that tariffs on imported agricultural products are low in Australia is no real measure of the 'open market' status of Australian agriculture.

Tensions in the Cairns Group became public during the WTO Doha Round. In March 2002 the Philippines government said it was considering withdrawing from the Cairns Group and the WTO over what it called discrimination between the developed and developing members (Dow Jones 2002). Then in September 2002 Indonesia refused to sign a Cairns Group paper calling for drastic tariff cuts in agriculture (TIU 2002). Australia, on the other hand, flatly rejected the developing countries' 'special and differential' claims for protection of strategic crops and 'counter-balancing measures', maintaining that it supports only 'efficient' exporters (DFAT 2003). This latter comment can be taken as a reference to capital intensive agribusiness.

At Cancun (Mexico) in 2003 these arguments came to a head, and to a halt. The 'market access' push confronted an intransigent, practical barrier. The agricultural protection of the EU and the US has effectively switched into 'green box' subsidy measures, which are immune to bilateral agreements and quarantined in multilateral negotiations. In contrast tariffs, as the major 'currency' of all 'free trade' agreements, are still heavily relied on by the developing countries both for revenue and for the protection of domestic production.

The UN's Food and Agriculture Organization had already recognized many of these problems. In a study entitled 'Agriculture, Trade and Food Security' the organization looked at the impact of WTO agreements on a select group of developing countries. It noted that agriculture was central to economic development in developing countries, where an average of 50 per cent of the population was engaged in agriculture, compared to 8 per cent in the developed countries (FAO 2000, table 1). It observed that 'tariffs play a much broader and more important role in developing countries for lack of other trade instruments and alternative safety-net measures'. There was a need for 'an appropriate safeguard mechanism' and, unlike the big powers, subsidies were weak (FAO 2000, 4). While many of the 14 developing countries under study increased their agricultural exports in the 1990s, this mostly built on trends in the 1980s. More significantly, the rise in agricultural exports was overwhelmed in most of the countries by a rise in agricultural imports. In 10 of the 14 countries the rise in imports was much more than that of exports (see Table 14.2). Poor, rural-based societies were increasing their food import dependence.

While the AOA had been in place for only a few years at the time of this study, the FAO report concluded that there was 'a general trend towards the consolidation of farms as competitive pressures began to build up following trade liberalization' and that there was a 'need for a more cautious approach to trade liberalization if social costs are to be minimized'. Because agriculture includes so many people in developing countries, 'the textbook solution of redistributing the gains

Table 14.2   Agricultural trade of select developing countries, 1990s

	Between 1990–94 and 1995–98	
	Change in agricultural exports, %	*Change in agricultural imports, %*
Bangladesh	−0.1	77.8
Botswana	32.0	37.4
Brazil	53.1	106.7
Egypt	21.6	41.6
Guyana	51.4	40.9
India	82.8	168.4
Jamaica	23.6	44.4
Kenya	46.0	49.3
Morocco	37.5	68.0
Pakistan	14.4	52.8
Peru	99.3	57.3
Senegal	−32.2	30.1
Sri Lanka	62.0	42.1
Thailand	35.4	71.1

Source: FAO 2000: tables 4 and 5

between winners and losers at the national level becomes impracticable' (FAO 2000, 11–12).

Floods of cheap imports are a serious concern for many poor countries. Jawara and Kwa point out that 'cheap European milk powder has displaced dairy farmers in India and Jamaica, and is threatening the livelihoods of Thai farmers. Corn farmers in Mindanao in the Philippines have been wiped out' (Jawara and Kwa 2003, 29). So the interest in accessing new export markets may be chastened if the means to do so involves exposure to greater vulnerability in domestic markets and domestic production. A wealthy country might contemplate dislocation of 8 per cent of its population and their livelihoods; it might even have the means to compensate for some of this dislocation. A poor country cannot contemplate the certain disaster of such dislocation among 50 per cent of its very poor, rural population.

In summary, while many developing countries share some of the interests of the wealthier agro-exporters, to access new markets for agricultural exports they differ in their approach to the means to be used. Both argue for reductions in export subsidies. However, countries such as Australia are able to provide a range of indirect subsidies and infrastructural support to their rural industries, while they demand the elimination of tariffs and quotas. Developing countries, on the other hand, generally want to maintain some level of tariff protection, as well as special mechanisms to protect strategically important rural production.

Food security and rural livelihoods

The globalization of agricultural markets has raised new food security dilemmas for developing countries. Underlying the concern to protect domestic markets and domestic production is a critical concern for food security. This is a concern also expressed by many wealthy countries, and used in support of their subsidies (e.g. ERS 2001). If domestic food production is smashed by a flood of cheap imports from large-scale, heavily subsidized agribusiness, precious foreign exchange will be required simply to replace subsistence food production. Most countries want to stabilize their domestic production as the central component of a food security strategy. No country is really happy to be import-dependent for its basic food needs as this could spell disaster in the event of trade disruption or war. However, few countries possess the capacity for expensive policies of subsidy and infrastructure which can circumvent the new forms of global trade regulation.

While the need for food security is universally recognized, the neo-liberal version focuses on commercial means, while the poor country version relies on a stabilization of domestic capacity. In the first version productivity and efficiency are measured as commercial returns. In the second the capacity of farming to contribute to food, security and rural livelihoods is taken into account.

In a 1996 report called Food Security and Trade, Australia presented the neo-liberal argument that trade liberalization leads to growth, growth leads to poverty reduction and poverty reduction solves food security. Distribution, not production, is recognized as the root of the problem; but open trade and participation in global markets is said to be the means of resolving that distributional problem. Food security is linked to poverty, and poverty is said to be best addressed through generalized growth.

> Food security... is about the distribution of food and ways to ensure that everyone has the resources or the capacity to access available food supplies through purchase, barter, growing food or other means... Poverty is the fundamental cause of food insecurity... how can poverty be alleviated?... [through] economic growth.... broad based trade liberalisation is an important vehicle for economic growth and the alleviation of poverty. It thus makes a major contribution to food security. (DFAT 1996, x)

Australia has repeated this theme many times since then and has linked both aid and trade to this version of 'food security'. In 2005 Australia's aid agency asserted that 'a more open trading system is central to food security', and that Australia's aid 'aims to advance Australia's national interest by assisting developing countries to reduce poverty and achieve sustainable development' (AusAID 2004, 1).

However, such an approach is regarded as inappropriate in most developing countries. India, Indonesia and several Latin American countries have provided input subsidies to small farmers – as well as food subsidies for poor urban consumers – as a type of social security system. Cheap seeds and fertilizers in the country – as well as guaranteed cheap basic grains and cooking fuels in the cities – have helped stabilize production, underwrite rural and urban food security, and have been an essential safeguard against starvation. But food subsidies have been attacked by IMF structural adjustment programs, while farming subsides have come under attack at the WTO. A past leader in these debates, India argued at the WTO for developing countries to maintain high tariffs for staple grains such as rice, wheat and maize, new special safeguard mechanisms to protect against surges of cheap imports, flexible domestic supports for agriculture, the elimination of export subsidies, and a reduction of agricultural tariffs in the wealthy countries (Kwa 2000, 2–3).

For its part, Indonesia has observed that it is too simplistic to assume that liberalization would help countries achieve food security – Indonesia's rice consumption alone is two thirds of the total world trade in rice – and has consistently stressed 'non trade concerns' (principally food security and rural development) in the WTO's agriculture talks (Hidayat 2002). Together with the Philippines, and 14 other developing countries at the WTO, Indonesia broke with the Cairns Group to form an Alliance for 'special products' and 'special and strategic measures', to help protect domestic agriculture (Glipo et al. 2003). The 'agriculture as multifunctional' group comprises rich and poor countries, including the EU, Japan, South Korea and Norway. In these circles, agriculture was said to be 'not only about food production but . . . non-trade concerns such as ensuring food security, environmental protection, [and] protecting the cultural landscape' (Kwa 2000, 4).

This is the theme developed by Marcel Mazoyer. In a report for the FAO he argued for the 'multifunctionality' of small farming – that small farms not only contribute market produce but also support food security, social security, productive livelihoods and more effective environmental management. Mazoyer says small farmers need 'sufficiently high' prices to be induced to plant crops, and to survive. On the other hand, the domination of global agriculture by large subsidized corporations is undermining small farming and food security.

> [It] will condemn hundreds of millions of small farmers and agricultural workers to stagnation, impoverishment, migration and hence to unemployment and low wages, especially in developing countries but also to some extent in developed countries. (Mazoyer 2001, 22)

Forced liberalization of agricultural trade would enhance the capital-intensive, corporate domination of agricultural production. This could well aggravate dumping, forcing down prices, destroying small markets and local food production, and pushing millions of small farmers from their lands. The resultant dispossession, unemployment and land clearing would create severe social and environmental problems in many developing countries.

Agribusiness in the wealthy countries is extending its dominance of global produce markets. The FAO points out that, while cheaper food imports have 'moderated the food import bills' of developing countries, they have also led to an increase in import dependence, which can damage local production and local markets.

Although lower basic food prices on international markets bring short-term benefits to net food-importing developing countries, lower international prices can also have negative impacts on domestic production in developing countries that might have lingering effects on their food security. (FAO 2004, s.5).

Developing countries are now, on aggregate, net food importers. This trend in recent years has been reinforced by the decline in Chinese grain production (FAO 2004, s.4–5). Distinct food grain trade patterns help explain different national approaches to food security. While all Cairns Group members export food, only five or six of the 18 members are food grain exporters. Access to food grains (principally rice and wheat) is at the centre of food security concerns. Most Cairns Group members are substantial importers of food grain (see Table 14.3).

Table 14.3 Cairns Group food grain trade, 2001

	net imports ('000 tonnes)		
	rice	wheat	cereals
Argentina	−683	−11590	−24153
Australia	−909	−18010	−22440
Bolivia	14	453	499
Brazil	875	7813	11149
Canada	376	−18966	−21655
Chile	105	514	1824
Colombia	113	1095	3230
Costa Rica	59	213	766
Fiji	43	99	132
Guatemala	41	260	662
Indonesia	2035	4197	6897
Malaysia	747	1081	4400
New Zealand	47	232	266
Paraguay	−16	82	−84
Philippines	992	2700	4145
South Africa	776	581	884
Thailand	−9421	649	−5137
Uruguay	−1042	−8	−573

Source: FAO 2002

In the year 2000 Brazil, Indonesia and the Philippines imported 20, 13 and 8 million tonnes of basic food grains (FAO 2002). These countries do not want even greater dependence on food imports. The African continent is also a net grain importer, to the tune of about 76 million tonnes per year (FAO 2002). Yet poor African countries hardly need to increase their vulnerability to food imports. Little countries like East Timor, in the name of food security, focus on strengthening their subsistence sector and local markets, so that they may be less reliant on rice imports (MAAF 2005). This is poorly understood by its wealthy, grain-exporting neighbour Australia (DFAT 1996; 2003). Sensitivity to food grain dependence strongly influences most grain importers to stabilize their domestic production so their dependence on staple grains does not worsen.

Concluding remarks

The globalization of agricultural trade is mostly a function of the rising power of global agribusiness corporations, backed by wealthy states, though in this chapter I have focused on trade arguments and the multilateral negotiations. The globalization process poses serious dilemmas for most developing countries. The opportunities for accessing new export markets are important, but probably limited in scope compared to parallel opportunities in labour intensive manufacturing and the pursuit of revenue and foreign exchange through global tourism. The intransigent nature of the wealthy countries' subsidies and infrastructural support for their rural industries imposes serious constraints on 'market access' opportunities and threatens the persistent dumping of cheap imports. This threat is at such a level that many farmer groups – faced with the elimination of their livelihoods – have demanded that agriculture be completely removed from WTO negotiations. The Mexican farmers group UNORCA says:

> The WTO does not consider the multifunctionality of agriculture, nor its importance in guaranteeing the sustainability of the rural environment; of biodiversity; of nature; of water; of air; of the earth and the soil; of culture; of traditional knowledge; of the sources of work; of food sovereignty; and of the cultural, social and environmental preferences of consumers – none of these things are the concerns of markets. The WTO only considers agriculture as a source of commodities for world markets... our position is that the WTO gets out of agriculture. (UNORCA 2003)

It may well be that the failure of the Doha Round has brought an end, for the time being, to the multilateral liberalization of agriculture; but the giant corporations have not halted their plans for expanded market share. The flurry of bilateral and regional agreements that has paralleled the WTO talks can do nothing to reduce wealthy country subsidies, as subsidy reduction can only be addressed multilaterally. However, this issue was not properly addressed at the WTO. Most wealthy country subsidies were effectively quarantined in the 'green box'.

At least in bilateral and regional agreements there will be a little more room to identify and support strategically important farm sectors. Tariff protection remains important, for many poor countries. Cheap seeds and fertilizer, and guaranteed cheap basic grains, have helped stabilize production and have been an essential safeguard against starvation. The imperative of food security, based in the first instance on domestic production and domestic markets, will continue to preoccupy most developing countries. Those countries with political will are likely to maintain some forms of protection, and to treat agriculture as something more than a global commodity.

References

Anderson, Kym and Rodney Tyers (1991), *Global Effects of Liberalizing Trade in Farm Products*, London: Trade Policy Research Centre.

ATO (Australian Taxation Office) (2003), 'Taxation Statistics 2000–01: A summary of taxation, superannuation and industry benchmark statistics 2000–01 and 2001–02: Total DFRS rebates paid', <http://www.ato.gov.au/taxprofessionals/content.asp?doc=/content/37484.htm&page=169&H24_2_1>.

AusAID (2004), *Food Security Strategy*, Australian Government: AusAID, Canberra, May.

DFAT (1996), *Food Security and Trade: a Future Perspective*, Department of Foreign Affairs and Trade, Commonwealth of Australia, Canberra.

DFAT (2003), 'Fact Sheets: Australia and the Doha Development Agenda', <www.dfat.gov.au>.

Dow Jones (2002), 'President Arroyo backs Philippines withdrawal from Cairns Group', 13 March.

ERS (2001), 'Food Security in the United States', Economic Research Service, US Department of Agriculture, <www.ers.usda.gov/briefing/foodsecurity/>.

European Commission (2004), *Report on United States Barriers to Trade and Investment*, Brussels, December.

FAO (2000), 'Agriculture, trade and food security: issues and options in the WTO negotiations from the perspective of developing countries, Vol II: country case studies', Rome, Commodities and Trade Division, Food and Agriculture Organization.

FAO (2002), 'Food Balance Sheet', <http://apps.fao.org/lim500/>.

FAO (2004), *The State of Food and Agriculture 2003–2004*, <http://www.fao.org/documents/show_cdr.asp?url_file=/docrep/006/Y5160E/Y5160E00.HTM>.

Glipo, Arze; Laura Carlsen, Azra Talat Sayeed, Jayson Cainglet and Rita Schwentesius (2003), 'Agreement on Agriculture and Food Sovereignty: Perspectives from Mesoamerica and Asia', September, Americas Program, Interhemispheric Resource Center (IRC), <http://americas.irc-online.org/wto/2003/0309aoa_body.html>.

Hidayat, Nur (2002), 'WTO, Indonesian agriculture, and food security', Institute for Global Justice, Jakarta, Indonesia, paper prepared for AFTINET seminar on Alternatives to the WTO, Sydney, 8 November.

Jawara, Fatouma and Aileen Kwa (2003), *Behind the Scenes at the WTO: the Real World of International Trade Negotiations*, London: Zed Books.

Kwa, Aileen (2000), 'Will food security get trampled as the elephants fight over agriculture?', Focus on the Global South, <www.focusweb.org>.

MAAF (2005), 'National Food Security Policy for Timor Leste', Indonesian Ministry of Agriculture, Forestry and Fisheries, draft for comments, Dili, 7 June.

Mazoyer, Marcel (2001), *Protecting Small Farmers and the Rural Poor in the Context of Globalization*, Report for the United Nations Food and Agriculture Organization, Rome.

Tangermann, Stefan (2004), 'Farming support: the truth behind the numbers', *OECD Observer*, March, <www.oecdobserver.org>.

TIU (Trade Issues Update) (2002), 'WTO Agricultural Negotiations', September, <http://canadaegg.ca/english/trade/reports/trade_issues_update_sep2002_e.pdf>.

UNORCA (2003), Statement on Agriculture and the WTO, Union Nacional de Organisaciones Regionales Campesinas Autonomas / National Union of Autonomous Regional Farming Organisations, 18 August.

Way, Nicholas (2005), 'Agriculture: Farmers lose debate', *Business Review Weekly*, 21 July, <www.brw.com.au>.

Windfuhr, Michael (2002), 'Little progress for liberalised trade: The agricultural exports of developing countries are blocked', *D + C Development and Cooperation*, 6, 31–4.

World Trade Organization (2003), 'The Agreements: Agriculture', <www.wto.org>.

Index

Printed in the United States
71134LV00001B/73-81